Ambiguity and Awareness
How Watching Movies Helps Us Think
About Art, Literature, Philosophy, Life and Everything

David Carl
© 2015

Contents

The mayor, at the urging of Bruno Crespi, explained in a proclamation that the cinema was a machine of illusions that did not merit the emotional outbursts of the audience. With that discouraging explanation many felt that they had been victims of some new and showy gypsy business and they decided not to return to the movies, considering that they already had too many troubles of their own to weep over the acted-out misfortunes of imaginary beings.

–Gabriel Garcia Marquez, *One Hundred Years of Solitude*

A spirited mind never stops within itself; it is always aspiring and going beyond its strength; it has impulses beyond its powers of achievement. If it does not advance and press forward and stand at bay and clash, it is only half alive. Its pursuits are boundless and without form; its food is wonder, the chase, ambiguity.

–Montaigne, "Of experience"

Movies for the Rest of Us

> Our sight has proved to be a source of supreme
> benefit to us, in that none of our present
> statements about the universe could ever have
> been made if we had never seen any stars, sun,
> or heaven. As it is, our ability to see the periods
> of day-and-night, of months and of years, of
> equinoxes and solstices, has led to the
> invention of number and has given us the idea
> of time and opened the path to inquiry into the
> nature of the universe. These pursuits have
> given us philosophy, a gift from the gods to the
> mortal race whose value neither has nor ever
> will be surpassed. I'm quite prepared to declare
> this to be the supreme good our eyesight offers
> us.

–Plato, *Timaeus* 47a (Donald J. Zeyl trans.)

I

It's not too late, and certainly not too early, to ask again the question of why, and in what ways, the movies matter to us today. What do the movies have left to say to us? And what do we have left to say about the movies?

Watching a movie is only half, and perhaps the less interesting half, of what we want from the experience of going to the movies. Along with the watching, we like to talk about what we've seen. This is one reason why we like to watch movies with other people. Talking about the movies is more than just a culture industry; like talking about sports, it's one of the things we like to do *together*.

Before the movies there were plays, photographs, sculpture, architecture, poetry, novels, dance, painting (all elements of what eventually came to be known as the cinema). Yesterday's salon has become today's book group. Starting with the 19th century German and British Romantics (from Goethe, Schelling and Schlegel to Wordsworth's *Prelude*), poets and artists began writing manifestoes about the goals and purposes of art. By the early decades of the 20th century so many manifestoes had been written that they started to develop into an art form all their own; an art form in which the *idea* became the content of the form. Idea (concept) became king, and art came closer to joining hands with theory, criticism (critique), and philosophy than it ever had before. This was a long way from the Leonardo's *Notebooks* and the letters of van Gogh. From the Futurists, Dadaists, Surrealists, and Situationists to artists like Kurt Schwitters, Marcel Duchamp, and Wyndam Lewis to Concept Artists like Joseph Kosuth, Sol LeWitt, and Mel Bochner, talk *about* art gradually became a kind of art in its own right. The UK-based Art & Language group made this explicit, as did Tom Wolfe's more critical evaluation of this trend in his campy critique *The Painted Word*.

Filmmakers from Eisenstein to the Dogme 95 group have penned their own manifestoes, issuing pronouncements about what film is, how it should be made, and what its goals should be. We have had poetics of cinema and phenomenologies of cinema, psychoanalyses of cinema and deconstructions of cinema. Now well into its second century (a young art in many respects, the oldest of arts in others), we have witnessed the various "posts" of cinema: post-modern, post-structuralist, post-colonial, post-gender; we have entered and surely within the next few years will emerge from the era of "post-human" cinema. But who will write a manifesto not for the artists of cinema (the future filmmakers, critics, historians and theorists), but for the audience? Who will reflect on the pleasures of cinema, what Roland Barthes might have called the "bliss" of the screen's sound and images? Where do we find a manifesto on the ecstasies of cinema rather than its theories?

Such a manifesto might ask us to think about a question as simple as, "Why do we go to the movies?" (Which is perhaps not a simple question at all, once we start looking into it.)

Before the movies there was literature. Before literature (or rather, at the birth of literature in the West) there was Homer. Before Homer there was already storytelling: myth, legend, song, oral poetry. And there was magic: paintings on the wall depicting animals, motion, the chase, the hunt. Movies are just the latest form that magic and storytelling have taken in a history that is already more than 10,000 years old. It's a story that's still unfolding.

II

For those of us who care about art, literature, film ("culture" in its broadest sense), nothing says "who we are" more than the books we read, the movies we watch, the music we listen to. I began writing this book several years ago in response to a chain of thought inspired by two simple questions: "What's your favorite movie?" "Who is your favorite director?"

We enjoy answering the question, "What's your favorite..." because it gives us a chance to define ourselves, to say who we are in terms of the things we care about.

John Ford influences Ozu; Kurosawa influences Leone and Lucas, Chaplin influences Fellini (along with everyone else)... Perhaps there is no such thing as International Cinema because at its best cinema forms of a nation of its own. Be that as it may, Jean Pierre Melville, Michelangelo Antonioni, and David Lynch are all deeply Western filmmakers, obsessed with a uniquely western response to the struggle between good and evil as a kind of spiritual crisis. Melville's heroes are often criminals, but they live by a code (like the bushido code of the samurai evoked in Melville's 1967 *Le samourai*) which allows them to live with a sense of honor and distinguish right from wrong, even in the moral gray of the criminal underworld. Friendship, loyalty, courage—these are the virtues of Melville's heroes, and these qualities add up to a certain "cool" that he may derive from American actors like Bogart, Dean, and Brando, but to which he gives a uniquely French twist (different from the kind of "cool" we see developed in later American actors like Steve McQueen, Lee Marvin, and Paul Newman). It is within this sense of "cool" that Melville explores his own sense of spirituality in the context of a kind of warrior ethic that is simultaneously an aesthetics of style. In Melville's hero the ethical and the aesthetic are gracefully blended in the notion of cool.

Antonioni's characters are also "cool", but bordering on the frigid (frozen in various ways). Although not criminals in the social sense, they may be so in the spiritual sense. And they are far from heroic; while they occupy striking aesthetic surroundings, they are wholly unethical—not because they are evil, but because they are weak. Melville's three virtues—friendship, loyalty, and courage—are wholly lacking in Antonioni's world. His characters are too close to pathetic to be tragic, but they are not contemptible because they are often too much like we are, and even in the fantasy world of the movies we find it difficult to hate ourselves. They are living through a kind of modern crisis from which all the heroics have been drained, and what is left behind is lush, indulgent, stylish and visually gorgeous, but spiritually bereft. It is in their response to this sense of bereavement that Antonioni's characters regain a kind of antiheroic charm, especially in the case of the female leads played by Monica Vitti in the four films she did with him between 1960 and 1964. Vitti affirms the possibility of a new kind of heroism in response to modern angst. In Antonioni, anything that can still be affirmed against this backdrop of modernity takes on a new significance and pries open to door to hope as if for one last time (as in the endings of *Blow Up* and *The Passenger*, in addition to his films with Vitti).

With Lynch, cool and despair join hands to occupy a landscape that is alien in direct proportion to how familiar it seems on the surface. Unreal things happen in everyday places (our homes, our neighborhoods, inside our heads), proving that these landscapes are not so familiar after all. What we thought was comfortable and commonplace is revealed as concealing dark, hidden corners. These may be the corners of our own imaginations, which tend to run away with themselves, at least if Lynch has anything to do with it. But here too there is a kind of spiritual struggle going on; a struggle between good and evil that is very real for Lynch, even if it is a rather specifically conceived western sense of good and evil. (It would be Manichean if it didn't keep doubling in on itself and implicating his films' various heroes with a sense of their own moral ambiguity.)

The devil, last seen in the works of Milton, Goethe and Dostoevsky, is still alive and well in the films of Melville, Antonioni, and Lynch. He is still charming, still tempting, and still leaves a wake of despair that demands some sort of spiritual response from those he encounters. For filmmakers, with all the resources of the audiovisual at their disposal, these responses, no matter how ethically grounded, must always be aesthetic as well.

III

The goals of this book are twofold: the first is to offer a series of close readings of a number of individual films; the second is to extract from these readings a more general theory of film that takes into account different aspects of the movies, from *mise en scène* to acting, camerawork to lighting, writing to editing; time and space, sound and image. Along the way I try to offer a sustained argument regarding the stakes of and challenges to taking cinema seriously in a world overrun by movies. Each chapter offers a different perspective on this larger question about the role of the movies in our lives today.

The book consists of a collection of essays, from that French word for "to try or attempt." An essay is the written record of an earnest effort that calls on the author to try his very best, no matter how inadequate the results. In this sense any essay that is not, on one level, a failure, is an essay that stopped too soon, when the writer was still feeling safe and secure in his own thinking. Often the point of failure is where things get interesting, where risks are taken and new possibilities emerge.

This book, in one sense, is following up on Adorno's idea that "Today art is hardly conceivable except as an orientation anticipating the apocalypse" (*Aesthetic Theory*).

This idea of the interesting failure is something the essay has in common with the movies. One distinguishing characteristic of great movie directors is that there is as much to learn from their failures as from their successes. Along with their masterpieces, Antonioni, Melville, Lynch, Peckinpah, Cassavetes, Sam Fuller, John Huston, Howard Hawks, Jim Jarmusch and Terrence Malick all made bad movies; but they are bad movies I've learned more from watching and thinking about that the "good" movies of many a lesser director. There is such a thing as a provocative failure.[1]

A "merely bad" work of art is one that is not even

---

[1] Who was it that said, "I would rather be a successful failure than a failed success"? I think it might have been a character in one of my novels, but perhaps it was just the author consoling himself after any number of his completed projects.

interesting in the way it fails. I care most about the work of those directors who not only risk going wrong, but actually precipitate themselves into the breach, knowing that the only alternative is to remain perpetually on the safe side of what they are comfortable and familiar with (what they are "good at"); the comfortable and familiar being antithetical to art however we choose to define it.

IV

Let's pretend. When we pretend, we use our imagination to engage in a particular kind of thinking. We think what isn't. We don't need to use our imaginations when we think what is. The imagination is reserved for thinking things that aren't true. For things that are true we can use the rational faculties. Sometimes we don't know whether something is true or not. In cases like these both the rational and imaginative faculties can be used to think about them.

Let's pretend that literature, the telling of stories in written forms of language, is the greatest art form ever developed by human beings. Music is a close second. The wide array of visual arts comes next. In this world of make believe fiction is an act of the imagination by virtue of which something that is not true is treated as if it were. The more powerful the fiction the more convincing the treatment. Those of us possessed by a particular love of literature never quite abandon the suspicion—natural in childhood—that a sufficiently powerful fiction might cross the invisible line and install itself as truth. This would be gratifying in the short run but ultimately uninteresting as we would soon want another fiction, always preferring the possible to the real, even when the real had its origins in a fiction, as in fact perhaps all reality does. Stories.

Imagination does not merely envision the false as if it were true. It also conjures up the possible. And when it comes to the possible, it's never simply a matter of *discovering*; it's a matter of determining, even expanding, certain limits.

The movies too are a realm that explores the limits of the possible. Some movies reinforce long-established boundaries and conventions. Other movies blow the doors wide open. It seems that virtually anything is possible; sometimes even the impossible.

One Door Opens and another Door Closes:
Michael Corleone's transformation in *The Godfather* (1972)

One hour, one minute, and 39 seconds into *The Godfather*, Michael stands outside the hospital where his wounded father lies. Seven minutes and 6 seconds later he stands outside the same hospital and lights a cigarette for Enzo the baker. In the course of those 7 minutes everything has changed in the life of Michael Corleone.

I'd like to move slowly through the hospital scene, lingering on a few specific images that provide us with visual clues to this transformation, and say a few things about the techniques Coppola employs to create what I consider to be the scene of maximum dramatic tension and suspense in the movie. It is significant that this moment of maximum drama is also the moment of transformation for the movie's main character.

Before examining the hospital scene in detail I should point out that, at one level, nothing really happens in this scene. Instead, the action is devoted to avoiding what *could* happen, or what *will happen* if Michael doesn't take firm and decisive steps to prevent it. We might say that the action in the hospital scene is internal, rather than external. The action takes places within Michael, and within us, as viewers and interpreters of this internal action. For other than brief interactions with a nurse who remains virtually faceless throughout the scene, with his speechless father lying in bed, and with the civilian baker Enzo about whom we heard but who we did not meet in the Don's office during Connie's wedding, Michael plays the scene alone.

Throughout the hospital scene there is no actual violence, though the end of the scene is punctuated by the brutal moment when Captain McKluskey, brilliantly played by Sterling Hayden,[2] breaks Michael's jaw. Coppola creates the moment of greatest suspense in the movie through suggestion and possibility, rather than through direct action. In comparison, the scenes in which Luca Brasi is garroted, Don Vito is gunned down in the street, Michael shoots Sollozo and McKluskey, Carlo beats Connie and Sonny beats Carlo, and Michael's hitmen eliminate the enemies of the Corleone family, are all more intense "action sequences," but they lack the suspense and excitement of the hospital scene created by the tension of the possible as opposed to the actual.

The hospital scene begins one hour into the movie and ends seven minutes later. This seven minute scene consists of a total of 72 cuts and shots. Walter Murch, who was a close friend of Coppola's during the shooting of *The Godfather* and worked as the editor and sound editor on several of his movies, said this about editing Coppola's *Apocalypse Now*:

> . . . at the end of it all, when the film was safely in the theaters, I sat down and figured out the total number of days that we (the editors) had worked, divided that number by the number of cuts that were in the finished product, and came up with the rate of cuts per editor per day—which turned out to be . . . 1.47! (Walter Murch, *In the Blink of an Eye*)

Granted, Murch's example from *Apocalypse Now* is offered as one extreme of the editing process; but if Murch's average did hold true for this particular scene in *The Godfather* it would mean that an experienced editor, working 8-hour days, would have needed 7 weeks to edit the hospital scene. That's a minute of film per week. Averaged over the entire movie, that would mean it would have taken 3½ years to edit the entire three-hour movie. These numbers help us appreciate that each of the 72 shots that comprise the hospital scene is part of a carefully

---

[2] Cf. John Huston's 1950 *The Asphalt Jungle*, Nicholas Ray's 1954 *Johnny Guitar*, Kubrick's 1956 *The Killing*, and Robert Altman's 1973 *The Long Goodbye* among others.

choreographed and well thought-out vision of the effects the scene is intended to achieve. Some cuts last nearly 30 seconds, others last an instant, but every one of them has been constructed to lend to the overall impact of the scene as a whole.

The scene starts with the hospital entryway: an archway framed by feeble but colorful Christmas lights offers virtually the only bright colors in the movie for the next 7 minutes. This façade may remind literary viewers of the arch under which Dante passes as he enters Hell, bearing the warning, *Abandon all hope, ye who enter here.* And for Michael this scene does represent the end of one particular kind of hope.

Of the 72 shots that comprise the hospital scene, this initial view of the archway framed by twinkling Christmas lights is the longest at 28 seconds. The scene opens with a view of this archway, allows a taxi to pull into frame and deposit Michael into the scene without cutting, and ends with Michael moving toward the building he is about to enter. The camera angle makes Michael look small in comparison to the looming, ominous archway and staircase he is about the climb. Small and virtually lost in shadow, Michael approaches the staircase. Seven minutes later, when Michael is again on the stairs, the camera angle is shifted and medium close-up shots are used so that Michael looks larger and more significant.

We linger for a full 28 seconds on this shot to build suspense, which the music in the soundtrack emphasizes, and because it is so artfully composed. The use of light, shadow, color and camera angle create an image that is both beautiful and threatening—a façade that Michael must penetrate as a first step in his own journey toward replacing his father and becoming the Godfather. This archway serves as a frame through which Michael will pass and, in the course of a few minutes, be transformed, entering into a stage of his life that his status as a "war hero" and his relationship with non-Italian Kay suggested he had escaped. His passage through this eerily lit archway into the hospital (and place of life and death) is also a passage into a life that neither he nor his father had ever wanted or expected him to take.

The first cut is to an empty hospital hallway. Throughout the hospital scene empty hallways are used to create tension and suspense. Some of these shots only last a few seconds, but they have a significant dramatic effect. (There's an interesting bit of trivia about how George Lucas helped Coppola add these empty hallway shots to the movie after the scene had been shot to build dramatic tension. This footage was found among originally discarded strips of film.)

As with the shot of the entryway, this second shot starts with a fixed view of a static landscape into which motion is introduced by means of a side entrance. In the first shot an arriving taxi; here, Michael who is now inside the hospital. The taxi's entrance is from the left of the screen; Michael's entrance balances this motion by coming from the right. These establishing shots first introduce the audience to the setting, and then allow action to move into the frame.

There is something beautiful about the nauseous hospital green of the cramped corridors through which Michael walks and through which he and the nurse maneuver the bed bearing his helpless father. The camera work is confined to these narrow passageways, which restrict our view, leaving us with the impression of the ominously unseen. This sense of the ominous is further increased by the eerie music of the soundtrack and the bizarrely repeated word "tonight" that echoes through the building, though whether as part of the external soundtrack or an inexplicable part of the ambient sounds of the hospital I can't say. (Is it a record player skipping somewhere in the nurse's lounge?) It is one of the strangest phonic devices in the entire movie. Although there is no dialogue in the movie for several minutes, these background sounds are accompanied by the ambient noises of an empty building with its eerie creeks, slams and footsteps.

When I watch movies I am particularly interested in walls and doorways. Doorways, of course, are obviously important: they are passageways for the entry and exit of characters in a scene and they are also excellent frames for action. (Perhaps most famously used by John Ford in his framing of John Wayne as Ethan throughout his 1956 *The Searchers*.) Just as the movie screen itself is a frame that allows the director to establish a specific shot for the audience's contemplation, so too are doorways frames-within-frames. They serve to further highlight a specific image or action that appears on the screen. The most famous example of this in the *Godfather*, and one of the most famous in the history of cinema, is the final image in the film, during which the door slowly closes between Kay and Michael as he is receiving the loyalty of his new mafia retainers who kiss his hand and address him for the first time as "Don Corleone." We see here most explicitly, if we did not realize it before, that the Godfather of the film's title is not the character of Vito played by Marlon Brando, but the new Godfather played by Al Pacino.

This closing door in the final scene of the movie is more than just a symbol—it is also a physical portrayal of one of the main themes of the film: the gulf between the realms of the personal and "business" that grows wider and wider over the course of the film as the old way of doing business is gradually overwhelmed by a new way which threatens the family values that underlay the criminal empire under Vito's control. Michael speaks of "my business" when talking to Kay, whereas Vito always spoke of "the family business." This is characterized in the film by the never shown but often alluded to drug business, which is the precipitating crisis in the Corleone family's fall under the old Don and rise under Michael.

Because doors are on hinges, they are not stationary frames, but swinging ones, which open (as in the scene in the hospital when Michael opens the door to his father's room) or close (as in the final scene with Michael and Kay) in order to build tension and suspense or introduce a sense of possibility or finality. One might say that the door Michael opens in the hospital, to reveal his father whom he must first help and eventually replace, finally closes in the final scene of the movie when Michael's transformation from "civilian" to "Godfather" is complete.

Once Michael enters the hospital we have a series of shots that start to build up a sense of dramatic tension; some stationary, such as the medium close-up of the half-eaten sandwich, suggesting a hasty departure, and some tracking motion, such as of Michael's increasingly rapid progress through the hallways. A realization is dawning on Michael, as it is on the audience, that all is not right here. What started out as a routine visit to the hospital has transformed into a crucial moment for Michael.

This realization is marked first by the close-up of Michael's face, in which Pacino's eyes and mouth express the initial signs of concern. This is immediately followed by a shot of Michael running. In all of these shots, the camera remains stationary, which means that characters move towards or away from it, coming in and out of focus and obscuring the camera's line of vision with parts of their bodies.

After his hurried motion through the hallways Michael slows to a walk as he approaches the fateful door to his father's room. Here we have the cautious opening of a door onto a new world which I have suggested is the compliment to the closing door between Michael and Kay at the end of the movie.

Until this point, the hospital scene has been silent except for the soundtrack and ambient noises. The first spoken lines, by a minor character in the film, are a question and a statement: "What are you doing here? You're not supposed to be here," the nurse says. Her comment is more right than she realizes. Michael is not supposed to be here. He has tried to stay free of the "family business," but the pull of family, and perhaps of business as well (the two at this point still held together by the force of Vito's leadership), is more powerful than he knew. In response to the nurse's question he must assert an identity which his military uniform during the wedding scene and his relationship with Kay, obviously strained in the scene immediately preceding the hospital scene, has tried to deny. "I am Michael Corleone," he says, as if acknowledging it for the first time. "This is my father."

As Michael and the nurse are moving Vito's bed, the soundtrack introduces the sound of Enzo's footsteps. Waiting for the person who these footsteps precede, we see the striking close-up of Michael's face, the right side obscured by another doorframe, as if to suggest the dual nature of the character who is being faced with a life-changing decision—a decision which will gradually lead to the eclipse of the "right" side of his character, as the left, "sinister" side comes forward; in literature the left is the side of "Satan and all his works" which Michael claims to denounce during the baptism scene at the end of the movie—at the very moment when it is most apparent. (Another possible nod to Dante here, who almost always turns to the left during his journey through Hell in the *Inferno*.)

This shot of the left half of Michael's face is followed by the gorgeously composed shot of an empty hospital corridor we first saw as the second shot of the scene. There is nothing unusual about this shot, which is precisely what makes it so striking. There is an exit sign, a bulletin board visible at the far end of the hallway, a fire extinguisher, a pair of benches and a hospital cart for wheeling patients. The shot is illuminated by hospital lighting that gives an eerie glow to the sickly green but immaculately clean walls and floor. (We are reminded, perhaps, of the eponymous hallway in Samuel Fuller's 1963 *Shock Corridor*.) At the end of the hall is a staircase, from which we expect, given the expectant tension on Michael's face, to see some unknown figure emerge at any moment. But the hallway remains empty. Again, nothing happens, but it is precisely this "nothing" that carries the tension and suspense of the scene.

Perhaps this shot feels so real because it is not a set, but an actual hospital. Seen with the added intensity created by this scene in the movie, it is a hospital corridor as we have never seen it before. It has become, due to the dramatic tension of the film, almost hyper-real, and we as viewers have been brought to a heightened sense of observational awareness. We are looking at the corridor of a hospital we might never bother to notice if we actually found ourselves waiting there for a doctor or a sick friend. As an object of dramatic and aesthetic contemplation the film doesn't merely ask us to look at this hallway, but educates us in the art of seeing as well, training us to become more observant and better seers of what we are watching and by extension, of the world around us.

Now the cuts come more quickly, building dramatic tension, and culminating in the shadowy figure of Enzo's back as it emerges from the staircase, his arm cocked and hand concealed as if holding a weapon. He is dressed in the long black coat and hat we've come to think of as the gangster's uniform in the movie (as opposed, for example, to the military uniform worn by Michael earlier in the film, or the tasteless civilian garb of characters like Freddo, Carlo, and Mo Green). But with the next cut we see the innocent face of Enzo, carrying not a gun, but a bouquet of flowers for the injured Don. Enzo has come to show his respect, and to express his gratitude for the Don's help in resolving his emigration problems. (He wants to stay in the U.S. and marry his boss's daughter.) And here Michael repeats the nurse's question from a minute ago, "Who are you?" It seems that the hospital scene is intent on confronting Michael with this central question of identity: who is Michael, and how will he come to realize who he really is? Enzo's offer to stay and help if there is going to be trouble, "for your father, for your father" he repeats, is the first sign of loyalty to Michael that we will see symbolized by the kissing of his hand at the end of the film. This gesture is mirrored by Michael as well, who kisses his father's hand after telling him, "I'm with you now" a minute earlier in the hospital room. Only Michael's kiss is quite different from the kisses of deferential respect he will receive at the end of film, or that which Vito received from Bonasera the undertaker at its beginning.

Michael's "I'm with you now; I'm with you" brings a tear to his father's eye, which in the context of this scene looks like a tear of paternal love for a son he thought had grown away from him. But by the end of the film, especially in light of the scene in which Vito confesses his aspirations for Michael—that he might have become a judge or a senator—may be read as a tear of sorrow that his favorite son was unable to resist the pull of the "family business" and make a new life for himself in America, just as the dreams of Bonasera the undertaker are dashed by the assault on his daughter and the impotence of the American justice system in the face of this crime. The movie opens with a reproach. Vito blames Bonasera for trying to live free of the world and influence of the Godfather. But eventually violence draws him in and Bonasera turns to Don Vito. In contrast, Vito had hoped Michael would free himself of the world of the "family business." But here too, violence draws him in. Those who use violence as a tool are not free to turn their backs on it when they wish to.[3]

One hour and seven minutes into the movie we have the beautiful shot of Enzo's face, waiting on the steps outside the hospital for Michael. Michael exits through the archway he passed under only six minutes earlier. Six minutes which, whether he knows it yet or not, have completely changed his entire life. Now the colors of the Christmas lights are complimented by the color of the flowers Enzo carries; flowers of gratitude for the Godfather's favors and protection, but also flowers which may remind us, because of the link between Enzo and Bonasera established in the first scene of the movie, of something ominous and funeral. Significantly, Michael will briskly toss them away when he comes out of the hospital to

---

[3] Violence is a kind of truth and here exercises the same kind of exigency that Wittgenstein recognized in truth when he observed, "The truth can be spoken only by someone who is already at *home* in it; not by someone who still lives in falsehood and reaches out from falsehood towards truth on just one occasion" (*Culture and Value*). Those who speak the language of violence (who are at *home* in it) cannot shut their ears to it when it calls.

prepare Enzo for the illusion of being a mafia bodyguard. Flowers have no place in this new world in which he is preparing to take up residency.

This transformation is given visible expression in the famous scene of Michael lighting Enzo's cigarette and noticing, without surprise or elation, but rather with a kind of detached observational objectivity, the steadiness of his hands. It is as if Michael is realizing, despite years of attempting to deny it to both himself and those around him, who and what he is. He is ready to answer the nurse's question, and ready too to live up the implications of that answer. His steady hands are a sign of his acceptance of this internal identity, brought forth by the crisis threatening his father's life that he is about to face and overcome.

Perhaps Enzo is framed so beautifully because he is the final image of the life Michael could have had and rejects, partially out of love for his father, and partially to fulfill a destiny he was born to and could not avoid. Earlier I referred to Enzo as a civilian. This is how other characters refer to Michael, despite the fact that he first appears in the movie in a military uniform, when they are preparing him for the meeting with Sollozo and McKluskey. But they are wrong and the uniform is right: by the end of the hospital scene, Michael is no longer a civilian, if he ever really was one in his heart. He is "with his father," and forever separated from the world of bakers and undertakers represented by the beautifully shot Enzo standing alone on the hospital steps. Enzo now represents the world that Michael can protect or exploit, do or extract "favors" for or from, but it is not the world he will occupy. Enzo is an image of the Michael who could have been.

Finally we reach the dramatic climax of the hospital scene, where Michael and Enzo stand on the stairway outside the hospital and Michael reaches into his coat for a gun that isn't there in order to scare off the hitmen who have come to kill his father. Here too we have a moment of suggestion rather than action. Michael scares off the men with his confidence—with the threat of violence rather than the act of violence.

At 1:08:45 the hospital scene ends, with the smoke from Enzo's cigarette partially obscuring Michael's face (as the right side of it was obscured by the door frame a few minutes earlier), as if to again emphasize the internal transformation with external visual cues.

In many ways *The Godfather* is a violent movie and also a movie about violence. (Which is another way of saying that it is a movie about a particular kind of truth.) But is there not another kind of violence, done to the movie itself, by the viewer who engages in the type of analysis I've been doing here? What about the hermeneutic violence performed on the film by the critic? We have lingered over details that would be almost invisible to an audience watching the movie as it was intended to be experienced, in a theatre, without the luxury of a "pause" button and the high resolution of DVD and Blu-ray technology. There is a sense in which this kind of analysis performs an act of violence on the film, tearing apart and looking in isolation at images which were intended to be seen as part of a smoothly flowing whole. But there is another sense in which this kind of artificial viewing attempts to recreate, in order to more deeply understand and appreciate, the acts of creation that gave birth to the film as a work of art in the first place.

When we recall what Walter Murch said about averaging 1.47 cuts a day while editing *Apocalypse Now*, and then think about the 72 cuts that comprise the hospital scene, we can appreciate the painstaking care and attention that goes into creating each scene in a great movie, a care and attention that both warrants and demands our own thoughtfulness and reflection at their most energetic and attentive. When we watch a movie we discover the same truth we encounter when we read a great work of literature or philosophy: there is great pleasure in the having of an idea. And it is in the service of this pleasure of ideas that we perform such acts of analysis and interpretation.

Barton Fink and the Life of the Mind (1991)

> If I had created the City of my dream, the City that is not, never was and yet manifests itself with acuteness, smells and loud sounds, if I had created *that* City, I would not only have been moving in complete freedom and with an absolute sense of belonging but also, most importantly, I would have taken the audience into an alien but secretly familiar world.
>
> —Ingmar Bergman, *The Magic Lantern*

Barton Fink presents us with an opportunity to reconsider that most magical aspect of the cinema, *mise en scène*. *Mise en scène* is nothing less than the visual world created by the filmmakers to tell us everything about the movie that is not conveyed by the dialogue, the story, the plot, the characters, and the acting. It is the physical setting of the movie, the very stuff of its visual being.

This is of central importance in any film, but in *Barton Fink* it is of particular interest because the world of the movie is such an unusual one. In most films *mise en scène* is created in the service of calling a particular world into existence. Often it is some version of the world we are already familiar with (either in our experience, our memory, or our imagination); for example, such and such a city in America in such and such a year. It may be a period piece: A suburb in the 1970s, New York of the 1920s, the Chicago of prohibition, the American West in the 1860s, Europe during WWI, or Vietnam in 1969. Sometimes it is a fantasy world that has been created expressly for the movie: a science fiction landscape, perhaps on a spaceship or another planet, or some fantasy version of our own world in the future. *Mise en scène* can be used to recreate the Wild West, the roaring 20's, World War II, an alien invasion, the Zombie Apocalypse, the town we grew up in, an all-too-familiar office building, a typical American high-school, an apartment complex, a jungle, a desert, or an urban wasteland. *Mise en scene* creates a world, whether it is the lush, visually brilliant Britain of Kubrick's *Barry Lyndon* or the rainy Los Angeles of Ridley Scott's *Blade Runner.*

Mise en scène tells us where we are. But the Coen brothers don't need *mise en scène* to tell us where we are as we enter the world of *Barton Fink* because they use a title to do it instead: "New York, 1941," even though everything about the setting would have conveyed the same information. But they're reserving *mise en scène* for something else; let's call it establishing a mood. What is this mood? What is "mood" in the movies? What else but how a movie makes us *feel.* Which, in the case of *Barton Fink*, is a very special kind of *creepy*; Poe would have called it an example of "the uncanny."

Consider just the first 10 minutes of *Barton Fink.* The movie begins with the credits appearing against a background of gold textured wallpaper. (We see later that it is the wallpaper from Barton's room at the Hotel Earle.) Wallpaper is important in the movie. It's a surface that hides another surface. The first shot after the credits takes us behind a surface, not of the wallpaper but of a stage. We're behind the scenes, listening to the over-acted, over-written, overblown lines of a "common man" in Barton's successful play:

"Dreamin' again," a woman says.
"Not anymore Lil. I'm awake now. Awake for the first time in years."

The movie's main themes are presented in the first few seconds: surfaces and what they conceal; actors and what they portray (or pretend to be); the tension between dreaming and being awake. The first shot in the movie is of something being lowered, descending on some sort of pulley. We are descending, from the very first image, going down, figuratively accompanying our characters on their descent into Hell. (Which, in a none too subtle way, is what L.A. will end up being portrayed as, with John Goodman's Charlie Meadows as a jovial, drinking Satan.)

These first few seconds also illustrate Barton's illusions about his work as an artist. Movies and the theatre are about creating illusions (not always illusions of reality), and Barton's illusions are largely "in his mind." On stage and out of sight wildly improbable lines are delivered—"I see the choir and I know they're dressed in rags, but we're part of that choir."—by a character meant to represent a "common man" (although the voice sounds strikingly like John Turturro's), while backstage a "real" common man works the ropes and pulleys that allow the fantasy to unfold. On the very line "we're part of that choir," we get our first shot of a human figure in the movie, bent over and working, completely uninterested in, unengaged with, and detached from the lines being delivered, lines that ostensibly give him, the "common man," a dramatic voice in the world.

The shot of this man walking away behind Barton is of someone who couldn't care less about the lies and fantasies of dramatic representation. A second stagehand sits nearby smoking a cigarette (beneath an eerily red-lit "NO SMOKING" sign, which is exactly the kind of sign you'd expect to see as a bad joke on your first day in Hell) and reading a newspaper, equally uninterested in Barton's paean to his fantasy version of "the common man." This is all the visual evidence we need to see that the movie wants us to think of Barton's play (and thus of Barton himself) as a pompous ruse (albeit a sincere one). A sincere ruse; that is: excellent raw material for Hollywood.

In the restaurant after the performance Barton says, "I can't kid myself about my own work. A writer writes from his gut. His gut tells him what's good." But throughout the movie Barton does nothing but kid himself about his own work. He's a bad writer who knows nothing about the people he wants to write about (ironically, since the implication is that he grew up with them in New York, and that his own background is working class). *The Herald* review of his play says that it's about people "whose brute struggle for existence cannot quite quell their desire for something higher"; but this describes not the people Barton thinks he is writing about so much as his relationship to his own writing. This relationship will unfold for the rest of the movie not in New York, but in Hollywood, a place that thrives on the tension between appearances and reality, aspiration and ambition, honesty and hypocrisy. A magical place of fantasy mixed with ruthless pragmatic business sense. (What darkness supports the light?)

At their first meeting Lipnick tells Barton, "The writer is king here at Capitol pictures. You don't believe me: take a look at your paycheck at the end of every week. That's what we think of the writer." And he's right: that is what they think of the writer. In Hollywood a writer, like anything else, is something you buy. Pay for it and it's yours.

But Hollywood is not simply a false mistress who erects a tempting but false exterior over a corrupt interior. Instead, She turns out to be the harsh mistress capable of telling Barton the hard truths he has tried to hide from. Ironically, Hollywood is the most honest character in the whole movie; the character so expert at disguise that She not only sees through everyone else's disguises, but forces the other characters to face and acknowledge them as well. And virtually every character in *Barton Fink* is pretending to be someone or something he or she is not. Charlie is not "really" an insurance salesman, Lipnick is not a colonel in the U.S. army, Mayhew is not a great writer, Audrey is "not just Bill's secretary"—and who, or what, the hell is Steve Buscemi's "CHET!"? Some minor demon in this infernal landscape? All of which leads us to wonder: just what is it that Barton appears to be but isn't? A writer? An artist? Someone interested in "the common man"?

Hollywood is a wonderful paradox: no place is more devoted to creating magic, but no place is more merciless in reducing it to a commodity that can be bought and sold. Hollywood is also the land where appearances are what is real. Obscuring the dividing line between truth and fiction, fantasy and reality, is the business of Hollywood. It's a place where dreams (or nightmares) come true, which means that the person who is the most duplicitous is, paradoxically, the most honest. (Lipnick tells Barton, "If I had been totally honest, I wouldn't be within a mile of this pool unless I was cleaning it.") Where does that leave Barton? Is he a real writer trying to pander his talent to the Hollywood beast? Or is he a hack who has to come to Hollywood to discover the truth about himself? What is truth in the movie? In the movies? In Hollywood? For any of us ever? What more do we want from a work of art than an opportunity to confront such puzzles concerning truth and fiction?

From the moment we cut from the final scene in New York to the opening scene in Los Angeles, we accompany Barton into a new world, a world that has never existed outside the imaginations of the filmmakers. This is where *mise en scène* comes in. Superficially, it looks like Hollywood in the 1940s, but in fact the Coen brothers have created a vision of Hollywood all their own, where nothing is as it appears to be, reality and fantasy are hopelessly confused, and truth and fiction are so entwined as to be virtually indistinguishable. The Hotel Earle, with its pealing wallpaper that seems to reveal something like flesh underneath and that appears to ooze or bleed when Barton presses on it (penetrating this "skin" with the thumbtacks provided by "Chet!" seems to provoke the sexual noises Barton hears through the wall) is a visceral embodiment of this vision of Hollywood.

Meta-portrayals of Hollywood as a city dedicated to ruthlessly profiting from creations of the human imagination are common. Hollywood—as we know from movies like Von Sternberg's 1928 *The Last Command*, Harry Lachman's *It Happened in Hollywood* (with an early writer's credit for Samuel Fuller), Preston Sturges' *Sullivan's Travels*, Billy Wilder's *Sunset Blvd.*, Curtis Hanson's *L.A. Confidential*, Robert Altman's *The Player*, David Lynch's *Mulholland Drive* and (perhaps culminating with) Thom Anderson's 2003 *Los Angeles Plays Itself*—is the place where fantasy and reality enter into the most bizarre of congresses. Nowhere else in America is the harsh reality of cutthroat business so seamlessly combined with the romantic luster of our dreams and fantasies. Hollywood is where people go to make their dreams come true, or, as in Barton's case, to encounter their nightmares.

Barton does not so much enter the Hotel Earle as magically materialize in its lobby as a result of a gradual but stunning fade that, at 7 minutes and 44 seconds, for a split instant creates the image of Barton standing before a surging body of water that has flooded the hotel floor. It appears as if he has split the rock and emerged out of it to stand, suitcase and typewriter in hand, on the shores of a new land. As the water recedes, Barton begins to move forward through the hotel lobby. This is one of the most beautiful shots in the film. Barton, backlit from the doors behind him, moves through a strangely empty (despite the many chairs) lobby of dusky browns and pinks that have a flesh-like character. This impression of the hotel lobby as something living is emphasized by the plants that give it a jungle-like feel. At first Barton is merely a silhouette moving through this strange new landscape.

The next cut lets us know we're not to be confined to the point of view of characters in the movie. We are above and behind Barton, but too far above for this to be the POV of a human observer, and as the camera pulls back we rise even higher to take in the lobby's chandeliers. The light has changed and we can see the chairs and the plants more clearly. The colors stand out more brightly and Barton himself appears in more detail. The pattern of the carpet resembles the pattern of the gold wallpaper against which the credits appeared at the beginning of the movie.

A few more things to notice about the Hotel Earle:

—the symbolism throughout the film not so subtly suggests that the Hotel Earle (like L.A. itself) is a kind of Hell ("Earle" and "Hell" are end rhymes)
—not just the fact that Chet emerges from below the floor (obvious symbolism), but the mottled color and texture of the trap door from which he emerges (carrying a shoe?)
—the overhead camera angle of the spinning hotel register Barton signs (a bird's, or God's, or Devil's, eye view?)
—the stains on the walls on either side of the elevator (the camera pans down though the motion should be up as the elevator rises/descends to floor 6)
—the impossibly long corridor Barton walks down to arrive at his room.
—the hotel's slogan, "A day or a lifetime" (ominous overtones)
—the broken pencil tip (more obvious symbolism for a sexually lonely and creatively sterile/impotent writer)
—the long row of shoes outside the doors of what otherwise appear to be unoccupied rooms in an empty hotel (except for Barton, Charlie, and the noisy lovers). (In *No Exit* Sartre wrote, "Hell is other people," but for Barton Hell may simply be himself and his solitude, cf. Pascal's "modern man's unhappiness stems from his inability to sit quietly in an empty room alone.")
—the (according to Geisler, impossible) mosquito as bloodsucker; L.A. as the natural habitat of vampires (cf. Joss Whedon's brilliant *Buffy* and *Angel* series)

In this movie, everything means something, which is as bad as saying that nothing means anything. That's the problem with symbolism, or rather its potential for fun in the hands of wry, dark comedians like Joel and Ethan Coen.

These early scenes establish the Hotel Earle as more than just a setting in the movie. It becomes one of the characters, living and breathing, sweating and groaning; it acts and interacts with the other characters in the film—the hotel, like Goodman's Charlie, is a living embodiment of Hollywood itself. (And Barton's room is the creepiest room in the movies since *The Shining's* Room 237 and Henry Spencer's room in *Eraserhead*, whose hairdo Barton's seems indebted to as well.)

At least this is one side of Hollywood. It would be pointless to try and identify which of the various settings (the Hotel Earle, Lipnick's office, the restaurant where Barton eats with Geisler, poolside at Lipnick's home, the beach at the end of the film) is the "real" Hollywood, for that is precisely what Hollywood is in the movie: the absence of a single unchanging truth. Hollywood is all surface. Peel back the surface, as the Hotel Earle peels away is epidermal wallpaper, and what is beneath is not the truth, but just a sticky mess, waiting to be covered by an appearance which will stand in for the truth. (It's a bit like the facelift scenes in Terry Gilliam's *Brazil*.) And what is a movie that is surface all the way down "really" about, if not the very question of what it means for a movie to be "about" something in the first place?

I'd like to add a few thoughts about what Charlie and Lipnick have to do with all this, and with Barton's nagging question about "the life of the mind."[4] Charlie and Lipnick

---

[4] Charlie tells Barton that he's in the business of selling peace of mind. In response, Barton speaks self-absorbedly of what he calls "the life of the mind." ("I got to tell you, the life of the mind, there's no

are doppelgangers, both for each other and for Hollywood. They do not "represent" or "symbolize" Hollywood; they embody it. They are large, dominating bodies. Bodies that embody, in different ways, what Barton calls "the life of the mind."

Think of Charlie and Lipnick as different aspects of the "entertainment" industry: Lipnick, in his Janus-like alternations between submission (licking Barton's shoe) and domination (firing and debasing Lou Breeze); Charlie in his peculiar relationship to make-believe and his own Janus-like embodiment of comedy and tragedy; the laughter-sobbing Barton hears through the wall (permeability of surfaces) representing both Thalia and Melpomene, the muses of comedy and tragedy respectively; and the friendly "guy next door" façade masking the "serial killer" interior. These ambiguities (submission / domination, laughter / sobbing, comedy / tragedy) find their way into the movie itself. Is *Barton Fink* a comedy, a horror movie, or a tragedy? Yes.

Lipnick tells Barton the only thing that matters is, "can you tell a story?" and Charlie repeatedly offers, "I could tell you stories," but Barton can't put these two sides of Hollywood together. He's so caught up in the idea of his "work" as an expression of "the life of the mind" that he can neither tell nor hear stories. He is both deaf and mute (more impotency) to the only thing Hollywood cares about: other people's stories. He's too busy trying to figure out his own.

---

roadmap for that territory.") At one point Lou tells Barton, "Right now, the contents of your head are the property of Capitol Pictures." After seeing Audrey's body, Charlie tells Barton, "We gotta keep our heads." Audrey of course doesn't get to keep hers, but Barton does.

When explaining his ear infection, Charlie says, "Can't trade my head in for a new one," and Barton agrees, adding "I guess you're stuck with the one you got." But later in the film the cotton in Charlie's ear reappears in Barton's (also symbolizing his deafness) and Charlie will literally give Barton a head, as if to suggest that, when it comes to the life of the mind, it's always possible to get a new one. And it seems to work, since it is after Charlie gives Barton Audrey's head in a box that his writer's block disappears and he begins to write (just as Audrey helped Bill Mayhew with his own writer's block). The results, however, only reveal the kind of writer Barton "really" is.

The Devil is the King of Lies, but he often appears to confront us with truths about ourselves we'd rather not admit. If he's able to tempt us, it's because the potential to fall is within us all the time. Why else would we be willing to accept the otherwise outrageous doctrine of original sin? "Look upon me, I'll show you the life of the mind," Charlie shouts as he rampages down the hallway. But he's talking to Barton, (or to us), not to the cops (one of whom is already dead). What is it Charlie wants to show us?

Is the movie an imaginary voyage (like Dante's) into a literary Hell? What is the "life of the mind" if not the life we lead in our imaginations, a life fueled by the products of Hollywood, which feed our imaginations? Though whether these products nourish that imagination or enervate it may depend on what it is we're digesting (or how carefully we chew). The life of the mind is about death and violence and man's journey into the depths of Hell. Barton doesn't seem to realize (yet) that there's no "common man" who doesn't carry his own Hell around with him. No vision of Hell that isn't derived from the dark imagination of the poet that dwells in each of us.

Charlie calls Barton, whose aspiration is to turn the suffering of the common man into art, a "tourist with a typewriter," but when Barton leaves the burning hotel he carries with him his script and the box, not the typewriter he arrived with. The box has replaced the typewriter. What's in it (besides Audrey's head)?

Charlie: "It's just a lot of personal stuff, but I don't want to drag it with me, and I'd like to think it's in good hands. Funny huh, when everything that's important to a guy, everything he wants to keep from a lifetime, and he can fit it into a little box like that."
Barton: "It's more than I've got."

Charlie tells him it will help him finish his script, but overcoming his writer's block is not the same as being able to write well (since what he writes appears to be the worst kind of self-plagiarism: a repetition of something that was a cliché to begin with). After gaining from his encounter with the police a pretty good idea of what's in the box, he holds it up to his own head, as if trying it on for size. Earlier he told Charlie, "My job is to plumb the depths," and he says to Mayhew, "writing comes from a great inner pain." (In response Bill speaks of wanting to rip his head off; a desire Charlie will help him accomplish later in the film). But by the end of the film Barton seems to have learned that even "great inner pain" isn't enough to make him a good writer. It just makes him a human being. Earlier he had asked Audrey, "What don't I understand?" Perhaps this is it.

At the end of the film Barton has been sentenced (damned?) by Lipnick: "You're under contract, you're gonna stay that way. Anything you write is gonna be the property of Capitol pictures and Capitol pictures is not going to produce anything you write. Not until you grow up a little." (Lipnick, with his contract, is another Devil in the movie, playing the buffoonish Mephistopheles to Barton's Faust, who indeed seems to be fighting ("wrestling") for his very soul, if only to discover whether or not he has one.)

Barton's writing has been reduced to "property." So much for the life of the mind. Like Charlie, he has to get into the business of selling "peace of mind"—Lipnick tells him, "they [the audience] don't want to see a guy wrestling with his soul" (it's not *that* kind of "wresting movie"[5]). Where does that leave him, or us, at the end of the film? Are we finally damned, or only left with a more honest sense of the real challenges (obstacles, temptations, and hazards) that stand between us and the "life of the mind"?

When Barton meets the girl from the painting above the desk in his room he asks her, "Are you in pictures?" She says, "Don't be silly." But she is a picture. She asks him, "What's in the box?" and he says, "I don't know." "Isn't it yours?" she asks, and again he says, "I don't know." What doesn't he know? The movie ends as it began, the same music playing as the credits roll against the wallpaper from Barton's room at the Hotel Earle. Is Barton's "I don't know" a note of agnostic despair, or the first faint rays of dawning awareness? Where does he go from here? The last shot of him is from behind, looking at the girl, staring out at the ocean, the box in the sand beside him. What happens next? I don't know, but no doubt someone could

---

[5] Notably, Akira Kurosawa wrote a wrestling movie before launching his career as a director, and his directorial debut was with a movie about a Judo fighter.

tell a story about it.

The Lineaments of Gratified Desire:
Reading Emil Jannings

Having celebrated their first century of existence only in the last few decades, one might think that the movies would be the one art form that wouldn't have to wrestle with that vexed question, "What is a classic?" But they're not.

There are movie fans interested in nothing so much as when the latest installment of *The Fast and the Furious* franchise is going to hit the local Megaplex, and there are cinephiles so versed in the abstruse details of the art and history of cinema that they can recite the complete filmography of Louise Brooks, tell you every movie on Jack Fisk ever served as Artistic Director, and lecture you on Samuel Fuller's influence on the camera work of Jean-Luc Godard.

Where does that leave the rest of us? Those of us who care about movies and would like to know more, experience more, and wonder more—without losing the joy and pleasure we associate with and experience when watching great movies—may well ask what role critical film writing can play in our movie-watching. If you do not disdain a good James Bond flick, but also thrill at the near-forgotten artistry of Chaplin, Welles, or Hitchcock, and if you believe as a general aesthetic principle that with greater understanding comes greater enjoyment and that the more you see the richer your experience (not just of movies, but of the world), then opportunities to see better are valued accordingly.

"Learning" is not a dirty word for people who still think becoming better at something, even something like "going to the movies," brings with it an array of rewards and is therefore worth working for. One either believes that pleasure comes in higher and lower degrees or one doesn't. For those who do, the idea that education can lead to higher pleasures is a maxim. Those who don't can safely be left to their own devices. Those who do are justified in asking, "How do we go about learning to see better?" The movies are one of our best teachers in this regard, if we are willing to learn not only about, but *from* our encounters with them.

The challenge is a simple one, to understand if not to accomplish: how can our encounters with media art and entertainment—with movies, television shows and video—increase our sensitivity and receptiveness to the world around us? How can these encounters encourage our intelligence and imagination rather than deaden them? How can we respond to these mediums so that they enrich our lives rather than replace them?

On the question of learning: if I were to recommend only five books to someone interested in learning to prepare for his or her encounter with the movies and in the interests of trying to "see better" what they were watching ("seeing" being in this context an active verb, "watching" a relatively passive one), I would start with: Robert Bresson's *Notes on the Cinematographer*; Andrei Tarkovsky's *Sculpting in Time*; Jean Renoir's *My Life and My Films*; Bela Balazs's *Theory of the Film*;[6] and the *Essays* of Michel de Montaigne.

---

[6] What does it say about the seriousness with which we take movies as an art form, even in the 21st century, that in 2015 (the 100th anniversary of Griffith's *The Birth of a Nation*) two of these four titles

This last work is not technically a work on cinema, but it is a work of such pleasure, observation, insight, questioning, and thoughtfulness that a careful study of its pages is guaranteed to enrich any viewer's encounter with the movies.

In his longest essay, Montaigne asks:

> What of the hands? We beg, promise, call, dismiss, threaten, pray, entreat, deny, refuse, question, admire, count, confess, repent, fear, blush, doubt, instruct, command, incite, encourage, swear, testify, accuse, condemn, absolve, insult, despise, defy, vex, flatter, applaud, bless, humiliate, mock, reconcile, commend, exalt, entertain, rejoice, complain, grieve, mope, despair, wonder, exclaim, are silent, and what not, with a variation and multiplication that vie with the tongue. With the head: we invite, send away, avow, disavow, give the lie, welcome, honor, venerate, disdain, demand, show out, cheer, lament, caress, scold, submit, brave, exhort, menace, assure, inquire. What of the eyebrows? What of the shoulders? ("Apology for Raymond Sebond")

What of the hands? Montaigne knew, some 320 years before James Williamson's radical one-minute eight-second film *The Big Swallow*, how incredibly expressive the human physiognomy can be. This is a truth, hardly a

---

are currently out of print?

secret, that silent films were built on. One of the last shots of Josef von Sternberg's *The Blue Angel* is a close-up of Professor Rath's hand clutching the edge of the desk where he used to teach in a final death grip. All the pain of his life, and his death, are captured in the image of that hand. In F. W. Murnau's *The Last Laugh*, when the doorman has stolen his old uniform and slinks in shame through the neighborhood where he once strutted with pride, he seems to have shrunk, and the uniform dwarves his, the sleeves hanging down so his hands are no longer visible. As Balazs observes in the above-mentioned book,

> The close-up has not only widened our vision of life, it has also deepened it. In the days of the silent film it not only revealed new things, but showed us the meaning of the old. . . . a good film with its close-ups reveals the most hidden parts in our polyphonous life, and teaches us to see the intricate visual details of life... ("The Close Up")

A good film "teaches us to see." Among the stars of the silent cinema, one of the masters of the close-up as described by Balazs was Emil Jannings, who plays the Professor and the Doorman in the above-mentioned movies. It says a lot about the current status of the silent cinema—one of the greatest cinematic art forms even to this day—that it is no longer surprising to hear even someone who "loves movies" ask: who is (or was) Emil Jannings? (Will we some day ask, "Who was Charlie Chapin, Harold Lloyd, or Buster Keaton?") The fact that this has become a perfectly reasonable question to ask is significant in itself. Of course there are still those among us for whom the asking of this question is a sure sign that the barbarians and philistines have joined hands and are dancing at the graveside of culture. But for the rest of us (raised in an age when John Wayne already seemed stiff and outdated in comparison to Clint Eastwood, Sylvester Stallone, Arnold Schwarzenegger, and Bruce Willis, and even the status of Steve McQueen and Lee Marvin is up for grabs) it's a perfectly legitimate question and deserves an answer.

If you already know who Emil Jannings is, chances are you're either a movie buff or a "cinephile" or you had some sort of Introduction to Film or Film History class at college or university. If you don't know, then you're probably a perfectly average 21st century moviegoer, who's been grouped in with the barbarians and philistines by those who do know and who seem to enjoy lamenting the fact that, even in the movies, the "classics" just don't get the respect they deserve. Well, why not?

By way of thinking about this question I will make an assertion about a handful of Emil Jannings movies that are readily available for anyone who cares to see them: they are a true pleasure to watch. Not because they are "classics" or because they are "seminal works in the history of cinema" or "important artifacts of our cinematic culture," but because they are as powerful, provocative, and delightful to watch today as they were almost 100 years ago. It's a pleasure we may have lost track of along the way, may have forgotten we ever enjoyed; but it's not a pleasure we've forgotten *how* to enjoy, if circumstances conspire to give us a chance.

Let's consider the question from this perspective: How will contemporary viewers trained up in notions of comedy by movies like Ben Stiller's 2001 *Zoolander* or

Adam McKay's 2006 *Talladega Nights* starring Will Ferrell (which are funny movies) respond to movies like Harold Lloyd's 1923 *Safety Last!*, Chaplin's 1925 *Gold Rush*, or Buster Keaton's 1926 *The General*? Will they even have a chance to find out? To decide for themselves? Or is the choice made for them by obscure cultural forces that influence or even determine the movies we watch? How do we make these choices for ourselves, as opposed to allowing them to be made for us? How do we free ourselves from the closing off of certain possibilities when it comes to the range of our viewing options (and our experiences more broadly)? And how do we expand our options, not out of a sense of intellectual responsibility or aesthetic duty, but in order to expand the horizons of our artistic pleasure—to experience things that the passage of time, the accumulation of cultural prejudices, and the overwhelming demands on our energy and attention, threaten to overwhelm and obscure?

For many of us great movies have been placed beyond our reach not because the are censored, forbidden, or no longer fun and interesting, but simply because they have been covered over by decades of cultural accumulation that have obscured their brilliance from eyes that have never been given a chance to see and judge for themselves. Who chooses—and why—to watch a movie from 1924 in the 21st century? If we are encouraged to do so, if we are told that we "really should" watch such a movie, what kind of a "should" is this? An aesthetic imperative? A cultural or historical one? An intellectual "should"? We watch movies for pleasure, but this notion of pleasure is a potentially rich and complicated one— and who knows what forms of pleasure we may be capable of but have never been given a chance to cultivate and develop?[7] If I assert, "You (and who is this "you"?) should watch F. W. Murnau's 1924 *The Last Laugh*." It is fair to ask, "Why?" And it's a question that deserves an answer, not a dismissive shrug implying the disdain of cultural superiority.

Let's start with the fact that it's a great movie, for lots of reasons. The face of Emil Jannings is one of those reasons. Or rather, the face of Emil Jannings is a whole range of these reasons, each time we see it (which, given his status as the most famous actor of his time, is quite often in this and in the other films mentioned below).

The range of this face itself is not enormous. In each movie the camera tracks a similar trajectory, from vain and proud to fallen. It doesn't matter if the fall is from a simple doorman, an exalted general, or a tyrannical schoolteacher. Taken together, the three movies discussed below suggest that all human beings are essentially the same in this regard. The doorman who becomes a bathroom attendant in *The Last Laugh* suffers as much as the Grand Duke who becomes first a victim of the Russian revolution and then a Hollywood extra in *The Last Command*, or the high-school professor who becomes a scorned husband and a drunk in *The Blue Angel* (under the watchful and sometimes scornful eye of Marlene Dietrich's stunning Lola-Lola). They all suffer, simply because they're human. And Jannings' face, in each of these instances, traces the history of this suffering.

---

[7] If we live in a world of hedonism, we must speak the vocabulary of hedonism, whatever our opinion of the virtues of such a worldview. Therefore when we speak of the cinema, we must do so in terms of the pleasures of the cinema. This is the only vocabulary the world today is likely to understand or respond to.

Outside of a handful of film students, scholars, and *appassionatos,* who still remembers or watches with pleasure the first actor to receive an Academy Award for Best Actor (at the very first Academy Awards ceremony in 1929)? According to the story, Jannings received the award even though he only received the second highest number of votes, because the highest number of votes went to a dog—Rin Tin Tin. Apparently the individual members of the academy were capable of greater audacity of opinion than the institution itself. Be that as it may, the pleasure of watching Jannings in his great movies is not a historic pleasure, nor "merely" an intellectual or cultural one—it is the true pleasure of the cinema: the pleasure of image, story, and character, of light and shadow, of motion and the nuance of human face and figure. Jannings is a remarkable actor, not for the era of the silent movies, not for the 1920s, but as timelessly as any great artist working in any field at any period of time or place on the globe.[8]

How many people who still read (with pleasure) Shakespeare, listen to (and enjoy) Beethoven, and feel a spiritual stirring (despite themselves?) when contemplating Giotto's *Ognissanti Madonna* or Bernini's *Escstasy of St. Theresa* will give themselves the opportunity to see Jannings in Murnau's 1924 *The Last Laugh,* Josef von Sternberg's 1928 *The Last Command,* or

---

[8] Although, according to von Sternberg's autobiographical *Fun in a Chinese Laundry,* Jannings was a tyrant (von Sternberg's reputation among actors, producers and other directors being quite similar) and a manipulative, egomaniacal bore. Jannings collusion with the Third Reich on pro-Nazi propaganda films in the 1930s and 40s raises its own set of (extra-aesthetic) concerns, and there is something darker than irony in the coincidence that the recipient of the first Oscar for Best Actor in 1929 also received the title "Artist of the State" from Joseph Goebbels in 1941.

his 1931 *The Blue Angel*, which not only featured Jannings in an early speaking role but introduced the world to Marlene Dietrich?

In 1929 Louis Armstrong recorded (with Bessie Smith) "St. Louis Blues" for OKeh records and in 1931 Virginia Woolf published her masterpiece *The Waves*. There is no mistaken opinion that these works have been "improved on" by John Coltrane or Anthony Braxton, Thomas Pynchon or David Foster Wallace, or that progress in jazz or literature has effaced the greatness of the works of the past. These are hallmarks of great art that people listen to and read today with the same surprise and delight they experienced when these works were first released. Why do far fewer people still watch the hallmarks of cinema made during these same years? Why does a different sense of "progress" tend to dominate and obscure the art of filmmaking?

Why otherwise aesthetically curious and culturally engaged people will pass over the rewards of silent film but grit their teeth through boring operas, or submit to forced marches through crowded museums for their 30 seconds before the works of the Great Masters are cultural mysteries I'll pass over here. But I would like to offer a few arguments in favor of taking the time to watch (and to see) the masterpieces of the cinema that are every bit as wonderful today as they were some 100 years ago (hardly a long time, in aesthetic terms).

Let's leave aside the kind of analysis that looks at Murnau's *The Last Laugh* from the angle of Marxist alienation, Freudian repression, or the manipulations of capitalist ideology and the symbolism of the military-industrial complex tied up in the old man's attachment to his uniform (a symbolism picked up and further exploited in von Sternberg's *The Last Command* four years later). Let's refrain from analyzing the attitude of the hotel manager, the niece, the neighbors, or the night watchman. Let's confine ourselves to a simple consideration of Emil Jannings' face.

What Montaigne knew three centuries ago is that the entire world is an occasion for reading. A glance at the table of contents of the 107 essays that comprise his 20+ year writing project shows that few things fell outside the scope of his roving eye and insatiable mind: smells, books, cannibals, impotency, cowardice, sleep, coaches, thumbs, cruelty, education ... the list goes on. Montaigne also knew that we can become better readers of the world through practice and effort. And what else were his own *essais* (attempts) than the record of such an effort? By dint of effort and attention we can increase our powers of observation and our sensitivity to nuance and ambiguity. And what is true of books is true of the world. And of movies. And of the many parts from which movies are made. We can read a camera angle. We can read the use of light and shadow. We can read a soundtrack or the use of ambient sounds used in conjunction with images. We can read an actor's face, his posture, and what we call "the language of the body" which is spoken, as with any language, more eloquently by some than by others. We can read, and learn to read, and read better through practice and effort. If we're attentive, the movies teach us how to read them, just as Montaigne tried to teach us how to read the world around us.

Balazs observes much the same thing when it comes to the close-up: "we see emotions, moods, intentions and thoughts, things which although our eyes can see them, are not in space," and "in the isolated close-up of the film we can see to the bottom of a soul by means of such tiny movements of facial muscles."

The bottom of a soul. Murnau's *The Last Laugh* was a miracle of technical innovation, special effects, and camera work for its time. Effects achieved with great effort and ingenuity in 1924 are easily replicated and exceeded by advances in technology today. But there is one tool the film relies on which seems to have become less, rather than more refined in the past 90 years: the human face.

How do we read a face? Can we in fact see "to the bottom of a soul" when watching the subtle motions of Jannings' face as it changes from vanity to despair and from love to anguish?

Can we see beyond the limits of time and space, into the soul itself? Can a movie show us that, for those of us with eyes to see?

Balazs writes, "Not only psychological subtleties or moving emotions can be shown in such close-ups, but greater things too, all the pathos of human greatness..." Jannings, at key moments in each of these three films, shows us this pathos, and this greatness. He is the anguished and despairing clown, the defeated general, the forsaken employee. He is the betrayed lover and the man left behind by history, hope, and life. We see all of this on his face, in each of these movies, more eloquently than any words could ever say it. We feel, at times, that we are looking at the facial equivalent of Kurtz's announcement of "the horror" at the end of Conrad's *Heart of Darkness*.

Of course Jannings doesn't act with his face alone. If he does not speak with words, his entire body is called on to speak for him. But he never really *does* anything in the way we've grown accustomed to seeing bodies act in movies today. He doesn't drive a car or ride a horse; he doesn't shoot a gun with preternatural accuracy, engage in carefully choreographed fistfights or leap through windows or off tall buildings. In *The Last Command* the most expressive thing he *does* by far is smoke his cigarettes. But in all of these movies primarily what he does is stand still, with such a sense of tremendous energy or defeat that when he does start to move it is only as a greater articulation of this state of being his mere standing was able to convey.[9] When he strides through the environs of his tenement building in *The Last Laugh* in his doorman's uniform, or lurks in the shadows after he has lost his job, his motion is the very distillation of the essence of "striding" or "lurking." His entire body creates the impression and speaks to us with far greater clarity than words ever do.

When we watch great examples from the era of silent movies (Chaplin, Lloyd, Jannings, Garbo, Lillian Gish, Louise Brooks, Evelyn Brent, George Bancroft, Gloria Swanson[10]) we see how much of spoken dialogue in

---

[9] Balazs described the "microphysiognomics" of the human face, expressive in its motion of the subtle changes *between* expressions by the tensing of a muscle, the twitch of an eyelid or the clenching of a jaw. To freeze an expression is, to a certain extent, to kill it, to read the line but not the subtleties between the lines. As Balazs writes, "In the early days of the silent film 'microphysiognomics' had already shown that one can read more in a close-up of a face than what is visibly written on it. On a face, too, one can read 'between the lines'."

[10] Who says, in her role as Norma Desmond in Billy Wilder's *Sunset Boulevard*, about this period, "we didn't need dialogue, we had faces." She may be crazy, but that doesn't mean she's wrong.

typical movies today is unnecessary and even detrimental to the effect the actors (or directors) are trying to create. So much can be said by standing still, by walking, by the power of the human face—so much that we're in danger of growing blind or deaf to in the face of the overwhelming speech and activity to which we're subjected by most (certainly not all) movies today.

Seeing the human body and the human face—witnessing the poetry of its movement and expressions—is a great pleasure of the silent film. It is not a duty. Not an intellectual exercise or a kind of cultural "homework"—it is an aesthetic pleasure of the highest order; a pleasure we should not be deprived of because we're tempted to overlook silent films as "old" or "boring" or "out-of-date" when compared to the miracles of modern technical production. The power, the truth, and the beauty of these works from a century ago are just as vivid today. One only needs eyes to see. Eyes, I might add, that these movies are quick to restore to us. We need go nowhere else for a better education in seeing than to the movies themselves.

Watching Jannings in these movies is a lesson in learning how to see the human face and body, because Jannings can show them to us with the skills of an actor trained up in the world of silent films. His face possesses a genius of expression that the introduction of dialogue to movies threatened to eclipse. But by revisiting these early classics we can see again a power of expression that has much to teach us about our own powers of observation.

What Jannings' movies show us is still as beautiful, powerful, and moving a century later. Just look at them and you will see. Learn how to read them and you will see even more.

This is one means of making our way back to the question, "What is a classic?" A work immune to the threat of progress. One that cannot be improved upon simply as a result of the passage of time or because of technological developments. Or, as Ezra Pound said, "News that stays news." Ninety years later, *The Last Laugh* is still news.

Why Don't I Want to Be Like Victor Laszlo? Some Questions about *Casablanca* (1942)

> We must close our eyes and invoke a new manner of seeing, a wakefulness that is the birthright of us all, though few put it to use. ... Do you see yourself in this state? Then you have become vision itself.
>
> –Plotinus, "Beauty" *Enneads*

> De gustibus non est disputandum est—that is, there is no disputing against Hobby-Horses; and for my part, I seldom do.
>
> –Laurence Sterne, *Tristam Shandy*

Some dates and numbers:

Between 1912 (3 years before D. W. Griffith's *The Birth of a Nation*) and 1961[11] Michael Curtiz made over 150 movies in Europe and America. It is one of the longest, richest careers in movie history (compare it with the 139 films made by John Ford between 1917 and 1966 or Hitchcock's 53 films made between 1925 and 1976), but one largely unremembered by contemporary audiences outside of his 1942 work on *Casablanca* (and, to a lesser, though no less deserved, extent, for his work with Joan Crawford in *Mildred Pierce* three years later). Curtiz is rarely listed alongside Ford, Hitchcock, Kurosawa, Ozu, Melville, et. al. as one of cinema's "great auteurs."

---

[11] The year of Resnais' *Last Year at Marienbad*, Kurosawa's *Throne of Blood*, Ozu's *The End of Summer*, Rivette's *Paris Belongs to Us*, Melville's *Lèon Morin, Prêtre*, and Buñuel's *Viridiana*.

When Ingrid Bergman starred in *Casablanca* in 1942, her work in *Gaslight* with George Cukor (1944), with Hitchcock in *Spellbound, Notorious,* and *Under Capricorn,* (1945-49) with Rossellini[12] in *Stromboli, Europa '51, Viaggio in Italia, Giovanna d'Arco al rogo,* and *La Paura* (1949-55), with Renoir in *Elena and her Men* (1956), and with Ingmar Bergman in *Autumn Sonata,* her final film (1978), all lay before her. Yet at 27, Bergman would seem "old" compared with the 19-year-old Lauren Bacall who starred with Bogart in her first film two years later: Howard Hawks' pseudo-*Casablanca* (not so much a remake as a charming rip-off), *To Have and Have Not.*[13]

Bogart's status as a "star" began one year before

---

[12] How often do we recall Bergman not only as the famous actress, but also as the mother of Isabella Rossellini? When you see *Casablanca* it is startling how similar the two women look, especially when you see Rossellini in David Lynch's *Blue Velvet.*

[13] *It's still the same old story, a fight for love and glory...* If you swap out Morocco for Martinique, Bergman for Bacall ("Kid" becomes "Slim"), and a bar owner for a ship's captain, you basically have the same movie, less canonical, but somehow even more appealing in an innocent sort of way. (Maybe it's Bacall's throaty singing.) There's the two piano players (Sam becomes Cricket (played by Hoagy Carmichael), the two fat Vichy cops (both played by Dan Seymour), the two married couples Bogart has to risk his neck to save, and even another appearance by Marcel Dalio. One significant difference between the two movies is Walter Brennan's role in *To Have and Have Not.* Brennan is one of only three men to win three acting Oscars, along with Jack Nicholson and Daniel Day-Lewis. Brennan, like Nicholson (despite compellin roles in *Easy Rider, Five Easy Pieces, Chinatown,* and *The Shining*), seems to have received the award for expertly playing the same role (himself?) over and over again. Daniel Day-Lewis, from playing a fascist homosexual in Stephen Frears 1985 *My Beautiful Laundrette* to Abraham Lincoln in Steven Spielberg's 2012 *Lincoln,* is perhaps the artist with the greatest range of any actor in the history of cinema.

Casablanca (though never before in a romantic lead) thanks to his work in Raoul Walsh's *High Sierra* and John Huston's *The Maltese Falcon*. (Huston also co-wrote *High Sierra* and was one of Bogart's drinking buddies). Bogart was 43 to Bergman's 27. He may be the male actor most responsible for the growing distinction, in Hollywood, between a "star" and a great actor. I'm never really sure whether there's much to admire in Bogart's acting, though there's no question about the charismatic power he manages to emanate from the screen to the viewer's imagination. Few actors have the screen-presence or power of Bogart. It's like watching a cliché come to life, a cliché we feel we're in the presence of as it is visually created. (Though from Paul Muni to George Bancroft, there were plenty of jaw-clenching tough guys famous for their repressed vulnerability before Bogart came along.) If that's good acting, he's got it in Spades. If it's something else, then there may be something we want from movie actors that's more (or less) than just acting.

In any event, Bogart on the screen, whether with Bergman, Bacall (not only in *To Have and Have Not*, but also in Hawks' marvelous 1946 *The Big Sleep*, Delmer Daves' 1947 *Dark Passage*, and Huston's 1948 *Key Largo*), or Katherine Hepburn (in Huston's 1951 *The African Queen*), has a power that inspires the viewer's imagination (as is perhaps best expressed by the adulation of Jean-Paul Belmondo's character Michel in Godard's 1960 *À Bout de souffle*). In 2003 the AFI listed Rick Blaine as the fourth most popular movie hero of the past 100 years (after Atticus Finch, Indiana Jones and Sean Connery's James Bond).[14]

---

[14] By way of contrast, in the same poll Anthony Hopkin's Hannibal Lecter topped the list of greatest movie villains, followed by Norman Bates and Darth Vader.

None of which tells us anything about what we might find perplexing (or troubling, or fascinating) about *Casablanca*, or why it might not be obvious that there's anything perplexing to find there in the first place.

Saying you don't like *Casablanca* is like saying you don't like The Beatles; it might be true (and there may be good reasons why it's true), but people you confess your dislike to will often look at you as if you're just trying to be contrarian for form's sake. But what does it mean to "like" something, in the aesthetic realm, in the first place? That it gives you a kind of unreflective pleasure and enjoyment? This tends to be what popular music, pulp fiction, and cult films do (the "cult" moniker often being a sign that we enjoy, rather than think about, a movie); and it is one of the reasons they gain their status as cult films in the first place. John Cage (who is rarely mentioned during conversations about *Casablanca*) significantly observed that he did not want the sphere of his experiences to be limited by his likes and dislikes. This is a good warning and a helpful corrective for those who are too quick to dismiss some movies as "difficult" (read: boring) and to accept (or dismiss) others because they are "easy" (read: entertaining).

It may be true that *De gustibus non est disputandum*, and certainly taste (or whatever forces and ideologies influence or determine our taste) guides us in our aesthetic preferences from the books we read to the music we listen to; but it can also shut down possible experiences, leading us to pass judgment not so much on the work as on ourselves. As Cage might have asked, "How do you know, when a work bores you, if the work itself is boring or if you're just not paying proper attention?" When it comes to certain works of art, this is not a question to be taken lightly or to be dismissed with a knee-jerk appeal to taste. Taste is something that can be formed (since it has already been formed, whether we realize it or not). It is something that can be cultivated and developed. It is something learning can improve. Since there *is* a difference between good and bad taste, there must be a certain amount of *disputandum* possible when it comes to taste after all. Which brings us back to the question of whether or not one "likes" *Casablanca*. (Which may be the least interesting question we can ask about the film.)

It's not a difficult film to like, if we let our guard down. But what is a "difficult" film, and in what sense is *Casablanca* a departure from the difficulties often associated with such films? Is *Casablanca* a guilty pleasure? Is it escapist cinema? If so, what are we escaping from (or to) when we give ourselves over to its manipulations? For there can be no doubt that the movie tries to manipulate us (and generally succeeds in doing so), starting with the gauzy soft-focus camera work that makes Bergman's face glow (not that it takes much to do so) and makes her eyes shine with that always-on-the-verge-of-crying look. But rather than resent this manipulation (which we usually do in other circumstances once we become aware of it), the film coaxes us into surrendering to it. We're persuaded to enjoy being carried along on this raft of absurd romance and improbable nobility, so thinly veiled under a mask of tough-guy callousness and self-sacrificing women, perhaps because we don't really want to accept the absurdity and improbability of it all in the first place. We want to be persuaded, so when it comes to *Casablanca*, most of us are easy marks.

Secretly (or not so secretly; cf. Belmondo's Michel or Woody Allen's Allan Felix in *Play it Again, Sam*) we all want to be like Ilsa or Rick (or at least work at his bar: as Captain Renault tells Major Strasser, "everybody comes to Rick's" (which is also the name of the play *Casablanca* was based on))? Despite his nobility (and that sexy scar over his right eye), I imagine few audience members wish they could be like Victor Laszlo. But why not? What's wrong with him, especially since he "gets the girl" (sort of) in the end?[15] But we prefer hard-drinking ("What nationality are you?" "I'm a drunk."), tough-talking (Ibid), cigarette-smoking (passim) Rick. Don't we all want to be the guy who everyone wants to have a drink with? Or the one woman he's willing to have one with? The guy for whom, when he's spotted in the bazaar, prices immediately drop? Whose suits and tuxedos fit perfectly? Who plays chess alone in a crowded bar while people drink and gamble around him? The guy men have instinctive respect for and loyalty to and women can't help falling in love with?

"He's the kind of man who, if I were a woman, and I were not around, I should be in love with Rick," says Claude Rains' devilishly charming Captain Louis Renault (which line may shed some light on the final two minutes of the film.) Don't we all want to be the woman who a man will give up everything for (even, it turns out, that very woman herself)? The woman who can tear aside his

---

[15] This isn't a rhetorical question, since understanding why audiences prefer the anguished Bogart to the noble Paul Henreid (and why Bergman's Ilsa apparently does too) helps explain what we find compelling about the film's predictable yet effective "chemistry." It might even help us understand ourselves, both as audience and as fantasy-obsessed imaginists as well.

tough-guy exterior to reveal the vulnerability that makes love possible (imagine "a guy standing on a station platform in the rain with a comical look on his face because his insides have been kicked out").[16] The movie's fantasies are our fantasies (even if we feel chagrined to admit them, even to ourselves), so of course we allow ourselves to be manipulated by them. It's only an extension of the self-deception we allow ourselves to be manipulated by whenever we let our imaginations run away with us. (Which, let's face it, is as often as the world permits, most of the time).

It's still the same old story. Yet oddly (I want to argue), despite its many manipulative qualities (from camera work to costuming and from studio-built sets to the use of newsreel images), *Casablanca* succeeds in being a movie that tends to liberate the imagination rather than enervate it, provoking it rather than controlling it. There may even be an opportunity for a kind of self-knowledge here, in the form of a better understanding of the way our illusions lead us to construct fantasy images of ourselves and our own (rather uncritically arrived at) ideals. The movie fulfills so many of our expectations (as Umberto Eco said, it combines so many clichés that it manages to avoid the negative effects that just one or two clichés tend to produce in inferior movies[17]), and yet in the end (and along the way) it still invites us to further wonder and speculation. In other words, it doesn't *really* answer all the questions it looks like it arrives at such certainty about.

---

[16] "Love you will find only where you may show yourself weak without provoking strength." Theodor Adorno, *Minima Moralia*

[17] "Casablanca: Cult Movies and Intertextual Collage" in *Travels in Hyperreality* (Harcourt, Brace, Jovanovich, 1986).

Flirting (or outright hopping into bed) with clichés and stock characters as it does, *Casablanca* might very well have been a relatively uninteresting movie (and some viewers still think of it as such). What saves it for me is a certain style that allows for more indeterminacy and ambiguity than appear on the film's surface. This style has a lot to do with Bogart's acting, heavy handed as it usually is. There's nothing subtle about Bogart on the screen. And yet strangely, something not quite one-dimensional emerges from this lack of subtlety. For example, consider the relationship between the personal and the political as motivations for Rick's actions in the film.

It's been said that, starting with an implicit debate between Heraclitus and Parmenides (who are rarely mentioned during conversations about *Casablanca*), the tradition of Western philosophy has been an investigation of the relationship between the One and the Many. (Conceived in terms of Being and Becoming by Parmenides and Heraclitus respectively.[18]) This One and/or Many debate reaches a high point in Plato's *Republic*[19] and in the 20th century it unfolds not so much in terms of the metaphysics of Being and Becoming (unless you're Heidegger) but rather in terms of the personal and the political. What is the relationship between the personal and the political, the one and the many, in *Casablanca*?

---

[18] In the East you might say the philosophical tradition has largely consisted of a debate between the "Some" (Hinduism in India, Legalism or Confucianism in China) and the "None" (Buddhism in India, China, Tibet, Japan) and (in some versions) Daoism in China).

[19] At this point it is traditional to include a footnote pointing out Alfred North Whitehead's remark about all Western Philosophy being a footnote to Plato. Footnotes about footnotes being a charming quirk of the sophisticated postmodern sensibilities we've apparently developed since the time of both Plato and Whitehead.

Here an interesting inversion takes place, for it is precisely during Rick's impassioned speech to Ilsa on the airfield ("I'm no good at being noble [ha!], but it doesn't take much to see that the problems of three little people don't amount to a hill of beans in this crazy world") that he reveals that there has been a redemptive moment (or so the movie would have us believe) of overcoming his personal bitterness and resentment ("one woman has hurt you and you take your revenge on the rest of the world"). He is now recommitting himself to the larger fight going on around him. The film also implies that this redemptive moment occurs shortly after Ilsa and Rick have sex.

Why is it that the movie's most personal theme, Rick's love for Ilsa, seems to reignite his most socially oriented self (his commitment to "lost causes")? Why does he rediscover his politically noble side (how often do we hear about his gunrunning to Ethiopia and his fighting in Spain against the Fascists?) as an extension of his personally romantic side?[20] Such questions reveal a more nuanced ambiguity to the film than its final resolution might suggest.

Regardless of whether or not *Casablanca* is a "great" movie (that this remains an open question on several levels reveals the many ways we use the word and the

---

[20] With the benefit of historical hindsight, we know that this time Rick will be on the winning side, but that outcome was far from certain in 1942 when the film was made. The German couple on their way to America who toast their new life might seem like an image of canned patriotism today (though their bumbling English pokes fun at even that simple idea), but when *Casablanca* was made, VE Day was still three years away, and America had only entered the war the year before.

concept "great" when talking about the movies—perhaps in ways more varied, diverse and complicated than we do when talking about works of art in other genres such as poetry, sculpture, painting, and classical music), there is no question that the movie moves us and gives us pleasure. Sometimes that pleasure is dependent on not thinking too closely about what we're watching and sometimes that pleasure depends precisely on our willingness and ability to think about things too often taken for granted or unexamined. The ability of a work of art to make us wonder and question may be a fairly low bar by which to evaluate it's aesthetic quality (if it can't do that, what can it do?), but it is hardly irrelevant (if it doesn't do that, what *is* it doing?). In the case of *Casablanca*, audiences may be divided into many categories (the naïve, the sentimental, the cynical, the tough; as well as along the lines of how they answer the question: does the movie have a happy ending?) and different questions emerge depending on how we read these possible responses to the film.

Where do we look for answers to inevitable questions, such as when certain key developments in the film first take shape?[21] The dialogue (with all its famously quotable lines) does not tell us. What does? Only the characters' facial expressions, carefully screened at key moments. For example the muscles in Bogart's face spasming during

---

[21] For example: Rick's decision to help the Bulgarian couple, and then later in the film not only to help Ilsa and Laszlo, but also to give up Ilsa to Laszlo; or Ilsa's realization that she loves Rick and not Laszlo (or perhaps Rick more than Laszlo); or Louis's decision to shift his loyalties from the Reich-sympathetic Vichy government to the Underground movement. Are these decisions examples of personal or political realizations and commitments? What do they say about the relationship between the personal and political as it is developed in the film?

his conversation with the young Bulgarian woman when he delivers the crucial line (in response to her speaking of keeping something "locked in her heart," an imprisonment Rick must think he knows a thing or two about): "Nobody ever loved me that much." But that's not the point; the point is, did *Rick* ever love anyone that much? It is only when he realizes that Ilsa does love him "that much" that he'll be able to sacrifice himself by giving her up (but what sort of sacrifice is this, in the context of the movie?), rather than ask her to sacrifice Laszlo so that they can be together. Which leads one to wonder, is Rick sacrificing himself or Ilsa, or are they both sacrificing themselves for Laszlo? Or is Rick not sacrificing anything at all, but simply acknowledging a truth about love and fantasy (and the fantasy of love): that it is often better to long for than to possess, better to desire than to consummate?

Why doesn't Ilsa pull the trigger when she has Rick at gunpoint? Because she loves him? Often in the movies (as in life) this is a reason *to* pull the trigger, not to refrain from doing so (cf. Billy Wilder's *Sunset Boulevard* or John Huston's 1985 *Prizzi's Honor*). Because Rick's seductive self-confidence and general world weariness ("go ahead and shoot, you'll be doing me a favor") make her fall in love with him all over again? Because she doesn't know what she wants? Or because this is the best way for her to get what she wants? A few minutes after pulling a gun on him, she tells Rick, "you have to think for both of us; for all of us"; and again Rick's face tells us that this is the crucial line which triggers the moment of transformation in his character, the moment when he realizes that being loved (and therefore being worthy of love) is even more important than being with the woman who loves. When Rick says, "All right, I will," again it's his face that tells us everything has changed; that it's a different man speaking than the one who said, a few minutes earlier, "I'm gonna die in Casablanca; it's a good spot for it." In this dance of faces, who's playing who here? To what extent is the film, like Rick's roulette wheel, a fixed game?[22] Or is it that we just need someone to tell us which number to bet on, and whether or not to let it ride?

In addition to such questions, there are interesting parallels in the movie, such as when Ilsa asks Laszlo a version of the same question the Bulgarian woman asks Rick ("Victor, whatever I do, will you believe that I . . .") or when she parts from Rick in his restaurant in Paris (La Belle Aurore) and then later from Laszlo at the door of their hotel room in Casablanca. In each of these scenes it is when the film is most intensely personal, and speaks to us most urgently (if not convincingly) about the heroism of individual sacrifice, that it (or its main characters) are also most political. Which is to say, the film is most political when it appears to turn to the personal, and it is most personal in those moments when the individuality of the characters recedes behind the manipulative ideologies fostered by the film's romanticism.

A final question. What happens to Rick at the end of the

---

[22] For movie fans there's a wonderful moment when Marcel Dalio, who plays Rick's croupier Emil (he also appears in *To Have and Have Not*), delivers the line, "les jeux son fait," reminding us of his central (though controversial, as a Jew playing a member of the French aristocracy on the eve of WWII) role three years earlier in Renoir's magnificent *La Regle du jeu*, though that movie's reputation would not gain its massive stature until many years later (it was originally banned by the Vichy government). He also starred in Renoir's *Grand Illusion* with Jean Gabin. As a Jewish actor, Dalio fled France for America after the Nazi occupation, where his career never again reached the heights promised by his work with Renoir in the 1930s.

film? Does he reveal himself as a Laszlo-like team player after all (as he perhaps has been all along, despite his efforts to deny it), or does he remain the tough loner that Hollywood cinema thrives on and that Bogart, along with John Wayne (cf. John Ford's *The Searchers*) and others, played no small part in helping to construct as an imaginative ideal? Can he be both? Does the end of the film endorse the political ideology of common cause espoused by Laszlo, or does it settle on a more subtle form of individualism that Rick represents without even realizing it? In the end, has politics justified the individual (giving him a reason to live (or die) and love (or renounce love for something higher?)? Or has the individual found a way to discover in politics the apotheosis of his individualism? Louis identifies Rick as a sentimentalist and a patriot, but he is quick to join him in these romantic impracticalities. Why? Because it makes for a good ending to the movie? But just what sort of a "beautiful friendship" does the movie's end promise us? Have two ostensibly selfish men found a reason to think of something other than themselves? Or is it this very selfishness that will be the basis of their friendship? (During their first conversation in the movie, Louis says, speculating about why Rick doesn't return to America, "I like to think you killed a man; it's the romantic in me.")

On the question of political ideologies in the film, both repressed and explicit, it's amusing (or disturbing) to recall (or learn) that the studio's first choice for the role of Rick was not Bogart, but B-movie actor Ronald Reagan (with Ann Sheridan to play Ilsa). And as odd as it is to imagine a former Richard Blaine as president of the United States, it's even less likely that popular culture would have continued to harbor the fond affection for Bogie that we currently have if we'd had to see him as our president. Some things are better left to the imagination; which in fact is precisely what *Casablanca* is about.

The Gillis-Monkey Trial:
Love and Madness in Billy Wilder's *Sunset Boulevard* (1950)

Lovers and Madmen have such seething brains
Such shaping fantasies, that apprehend
More than cool reason ever comprehends.
The lunatic, the lover and the poet
Are of imagination all compact.

–A Midsummer Night's Dream V.i.5

As is so often the case, Shakespeare got there first. Norma Desmond, lunatic, lover, and poet, with her shaping fantasies will shape the destiny of poor Joe Gillis, whose cool reason scarcely comprehends what's happening to him. He wanders into Norma's dilapidated mansion one day to take the place of her recently dead chimpanzee, and finds himself drawn into a world of love and madness not of his own making but all too familiar, from which he cannot escape. How could he, if he is a lover, a madman, and a would-be poet himself?

This is what strikes me most about *Sunset Boulevard*: the love and the madness. Love is a necessary ingredient of any film noir. But the madness is a bonus, which, as the poet knew, is always part of any true love. And this time maybe Shakespeare didn't get there first. Plato said (or has Socrates say), "Love is madness Heaven sent." Norma's madness may not come from Heaven (or perhaps it does, depending on one's view of Hollywood), but it is certainly a kind of love.

Gillis's first glimpse of Norma Desmond's house makes

him think about "crazy movie people" of the 1920's. *Sunset Boulevard* is about the madness of love, and the love of Hollywood which may also be a kind of madness, as it becomes for Gloria Swanson's brilliantly played Norma Desmond. Stars (those celestial bodies that captivated the first philosophers and turned their eyes upwards), like love, also come from heaven, and it's Norma's obsession with being a star that leads to her madness.[23]

There are many forms of love in the movie: Norma's for Joe, Max's for Norma, Joe and Betty's, Betty and Artie's, even Joe's for Norma, which must exist at some level. Why else does he rush back to her after her suicide attempt on New Year's Eve (a kind of Walpurgisnacht)? Why does he submit, again, to the spell—the magic and the madness—of Hollywood and its mad dreams of the past that seek to control the future?

For along with love and madness, the movie is also about the forgetfulness of Hollywood and about the adamancy with which it insists on the "now" to the exclusion of acknowledging its own past, its traditions, and its history. In Hollywood (a microcosm of the U.S. in this regard), everything must be modern, and everything must be new, because you can only sell something that's new. But of course, Hollywood's power depends on a relationship it

---

[23] One thinks of Van Gogh: "It is possible that these great geniuses are only madmen, and that one must be mad oneself to have boundless faith in them and a boundless admiration for them. If this is true, I should prefer my insanity to the sanity of the others" (*Letters*). Or perhaps of Kerouac's Sal Paradise: "The only people for me are the mad ones, the ones who are mad to live, mad to talk, mad to be saved, desirous of everything at the same time. The ones who never yawn or say a commonplace thing, but burn, burn, burn like fabulous roman candles."

has with its past as well. In business, technology, and industry (from automobiles to medicine and from computers to agriculture) progress is the norm and a financial imperative. In the arts (as I have argued before) it is a dangerous illusion. Hollywood is that strangest combination of art and industry, business and culture, and culture *as* business. So, does progress reign in Hollywood, in which case Norma Desmond must be left by the wayside? Or do timeless aesthetic qualities trump transience? Hollywood is confused about its own past— longing for it, regretting it, embarrassed by it, by turns celebrating then denying it—but who among us isn't?

Norma has inscribed Joe's cigarette case, "Mad about the boy," stating explicitly the film's theme that love is a kind of madness, and for her, madness a kind of love. Her love for Hollywood, for acting, for an unattainable perpetual youth, and for Joe himself: all these loves are either unattainable, or attainable but unsustainable.

Her brain may be seething, but as a true scion of Hollywood, Norma has learned how to shape fantasies. She starts with her own, building a world of functional illusion around her, and then she draws in others: Max, her ex-husband butler, and writer Joe Gillis, who has dreams of his own. He has to. Without those dreams, what power would Norma (standing in for all of Hollywood here) have over him? It's Joe's dreams more than his economic straits (not quite greed, but a close cousin: maybe nothing more ominous that a simple desire for "the good things" in life (champagne, caviar, nice clothes, a gold cigarette case, cufflinks, a pool)) that entangle him in Norma's fantasy world. One dreamer reels in another. To put it another way: Norma tells Joe she wants to stage her return (not "comeback") to Hollywood by playing

Salome, which would make Joe an odd sort of John the Baptist. But the film suggests that what she should really be starring in is a remake of *Faust*, with her in the role of Mephistopheles,[24] tempting Joe to sell his soul. But in exchange for what?

Sunset Blvd. reminds me of Faust more than of Salome[25] (although Norma dances with a variety of veils throughout the movie) not so much because of the love and the madness (themes in Salome as well), but because of the ever-popular trope in Hollywood movies about Hollywood: the perennial question of "selling out." Why is Hollywood so fascinated with this phenomenon, and what does it really mean to sell out? Is it a form of giving in to temptation? But the temptation to do what? To make some sort of compromise? To reveal one's "true self"? Does Joe Gillis "sell out" in the movie? Does he compromise his moral standards or his (admittedly questionable) talent in the service of Desmond's money? The scene with the repo men who show up at his apartment looking for his car suggests he's not giving up his high ideals or youthful naiveté–that happened long

---

[24] Norma Desmond is played by actress Gloria Swanson, a huge star of the silent movie era, who would have been just about the right age (she was born in 1899) to play Gretchen in Murnau's 1926 *Faust*. Camilla Horn played the role instead, with Emil Jannings in the role of Mephisto.

[25] And also a bit of Cervantes' *Don Quixote*, with Norma in the title role. In Norma Desmond, Hollywood created the ultimate tribute to the power of the cinema: a character incapable any longer of distinguishing between fantasy and reality. By the end of the film, "the dream she had clung to so desperately had enfolded her," and she's come as close to transforming reality into fantasy as any fictional character since this theme was explored by Cervantes in 1605. Is it madness, or the power of the imagination to shape reality? Cervantes and *Sunset Boulevard* both ask us to consider this question in light of the power of the human imagination.

before he wandered into Norma Desmond's driveway.

Norma isn't the only temptress in the movie. There's Hollywood too. The greatest temptress, and the most fickle mistress, of them all. And then there's Betty Schaefer. What's she tempting Joe to do? (Other than steal a good friend's fiancé?) On several occasions Betty is shown eating an apple. The second time, Joe is eating one too. If Norma is a kind of Mephistopheles, is innocent young Betty a kind of Eve, tempting Joe's Adam to a fall he doesn't even see coming? Norma may tempt him with money (but tempt him to what? What's he giving up exactly in order to be with her?), but it's Betty's role in his life that ends up getting him killed.

What's being sold when a person sells out? This is one of the oldest questions in Western literature. (Even Achilles faces a version of it.) In the Faust legend, the Devil offers Faust his every earthly desire in exchange for one small thing: his soul. Is this what the characters in the movie, from Joe to Norma and from Max to Betty Schaefer are playing for? What does it take to lose a soul? Joe is trying to hold on to his, as his various attempts to escape Norma's mansion make clear. But how strong a grasp on it did he have, even before the events of the movie began? As we see in the first minutes of the film, Joe is a dead man before the movie even begins. What sort of a warning is that?

Is Joe Gillis a sell out? Does Hollywood, which I think stands in for the world here (since what else does Hollywood aspire to be but the whole world in miniature, as the scene with Joe and Betty on the Paramount Studios lot makes clear), tempt each of us to "sell out" and to compromise on a different kind of madness—the madness of our dreams and ideals? We get a sense of this in the scene in Sheldrake's office when Gillis is trying to sell the script to *Bases Loaded* and first meets Betty Schaefer, but we really feel its weight about 15 minutes into the movie shortly after Gillis has met (and insulted) Norma Desmond. (The best two lines in the movie: "You used to be big." "I am big; it's the pictures that got small.") She offers him a job. A job he doesn't want, working for a woman he's already suggested may be a bit like Dickens' Miss Havisham. (And in fact Norma will prove to be more like her (someone who's been "given the go by") than he could have realized; just as Joe proves to be an interesting version of Pip as his own "great expectations" are gradually dismantled throughout the movie.) But he takes it because he needs the money. Money is just one of the ways Hollywood (again, standing in for the world here) gets at us; one of the ways it persuades us to start making compromises and pries our dreams from our fingers.

Of course in Norma Desmond's case, it isn't money (or the lack of it) that threatens to pry her dreams away from her. In fact, it's one of the things that help her hold on to them so effectively long after they're gone. She's rich. But that only allows her to see more clearly what can and can't be bought. "I own three blocks downtown; I've got oil in Bakersfield . . . what's it for but to by us anything we want?" Anything we want? That depends on whether what we want is for sale. And the question of what is and what isn't for sale is another aspect of the question of what it means to "sell out."

That leads to another question the movie hits us with: what's the difference between a Betty Schaefer, whose aspirations all lie before her (and may never be realized), and a Norma Desmond, whose dreams, having been realized, can neither be maintained nor recaptured? Aren't they both the same kind of person (and in that sense like all of us): a person with dreams, which Hollywood (the world) will either dash or help make true? But what happens when all your dreams come true and you're still the person you always were? Where do you go then?

In response to some cynical remark he makes about the writing process, Betty asks Joe, "Don't you sometimes hate yourself?" "Constantly," he replies, and he's joking, but he's not. Selling out means doing something that makes you like yourself less than you did before. But how expensive is it to live a life that allows you not to hate yourself? It's not clear that Joe was managing that even before Norma Desmond came along.

One thing it might mean to "sell out" is illustrated by the oft-repeated anecdote involving Oscar Wilde, who once asked a British lady if she would go to bed with him for one million pounds. When she replied that she would be a fool not to, he asked her if she would go to bed with him for 2 pence. "Mr. Wilde," she replied indignantly, "what kind of a woman do you think I am?" "We have already established that," Wilde answered, "now we're merely haggling over the price." And that's what selling out often involves: distinguishing between what aspects of your life can and can't be haggled over. Is there anything in your life that can't have a price put on it? That's what Hollywood (the world, Mephistopheles) wants to know: what's your price? Once the system (whether it's Hollywood, Wall Street, or Dayton, Ohio) helps you discover "what kind of a person you are" (on the phone Norma asks Betty if she knows what sort of man Gillis is), it will also help you discover the price. (Either the price the world will pay in exchange for your being that kind of person, or the price you'll pay as a result of being that person.) But that's just haggling. The real insight, if we're paying attention, comes with that initial moment of self-realization. This is a gift really, if we're in a position to learn from it. It's a gift that a place like Hollywood bestows by stripping away all kindness and illusion (unless you can afford to keep an ex-husband like Max around), and forcing us to see and experience things we might prefer to ignore and avoid. That is, not the kind of gift we're always eager to accept, any more than Joe seems eager to accept the solid gold cigarette case we see him carrying a few scenes later.

Perhaps Gillis experiences the initial moment of self-realization when he realizes it's time to go back to the copy desk of the Dayton Evening Post. But then given the chance for some "easy money" by working for Norma Desmond (at a job he doesn't respect and for a woman he thinks is half crazy), he decides to stay. He's reeled back in. He thinks, in a hardnosed way, that he's selling out, but he doesn't even understand what he's selling until he's floating face down in a swimming pool. But that too, of course, is just a symbol. What he really sold was lost long before that fatal moment (as his final scene with Betty makes clear not only to him, but to the audience as well).

The symmetry of the movie is delightful. Joe Gillis arrives at the decaying mansion of Norma Desmond just in time to bid farewell to her former companion, a dead chimpanzee, and to quickly take his place. The chimp's luxurious coffin finds its compliment in Joe's tailored clothes and the gifts of expensive jewelry. (For that matter, what's more luxurious than being buried in a swimming pool?) Joe's death at the end of the movie is just the loss of one more companion for Norma. She has lost so many things one wonders if she'll even notice this most recent one. And indeed in her final scene, the glorious descending of the staircase, the implication is she doesn't. It isn't Joe she's killed, but the threat that anyone or anything could deny her status as a star. Or fail to love her for it. This too is a kind of madness that seems to go along with love.

Hollywood, for all its sins, is still a place that tells the truth. That's what the successful selling of its lies is based on. If Joe Gillis's writing is as hackneyed as his interior monologue ("that story of mine kept going through my head like a dozen locomotives"), it's no wonder he can't sell a script. Everyone knows Hollywood isn't a place where everyone succeeds (but what place is?). Even worse, *Sunset Boulevard* shows us that even when someone does "make it" in Hollywood it's only temporary (but what isn't?). Notwithstanding the idealistic portrait of Cecil B. DeMille (one wonders if he would have agreed to play himself in a less sympathetic role?[26]) as a kind, generous, father-figure director with a conscience (sort of: it may just be his inability to tell a hard truth), Wilder's movie certainly leaves us asking who's better off: the guy who runs back to the Ohio newspaper, or the star who,

---

[26] Though in light of his paternally protective line, "I'll buy him five old cars if necessary," it's amusing to learn that DeMille agreed to play himself in the movie only in exchange for a large salary and a new Cadillac. Nor is it insignificant that Joe encounters Norma through an effort to save his car (a convertible of course). The car has long been a symbol of L.A. and of California in general. Unlike London, Paris, New York and San Francisco, cities where the automobile has always seemed somewhat out of place—a cumbersome intrusion in a more intimate urban setting—L.A. was build for the automobile. The movie, after all, is named after a street the runs from downtown L.A. to the Pacific Ocean.

like her celestial namesake, burns out long before news of the event reaches home.

And what are we to make of 22 year-old Betty Schaefer's question, "What's wrong with being on the other side of the cameras? It's really more fun." Fun for whom? What kind of fun? This is an ominous moment in the film, especially for women in the 1950's, because the movie shows us that DeMille can age gracefully in his career whereas Desmond can't. It may be true that Norma Desmond helped make Paramount Pictures, but she's through now, whereas DeMille is still a powerful director (cf. the chain of command by which news of Norma's visit to the studio eventually reaches his ear). Age hasn't compromised his value to the studio, in part because he works behind the scenes, and in part because he's a man. Joe Gillis can say with impunity, toward the end of the movie that "there's nothing tragic about being 50", because (if he lives that long) he could still be writing at 50. But there's something very wrong with being 50 if you are an actress whose career is built on youthful beauty, energy, and charm (the qualities associated with a Salome).

Gillis's dream about the organ grinder whose face he can't see (ironically, since Norma Desmond's face surrounds him in the mansion in the form of innumerable photographs, autographed pictures she sends in response to forged fan letters, and the movies they watch starring her in the old silent classics) and the chimp dancing for pennies wouldn't pose much of a challenge for Freud. But Gillis's isn't a complex psyche. He's aware of what he's doing, and just moral enough (like many of us) to be bothered by it, but not moral enough to stop (if what he's doing is in any sense immoral—after all, he's not hurting anyone but himself). When Betty Schaefer tries to reach Gillis by phone at the mansion, Max tells Norma it was just someone inquiring about a stray dog. This is the second animal Joe is compared to in the film. And the mansion, first a funeral home (the chimp will be buried in the garden, "any city laws against that?"[27]), is now compared to the pound, where stray dogs are locked up.

"There's nothing tragic about being 50." Unless you're a star who knows that "the stars are ageless," or at least must appear to be so. Hollywood operates on a somewhat sickly form of meritocracy (with a whole lot of luck, favoritism, and nepotism thrown in)—it's not fair, but it's strict as hell. Joe isn't a good enough writer to make it there, and Norma has gotten too old. In the end, perhaps Joe had no more control over his talent than Norma does over the passage of time that is her greatest enemy. We want to believe that if the hero (since we tend to see ourselves in this role in one way or another) only tries harder, success will come eventually. But that's not the lesson Joe learns. He's going back home, giving up on his dreams. Norma is the alternative possibility: she refuses to give up her dreams, and chooses madness instead (though it isn't so much a choice as a consequence of the passion with which she clings to those dreams).

Between madness and mediocrity, which is better, which is worse? Who's the tragic character here? Max, who gave up a successful directing career to work as a butler for the wife who threw him over only to become a faded actress? Betty, who fell in love with one man while engaged to another? Artie Green, who hasn't a clue what's going on

---

[27] Not that it matters. We see at the end of the film that Norma is not particularly interested in what the law does or doesn't allow. Whether it's burying a man or a monkey, Norma is a law unto herself.

around him; "as nice a guy as ever lived" off filming in Arizona while his fiancé falls for a tough-talking writer living as a gigolo? Or poor Joe Gillis, just an ordinary joe, caught up in the inexorable logic of love and madness?

What is "Hollywood" in the movie? The entertainment industry? The realities of capitalism? A manifestation of human greed? A symbol of the world? Or is it Time itself, inevitable and relentless, consuming all in its path: the actors; a bit more slowly the directors, and eventually the movies themselves? On the surface (on the surface of *Sunset Boulevard*) it looks like 1950's Hollywood has been kinder to Cecil B. DeMille than it has to Norma Desmond (or was to Gloria Swanson), but 65 years later, how many audiences are interested is seeing DeMille's *Cleopatra, Samson and Delilah, The King of Kings, The Ten Commandments*, or any of the other 80+ movies he made between 1914 and 1956? Eventually, DeMille went the way of Norma Desmond—it just took him a little longer to get there. If Hollywood is a representation of Time itself, we'll all get there eventually.

I learned in a college logic class that if A=B and B=C then A=C. Therefore, if Norma=Hollywood and Hollywood=the World, then Norma Desmond=the World: mad, exuberant, and full of a type of love which looks like the most destructive force in the World. A Love that destroys the World (which means that ultimately it destroys itself). And Joe Gillis is just a man in the world. Maybe it's not really a question of selling out at all, but merely a matter of how long any of us, with the feeble powers we can muster, can hold out against the world. When even love is against us, what hope do we have?

It's only at the end of the film that Max for the first time refers to his ex-wife-employer as "Norma" rather than "Madame", during what may be the most moving scene in what is, in fact, a poignant movie (a fact which Joe's overblown voiceover and the often corny dialogue between him and Betty sometimes threatens to obscure): "Are you ready Norma?" he asks, delivered with von Stroheim's most eloquently solicitous expression. Something has been recaptured, if only for a moment, when he returns behind the camera to direct what will surely be Norma Desmond's final scene.[28]

But Norma is right when she says, "After *Salome* we'll make another picture, and another picture"; it's just a matter of understanding this "we" broadly enough. Movies keep getting made (for better or worse). Hollywood will consume an untold number of actors, writers, producers, electricians like Hog-Eye, makeup artists, editors, composers, readers like Betty Schaefer, and directors, but there will always be another movie. When it comes to human beings, the old must make room for the new. The only thing that might last, if we're lucky, are the great films they will produce through the miracle of collaboration that making a movie demands (unparalleled by any other work of art unless it's the great cathedrals of the Middle Ages). Hollywood may be cruel (like Nature itself), unrelenting, and all-consuming (like Time itself), but there is no greater example of the collaborative possibilities of human creativity than what takes place when Norma's "we" makes another picture.

---

[28] And for those of us familiar with von Stroheim's own vexed relationship with Hollywood and the movies, seeing him behind the camera again, if only for a moment and only as part of the "make believe" role he's still playing for Norma, extends this poignancy beyond the film into our sense of the history of cinema itself, as do the cameos by Buster Keaton, Anna Nilsson, and H. B. Warner.

And this is true even for those of us who are just "wonderful people out there in the dark." And frankly, where else would most of us rather be?

Here's Looking at You Angel:
Looking at Marlowe Looking in Howard Hawks' *The Big Sleep* (1946)

I have wrestled with death. It is the most unexciting contest you can imagine. It takes place in an impalpable grayness, with nothing underfoot, with nothing around, without spectators, without clamor, without glory, without the great desire of victory, without the great fear of defeat, in a sickly atmosphere of tepid skepticism, without much belief in your own right, and still less in that of your adversary. If such is the form of ultimate wisdom, then life is a greater riddle than some of us think it to be.

–Conrad, *Heart of Darkness*

I'm surprised when people complain about not liking *The Big Sleep* because the plot is difficult to follow. It's a mystery movie. A mystery is a kind of puzzle; it requires solving. The movie is constructed so that the audience must play detective along with Marlowe. The movie doesn't do all the work for us. It gives us clues, not answers. We have to do some detecting of our own if we want to understand what's going on. Such detecting, when it comes to watching movies, is a form of reading.

Along with the gangster, the cowboy, the samurai, and the vampire, the detective is one of the great characters of the classic movie genres. But the detective is more than just another stock character, because in his search for a truth hidden below the surface of things, the detective is also a model for each of us when we're engaged in the act of watching. Good audiences are always like detectives when it comes to seeing what's really going on in a movie.

For a movie justly famous for its fast-paced edgy dialogue,[29] *The Big Sleep* is very much a movie about looking, which is what we do when we watch a movie. And when it comes to watching movies few things are more important than the difference between looking and seeing. Any detective worth his $25 a day (plus expenses) knows that when you watch without seeing, you're not really looking at all. And for those of us with eyes for the job, Bogart's Marlowe shows us how to really *see* when we look. It's what a good detective does.

Before the movies, there were the novels. *The Big Sleep* was the fourth Raymond Chandler story adapted for film and the second to feature the character of Philip Marlowe (the first being Edward Dmytryk's 1944 *Farewell, My Lovely* starring Dick Powell).

Chandler had in common with Philip K. Dick and John le Carré the uncommon ability to work in a form of genre fiction (the detective mystery, the sci-fi novel, the international spy thriller) and transform it into the kind of literature that only the greatest novelists are capable of writing. No doubt there are other writers capable of literary alchemy at this level, but there aren't many, and these three strike me as the absolute masters of the feat.

Le Carré has George Smiley and Chandler has Philip

---

[29] One of the best scenes in the movie is the conversation between Marlowe and Vivian Rutledge in which sexual innuendo thinly disguised as talk about horse racing ("a lot depends on who's in the saddle") was somehow passed over by the Hays Code.

Marlowe—detectives to rival, in the annals of literature, Doyle's Sherlock Holmes and Chesterton's Father Brown. Marlowe is the very prototype (along with Sam Spade, who Bogart played in Huston's 1941 *Maltese Falcon*) of the hardboiled detective: tough talking, self-possessed, bourbon drinking, good with the ladies, and quick with his fists. Smiley is the opposite in every way. Side by side they express nearly every aspect of fiction's ability to vividly portray and comment on those aspects of greed, lust, manipulation, deceit, and violence that characterize the darker side of modernity.

In Chandler's novels, Marlowe is the last Knight in a world long deprived of chivalry. He holds himself to standards and ideals (things like friendship, valuing integrity over money, the duty of his profession) that those around him seem to have given up on long ago. He is a philosopher for the modern age who plays chess alone, drinks alone,[30] reads poetry, and passes up the opportunity for a quick buck if he doesn't like the smell of where the money's coming from (like that epitome of virtue, George Eliot's Caleb Garth in *Middlemarch*). He doesn't take what he hasn't earned, and his standards for what it means to earn something are high indeed. In his sense of integrity, independence, and dry humor he generally reminds readers of his namesake, Joseph Conrad's Charles Marlow from *Heart of Darkness*.[31] He's a

---

[30] Despite his attractiveness to women he seems inevitably always to end up alone.

[31] I can imagine Chandler's Marlowe saying along with Conrad's: "No, I don't like work. I had rather laze about and think of all the fine things that can be done. I don't like work – no man does – but I like what is in the work, – the chance to find yourself. Your own reality – for yourself, not for others – what no other man can ever know. They can only see the mere show, and never can tell what it really means." (*Heart of Darkness*)

romantic figure and a made-to-order hero and he's as unlike Smiley (who's admirable and sympathetic in completely different ways) as Ian Fleming's James Bond is, but he's far more nuanced and compelling a character than Bond. He's an anachronistic Socrates who haunts the bars and restaurants of L.A. instead of the Athenian Agora, and drinks gimlets instead of hemlock.

That's Marlowe in the novels. Who is the Marlowe we meet in Hawks' version of *The Big Sleep*? As with so many things in life, the movie opens with a door that does the same.

First shot: impressive plaque on the front door of what we'll soon see is a family mansion. Shadow of a man in a hat falls across the plaque and the camera pans down to the doorbell. A man's hand, one ring on the ring finger, rings the bell with its thumb. Fade cut to the interior side of the same door flanked by two candelabra on large marble pedestals. Persian carpet on the floor in front of the door. No coat rack (Marlowe has to find a table for his hat). The top edge of two heavy tasseled curtains frame the door, and the shot, on either side. Back of a man (Norris the butler) approaching the door.

First line of the movie: "My name's Marlowe," delivered by the character before we even see him. A moment later our first sight of Marlowe as he enters the house is of him looking, taking in the surroundings, silently appraising the world he's just entered. Not reaching any conclusions, just looking: at the walls, the statues, the furniture, and then at the pretty girl who comes down the stairs.

That first cut of the film, from the plaque on the front door of the Sternwood mansion to the backside of that same door, is unusual because it is one of only a handful of shots in which we are not looking either directly at Marlowe or looking at what he's looking at. Generally, the camera either shows us Marlowe or shows us what he's seeing. This is how the opening scenes play out: first between Marlowe and Carmen Sternwood, the ensuing scene with General Sternwood, the following brief scene with Norris, the next scene with Mrs. Rutledge, the fade cuts to the sign for Hollywood Public Library and then to the book Marlowe is looking at, and so on throughout the film. We're always with Marlowe; we see what he sees or we see him as others do. We have the same information he does when it comes to solving the mystery.

After that early exchange, we'll never see the General again, though he'll frequently be referred to. But this isn't unusual. The film is full of characters who only appear in a single scene, from the General to the girl at the library ("I collect blondes and bottles too," Marlowe tells her), and from the cute taxi driver who tells Marlowe to call her if he can use her again sometime ("night's better; I work during the day") to the Acme Bookstore clerk who nearly steals the show from the Sternwood sisters' sultry seductiveness.[32]

The prevalence of characters who only appear once in the movie forms an interesting contrast to *Casablanca*, where a relatively large cast of minor characters, including Ferrari, Major Strasser, Sascha the bartender, Carl the waiter, Yvonne the barfly, the nameless pickpocket, and the Bulgarian couple, appear repeatedly throughout the

---

[32] Agnes, who appears in four different scenes in the movie (making her virtually one of the main characters of the film), hits the nail on the head when she says, "There's some people you don't forget even if you only see them once."

movie. In *The Big Sleep*, Marlowe appears in every scene, and only a few other characters appear more than once or twice (Vivian, Carmen, Agnes, Eddie Mars, Bernie Ohls). Two of the most important characters in terms of the development of the plot, Sean Regan (who does the General's drinking for him) [33] and Owen Taylor (the mysteriously murdered chauffer), are never seen at all, only referred to again and again. The movie is full of absences, except for Marlowe, who's always present. We're always either watching him or watching what he's watching.

This watching is related to one of the first things we learn about Marlowe: people respond to the way he looks (as both an active and a passive verb). Like Carmen Sternwood ("you're cute"), the librarian ("you don't look like a man who'd be interested in first editions"), the cab driver, the girl in the bookstore, and even the cocktail waitress at Eddie Mars' place (who gives Marlowe an almost possessive onceover as she jealousy notices the eye-play between him and Vivian), we form our opinion of Marlowe as a result of what we see, gradually developing our respect, our admiration, perhaps even our secret desire to be "just like him" through these acts of looking. The visual impression the camera gives us communicates his cool, his confidence, his competence, and his attractiveness to women (despite the fact that he's "not very tall."[34]

---

[33] Regan is referred to by nearly every character in the movie (Sternwood, Vivian, Carmen, Ohls, Harry Jones, Agnes, Eddie Mars, Mars's wife) but we never see him. How could we, since we eventually learn that he's been dead since before the opening of that fateful door with which the movie begins?
[34] Bogart stood 5'9" to Bacall's 5'8".

The movie is all about looking: looking for, looking at, looking through or under or into, and even overlooking when it comes Vivian's indiscretions apropos her sister's faults and flaws. That's what detectives do: they look for clues, for patterns, for explanations. They look at the surface of things, where things are rarely what they appear to be, and try to divine what's really going on beneath that deceptive surface. Thus Marlowe is able to see the truth behind the lies told by characters like Agnes, Joe Brody, Vivian Rutledge, and Eddie Mars to throw him off the various tracks he's on throughout the movie.[35]

The story everyone (including Chandler in a letter he sent to his British publisher Jamie Hamilton in 1949) tells about the movie version of *The Big Sleep* is that at one point Hawks and the screenwriters (the impressive trio of William Faulkner, Leigh Brackett and Jules Furthman) couldn't figure out who killed the Sternwood chauffer Owen Taylor, so they asked Chandler, who said he didn't know either.[36] But Marlowe knows, and we do too. It's all a matter of seeing what's happening in each scene of the movie. "Try looking at me when you're talking," Marlowe tells Joe Brody when he's grilling him for information

---

[35] The two characters he seems to sincerely like, General Sternwood and Harry Jones, are virtually the only characters in the movie who tell it like it is, "one right guy to another."

[36] 'I remember several years ago when Howard Hawks was making *The Big Sleep*, the movie, he and Bogart got into an argument as to whether one of the characters was murdered or committed suicide. They sent me a wire (there's a joke about this too) asking me, and dammit I didn't know either. Of course I got hooted at. The joke was in connection with Jack Warner, the head of Warner Bros. Believe it or not he saw the wire, the wire cost the studio seventy cents, and he called Hawks up and asked him whether it was really necessary to send a telegram about a point like that." –Raymond Chandler, Letter to Hamish Hamilton, March 21st 1949.

about what happened the night Geiger was killed (and moments before Brody himself will be killed). Marlowe knows Brody is lying and so do we. Brody looks directly at Marlowe when he's telling the truth, but starts shifting in his chair and averting his eyes when he begins to lie. Marlowe keeps moving in order to see his face, stalking him with his gaze. Looking is how Marlowe figures out what's going on, who's lying and who's telling the truth, and what the truth really means when it is being told, or, as is so often the case with Vivian Rutledge, when it isn't.

Marlowe sees through Brody's lies, just as earlier in the movie he saw through Carmen Rutledge. One of these acts of looking—which in fact are a kind of reading (books and reading are featured prominently throughout the film, as are libraries and bookstores)—is how the whole movie begins.

Other than the polite exchange between Marlowe and Norris at the front door, Marlowe's dialogue with Carmen Sternwood is the first real interaction in the movie. As Norris moves to the back of the frame, Carmen moves to the center, taking his place as the focus of our, and Marlowe's, attention. He watches her come down the impressive staircase in an equally impressive and provocatively short pair of shorts, in stark contrast to Norris's bow-tied tuxedo and Marlowe's coat and hat. First he looks her up and down, appreciatively, and wishes her "good morning." Then it's her turn to look him over, which she does by turning to face him and uttering her first line of the movie, "You're not very tall, are you?" This appraisal leads Marlowe to look at himself: "Well I try to be." First Marlowe looks and appraises Carmen Sternwood; then Carmen looks over Marlowe, and finally Marlowe looks at himself, all in about 10 seconds.

Marlowe's response prompts Carmen to move in for a closer look. Only now she's not just looking; she's also showing. She wants Marlowe to look at her and she invites him to do so by the way she looks at him.

"Not bad looking; but you probably know it," she says, playing with her hair in a way that says, "I know I'm not bad looking either." She's flirting; he's evaluating. His looking is intended to help him reach conclusions about the person he's talking to. Her looking is intended to help him reach those conclusions. She wants him to know she's flirting with him (she probably thinks it's a way of gaining control of the situation by making him want something she's in a position to give or withhold), whereas he simply wants to know: Who am I dealing with here? He's not trying to make an impression on her; he's trying to lead her into revealing herself to him.

When he tells her he's a shamus she says, "You're making fun of me," and he agrees, which surprises her, only she doesn't realize in just what way he's making fun of her.[37]

---

[37] There's a moment in the film where Marlowe may be making fun of Vivian Sternwood-Rutledge as well. When Vivian says, "I was beginning to think you worked in bed like Marcel Proust," he asks "Who's he?" This parallels a moment later in the film when Marlowe finds Carmen in his apartment and tells her, "you came in through the keyhole like Peter Pan" and she asks, "Who's he?" But it's just as likely that Marlowe knows who Proust is as it is that Carmen knows who Peter Pan is. When the General asks Marlowe about himself Marlowe says, "There's not much to tell. I'm 38, I went to college." We know he's educated, so Vivian's "you wouldn't know him," tells us more about how superficially she reads Marlowe than it tells us about his put-on lack of literary sophistication. (Marlowe is a reader, as the shot of him in the L.A. County Library shows us, and as his behavior throughout the movie demonstrates repeatedly.) He knows she's putting on an act for him. She doesn't know he's doing the same for her. A moment later they're both putting on an act, this time for

He's not lying about being a private detective; he's just pretending an interest in her he's already lost now that he's had a chance to size her up. As soon as he sees her tilt her head, toss her hair and allow her tongue to play in the corner of her mouth, he realizes she doesn't warrant more than a lie about his name (Doghouse Riley). She wants to lead him on; he wants to see who she is. In the exchange only one of them gets what he wants, and Marlowe says to Norris as he's led in to see the General, "You ought to wean her; she's old enough." Norris's, "Yes sir" is a brilliant moment of urbane deference. (As is his line, "I make many mistakes," after Marlowe's brief meeting with Vivian Rutledge).

Later in the movie (after Marlowe has recovered the incriminating photo of her from Joe Brody), Carmen again tells Marlowe, "you're cute" (for the third time), and this time adds, "I like you." Marlowe tells her the truth, "What you see is nothing," adding, for good measure, "I've got a Balinese dancing girl tattooed across my chest." Even when she's not drugged up, Carmen can't see what's happening around her and can't even accurately read the surface, much less below the surface, of things. But seeing what's really going on is what Marlowe's paid for.

The looking game continues when Bacall's Vivian Sternwood-Rutledge makes her first appearance. She's pouring herself a drink and gives Marlowe a split-second look of appraisal before returning her eyes to the glass she's filling. When she turns her attention to him again, it's to announce, "My you're a mess aren't you," again appraising him with a quick look. The ensuing verbal exchange is charged by their glances, which duel with the

whoever's answered Vivian's call to the Police Station.

same ferocity as their words. Whereas Carmen melted into Marlowe's arms ("she tried to sit in my lap while I was standing up"), her big sister tries to manipulate him verbally, and pushes back where Carmen succumbed. We see right away which of the two sisters is the more interesting, self-possessed, and potentially dangerous one.

Since the movie is so much about looking, and about the conclusions people reach based on what they see, Marlowe adopts a simple but effective disguise a few scenes later when he enters Geiger's Rare Books to encounter Agnes for the first time. He changes the way he looks by putting on a pair of glasses and tipping up the brim of his hat. It's a rare bit of acting for Bogart, who gets to step out of the tough-guy routine to play an effeminate book collector just long enough to bait Agnes and confirm his suspicions about the nature of Geiger's business. Again, appearances are misleading; Agnes is no bookseller, Marlowe no book collector (the librarian had it right), and Geiger no bookstore owner. Solving the mystery lies in bridging the gap between how things look and how they are, being versus seeming, the oldest question in the philosophical handbook. Which is why Socrates was a kind of detective (hot on the trail of the True and the Beautiful), and why the detective always has to be a philosopher at heart.

On the heals of his exchange with Agnes, Marlowe walks across the street and into one of the most charged scenes in the movie, which unfolds, despite the terrific energy between Bogart and Bacall, between Marlowe and the bookshop girl (wonderfully played by Dorothy Malone): "You begin to interest me, vaguely," she says, in response to Marlowe's line of questioning, but also in response to how he looks, and perhaps more importantly, how he looks at her. As she describes what Geiger looks like she looks Marlowe up and down, indicating with her eyes all the points of distinction between the two men, and decidedly in Marlowe's favor. The more she speaks of Geiger, the more appreciative her glances at Marlowe become. As the visual exchanges become more intense, Marlowe breaks out a bottle of "pretty good rye" he just happens to have in his pocket, asks the girl to take off her glasses, and the reverse-transformation that Marlowe underwent when he put on a pair of glasses to enter Geiger's shop occurs. Their mutual "hello" marks a moment of true seeing, of recognition on Marlowe's part, and of appreciation for that recognition on the part of the girl.

They're both fully clothed after the fade that cuts to the shot of the rainy street outside the shop window, but the music suggests both the passage of time and something romantic (sexual) that Marlowe's friendly pat on the shoulder and his "so long pal" undermine. We're left with an odd sense of unconsummated potential, despite the charged nature of that "hello" they exchanged, the paper cups of rye on a rainy afternoon, the discreetly pulled-down shade over the front door, and the glances that have fueled the scene since Marlowe entered the shop. Her "if you ever want to buy a book" is an open invitation that somehow we know Marlowe's fraternal pat rejects.

And yet despite the emphasis on seeing, the movie is still primarily driven by its dialogue. A few punches are thrown. A few shots are fired. Several people are killed. A few kisses are exchanged. But by and large, this is no action movie (despite the plethora of dead bodies). The plot unfolds through a series of conversations: Marlowe and Carmen, Marlowe and General Sternwood, Marlowe and Mrs. Rutledge, Marlowe and the woman in the bookstore, Marlowe and Joe Brody, Marlowe and Eddie Mars, Marlowe and Mrs. Rutledge again. This is a talking movie, accompanied by the looking that goes on (and all that looking implies) when two people talk to each other.

In between the talking, Marlowe has plenty more looking to do as part of his work: stakeouts, house searches, cracking codes, sizing up (and taking down) various bad guys—all forms of looking which he does in the line of duty. But duty to whom? Half an hour into the movie, it's not even clear who he's working for any longer. (This is characteristic of Marlowe in most of Chandler's novels and certainly true in Paul Bogart's 1969 *Marlowe* starring James Garner.[38]) He's on the trail of something, something he doesn't quite see yet, but has caught a glimpse of, and is going to pursue to the end.

Marlowe gets there by looking. In his second conversation with Vivian they're talking about Carmen's forgetfulness. "Just what did she forget about Sean Regan?" he asks. "What did she tell you?" Vivian counters, and his response, "Not half so much as you just did," refers entirely to a play of expressions that crossed Vivian's face in response to his question. She so put off by his cheeky perceptiveness she almost slaps him. Marlowe doesn't just look; he reads the people he sees, and reads them more accurately then they read him, which gives him an edge he knows how to take advantage of. Marlowe's skill as a detective comes down to shades of this: his ability to look, to see, and to read. The same skills we need when

---

[38] A role which no doubt taught him how to say "200 dollars a day plus expenses" with considerably more conviction when he went on to play Private Eye Jim Rockford between 1974 and 1980.

watching a movie. As audience we're playing detective along with Marlowe; it's an opportunity we have every time we sit down to watch a movie.

It's because he's a good reader (again, see the shot of him pouring over a book in the L.A. County library, or a later shot of Marlowe at his desk with a stack of books in front of him trying to crack the code in Geiger's notebook) that Marlowe knows Mrs. Rutledge is lying to him when she phones to say she hasn't heard from Agnes, and it's how he knows Eddie Mars has "got something" on her. It's because he's a good reader that he knows how far he can push Mars when they meet in Geiger's house for the first time. It's because he's a good reader that he knows the roulette game Vivian plays at Eddie's club is a set up. For Marlowe being a detective means being a good reader. He reads people; he reads situations; reading and detecting both require the same set of skills. Just like watching movies. For the thoughtful audience, such watching is always a kind of reading.

Learning must be preceded by the belief that it is possible to be better than we currently are. This belief (an acknowledgement of a certain degree of ignorance) is the precondition of education. Reading well is a form of seeing well. To see more, to see better, to be more sensitive, nuanced, perceptive, aware . . . this is why we read. It's a reciprocal relationship: the better we read, the more we see; the more we see, the better we read. This better reading is one of the things the movies can teach us.

Marlowe's Odyssey: Robert Altman's *The Long Goodbye* (1973)

When Howard Hawks made *The Big Sleep* with Humphrey Bogart in 1945, Chandler's *The Long Goodbye* wouldn't even be written for another eight years, and Altman would wait another 20 before making (and setting) it in 1973 L.A. The time and place are important, because the movie is more about a particular moment in time and space (California in the early 1970s) than it is about the mystery of an unsolved murder.

It's a sometimes-underappreciated truism about works of narrative art that in order to successfully express universal themes, they must be rooted in great specificity. There are no great novels directly *about* jealousy, revenge, madness, obsession, friendship, democracy, man's relationship to God, or "the search for meaning"; instead there's a novel about a maimed ship's captain hunting a big fish, or a lonely guy about to be cuckolded wandering around Dublin, or a woman getting ready for a party, in which all these themes burst forth from marvelous depths. If you want to tackle universal themes, you have to set your story in a very specific time and place and make your hero a very specific man or woman; otherwise you just go spinning off into the vagaries of dull assertion. In art, you get to the general through the specific or you don't get there at all.

One of the ways movies can achieve this specificity is through the details of realism. Writing about the realism in Hitchcock's 1930s British films, Raymond Durgnat observed,

> realism in the '30s was a rarer and more difficult achievement ... the director couldn't just point a T.V. camera in the street. He had first to notice certain details, love them enough to remember and to recreate them, and lastly to slide them deftly into a thriller context.

I think we see this kind of love for the realism of the everyday in Altman's eye for detail. A very different eye, a very different realism, and a very different kind of love than we find in near-contemporary Cassavetes' films (the toughest love in cinema) like *Husbands* (1970), *A Woman Under the Influence* (1974), and *The Killing of a Chinese Bookie* (1976). Examples: the items in Marlowe's kitchen, the "Specials" signs in the windows of the 24-hour Thriftymart (as well as the security guard reading a magazine on the job and the red bowtie, green vest, and haircut (or lack thereof) of the clerk working the checkout counter), the Customs sign between California and Tijuana, the enormous bronzed baby shoe in Marlowe's apartment, the automatic photo machine at the police station, the roll of toilet paper handed to Socrates in his jail cell, the sandwich menu on the wall of the bar where Marlowe gets his phone messages, the woman selling snacks through the windows of the bus in Mexico.

It's this kind of attention to detail that Altman uses to highlight his anachronistic version of Chandler's hero in his 1948 Lincoln Continental (a convertible the top of which never comes down during the course of the entire sun-drenched movie) and ubiquitous black suit. While the people around him are naked or in the flowing robes of 1970s California Counter Culture, Marlowe wears this suit in every scene in the movie:[39] to the Thriftymart at 3:00 a.m., in prison, on the beach, on his two visits to Mexico. Drinking on the beach with Roger Wade, Marlowe refuses to remove his tie. He's the one thing in the movie that constantly looks out of time and place against the backdrop of all these period-specific details. He's been transplanted from L.A. circa the 1950s to L.A. in 1973 so that we can see through his eyes just how deeply bizarre and alien this moment in American culture really is. Eliot Gould's constant refrain, "It's OK with me," rings like some kind of mantra: the stranger the world around him becomes (curiouser and curiouser), the more he affirms his bland acceptance of it. By the end of the film, however, it's clear that the way things are is not "OK" with Marlowe. He's something of a stranger in a strange land, but not because he's been displaced by 20 years from 1950 to the 1970s. Things are even more out of joint than that.[40]

Diderot wrote, "Foreigners, because they never have enough words to express their ideas, often invent remarkable new modes of expression. Poets are all foreigners." One of the beauties of Altman's film is that it has the effect of making us feel like foreigners in our own country, giving us that eerie "out of time and place" feel that lends new vitality to our acts of seeing. We see more when everything seems alien and strange. In *The Long*

---

[39] Unshaven and in his rumpled suit Gould's Marlowe makes fellow 1970s detective Columbo look like a fashion model.

[40] One thing that's changed in the 27 years since Hawks' movie is that Marlowe's fees have doubled: "50 dollars a day and expenses." Not bad considering inflation (and considerably less than Jim Rockford would start charging only a year later). Another difference is that Hawks' Marlowe went to college and Altman's didn't. In the 1940s having a college education probably set a man apart as much as not going to college did in the 1970s.

Goodbye, this strangeness is intensified by the fact that Marlowe isn't out of place by a mere 20 years. In fact he's coming to us from a past nearly 3,000 years old.

Generally speaking, I dislike reading any work of art as a series of symbols that point to or represent something else. I tend to dislike allegorical readings, overt symbolism, or speaking of art in terms of a "key" that will lead to the discovery of some deeper hidden meaning. So when I suggest that understanding Marlowe's relationship to his nubile neighbors is the key to understanding some of the larger themes in the film, I'm doing so under advisement. Perhaps it would be better to say that it was puzzling over Marlowe's relationship to the "girls" that first opened my eyes to a realm of possibility presented by the movie. In particular, the possibility that Marlowe is the most recent in a long line of avatars of a 3,000 year-old literary figure named Odysseus introduced to us by a possibly blind poet named Homer.

It's warm enough in L.A. for these girls (who never seem to sleep; one of the first clues to their "true" identity) to comfortably go about in various states of undress (another clue), but Marlowe puts on his coat and tie in order to drive to the 24-hour Thriftymart to buy cat food. It's while he's on this first odyssey in the movie ("Cat gets me to go out at three in the morning to get him a special kind of food; I gotta be out of my fucking mind,") that Marlowe encounters his first Odyssean nemeses, the Sirens. Their apartment is a kind of island suspended above the street below (and oddly protected by a transplanted traffic light) and the girls sing to him as he passes by, calling him over. One of the girls asks him to buy her two boxes of fudge brownie mix. These Siren neighbors are calling Marlowe to join them on their version of the Isle of the Lotus Eaters, but Marlowe is immune to the charms that captivate visitors to his own island-like apartment from both sides of the law (the two cops, Marty Augustine and his henchmen), even refusing a brownie one of the Sirens offers to save for him (they hurt his teeth). He has lashed himself to a sense of duty to (and affection for) his cat, and sails on past. This sense of duty and affection (which add up to a kind of loyalty) are early clues to Marlowe's character. They allow him to resist the Sirens' call, but not an appeal for help in the name of friendship from Terry Lennox.

If the first Odyssean characters Marlowe encounters are the Sirens, later he will confront a kind of Cyclops character in the figure of Roger Wade. Or is Wade more like Hephaestus, the lame creator god (in Wade's case impotent, though there's also Wade's cane, rescued by the dog (Cerberus?) from the ocean after Wade's suicide (in Chandler's novel a murder))? Hephaestus is married to the beautiful but untrustworthy Eileen Wade as Aphrodite, who doubles in the movie as a kind of Circe. Circe/Aphrodite welcomes Marlowe into their home. Cyclops/Hephaestus threatens to devour him but ends up drinking with him instead. Circe tempts him with lulling drugs: the lies of a beautiful woman, but also the dried apricots. Perhaps his camel cigarettes are the Moly he takes to protect himself from the spell she tries to cast on him. Later the gangster Marty Augustine, with his accompanying thugs and the litany of his expensive lifestyle, presents himself as an all-devouring Laestrygonian figure, brutal and voracious. Verringer's clinic (and for that matter, all of L.A.) is a land of Lotus Eaters. The cat may even be a kind of Penelope figure, representing a sense of home that is lost early in the movie and which Marlowe is struggling to recapture throughout the film.

And then there's that most pervasive of Odyssean nemeses, the Wine Dark Sea, which claims the life of Roger Wade (more convenient, and more Californian, than the novel's added level of complexity of having him murdered by his wife). Marlowe doesn't even seem to know he's sailing past the Scylla and Charybdis of Eileen Wade and Marty Augustine. There are casualties along the way, but like Odysseus, Marlowe will make it through only to face his ultimate challenge at the end of his final journey (which he makes by cheap Mexican bus rather than dark-prowed sailing vessel).

The analogy, of course, is not perfect, though it's fun to play with the possibilities. For example, the police chief in Mexico drives a "gold chariot." Is Terry Lennox a kind of wayward Telemachus? Why is there no female Penelope giving Marlowe a sense of home to return to? Which Homeric figure does the gatekeeper with a penchant for bad Hollywood impersonations represent? And the theory is all the more interesting if Altman was wholly unaware of any possible parallels and if all of the above is merely coincidental. In his own retelling of the *Odyssey*, James Joyce was quite explicit about making his modern-day Nobody an avatar of the Homeric hero (the novel opens with a discussion of metempsychosis between Molly (a different kind of Moly) and Bloom).

In Homer's poem, Odysseus names himself "Nobody" while trapped in the Cyclops' cave. In Joyce's *Ulysses* it's the world around Leopold Bloom that tells him, again and again throughout the long day of June 16, 1904, that he's a Nobody. Altman's Marlowe is something else altogether, an outsider who occupies the same landscape as the people around him, but on very different terms. As he says to David Carradine's character Socrates (another big fan of Homer), with whom he shares a bunk in jail: "Remember, you're not in here; it's just your body." If Homer intended Odysseus as a kind of Nobody-Everyman, it should hardly be surprising to encounter different versions of him popping up over the past 3,000 years on odysseys of their own.

Over-emphasizing any strict parallels between the *Odyssey* and *The Long Goodbye* would be pointless. It's a muddled affair at best; in the *Odyssey* the Sirens have nothing to do with the Lotus Eaters nor does Aphrodite have any obvious connection with Circe (though she is married to Hephaestus, to Ares' regret), but certain affinities are there. Not necessarily because Altman consciously put them there, but because such similarities are inevitable when a great attention to specificity gives rise to an exploration of more universal themes.

And while Los Angeles can hardly be considered a universal theme, it's true that the movie is more about L.A. (a place where people seem particularly prone to being adrift) than it is about solving a murder mystery. And why, after treating viewers to a half-dozen different renditions of John Williams' song "The Long Goodbye" (performed as part of the ambient sound of the film by hippie bongo drums, a doorbell, a Mexican funeral band, a lounge singer, and piped in as Supermarket Muzak) does the film end with the song "Hooray for Hollywood"? The song arises not from within the ambient space of the film, but as music that suddenly appears from nowhere as Marlowe inexplicably celebrates (by dancing with an old Mexican woman in the street) the fact that he's just murdered the man he thought was his friend. Why does a movie about L.A. end with a paean to Hollywood sung in Mexico? Why does a movie about friendship end with the murder of a friend? These questions are closer to the true mystery of the movie than the question of who killed Sylvia Lennox (the murder victim who, like Sean Regan in Howard Hawks' *The Big Sleep*, we keep hearing about but never see, since she's dead before the movie even begins).

3:00 in the morning is the perfect time to begin a movie about a man out of time. Even people who get up early don't get up at 3:00 a.m., and even people who stay up late don't usually stay up that late. (Bars in L.A. generally close at 2:00.) But everyone is up in this movie: Terry Lennox, the guard at the Malibu Colony (who seems to be on duty 24 hours a day; he says as much: "duty, duty, always on duty"), the employees at the Thrifymart (who know Marlowe by name), and of course Marlowe's neighbors. The movie opens with a shot of Marlowe fully clothed (except for his tie and jacket) asleep on a rumpled bed without pillowcases next to a plate of half-eaten food and a discarded magazine under a glaring light bulb that makes it look as if, even while asleep, he's under interrogation. The wall is marred from marks left by matches he strikes on the most improbable surfaces (Marlowe is the only person I've ever seen light a safety match on glass) to produce the most improbably large flames to light his ubiquitous cigarettes. No one else in the movie smokes; even the girls next door bake their marijuana into brownies rather than smoke it; even alcoholic Roger Wade refrains from the vice of smoking and he calls Marlowe the Marlboro Man at least in partial reference to his smoking (although Marlowe appears to smoke rather poorly rolled Camels).

Enter the cat. Throughout the movie, Marlowe keeps up a muttering monologue with himself, commenting on the events and people around him ("it's OK with me"). We know he's just talking to his cat, continuing a conversation he began in the opening scene of the movie and which he never finishes, in part because the cat has run away. The whole film might be read as nothing more complicated than Marlowe's search for his lost cat, another sort of Odyssean theme strained through a few dozen centuries of transformation. (Joyce's *Ulysses* also opens with a scene between Bloom and his cat. In the *Odyssey*, Odysseus comes home in time to see his dog Argos die, perhaps from the joy of seeing his long lost master one last time.) In place of the lost cat, Marlowe encounters a number of dogs along the way (the Wade's Doberman, the dogs that get in the way of his car, the ubiquitous dogs in Mexico). Dogs and cats. Cat and mouse: the game Marlowe is playing with Terry and doesn't even know it.

Before writing the screenplay for *The Long Goodbye*, Leigh Brackett co-wrote *The Big Sleep* with William Faulkner and Jules Furthman[41] for Howard Hawks. As with Bogart in its 1946 predecessor, Altman's Marlowe appears in every scene in the movie. The one exception, about an hour into the movie, is the conversation between Wade and his wife, while Marlowe stands out on the beach "counting waves." And even this scene is shot with a kind of double exposure effect to make it look like

---

[41] Hollywood trivia: Brackett also collaborated with Furthman on the screenplay for Hawks' 1959 *Rio Bravo* and co-wrote the 1980 *The Empire Strikes Back*, making her contributions to great examples of noir, neo-noir, the Western, and science fiction among the most far-ranging and impressive in the annals of Hollywood screenplay writing.

Marlowe is present (his figure is on the screen) even though he's not in the room and not party to the conversation. It's the only thing that happens in the movie that the audience sees and hears that Marlowe doesn't. Otherwise, in terms of clues (to a mystery that doesn't really even exist) we're in possession of the same facts that Marlowe has himself. Of course it's an important conversation for him to miss, since it provides the crucial clue to the fact the Eileen Wade doesn't want her husband back home ("saved" from Dr. Verringer) because she's worried about him, but because she wants to continue taunting him into drinking, pushing him towards the suicide she knows he's on the brink of.

In the scene where Roger wades into the ocean, does Sylvia chase after him to try and save him, or to prevent Marlowe from being able to do so? Verringer may be a mincing quack and a "little jerk" (Wade calls him "the albino turd" and Marlowe observes that writers have an interesting way of describing things), but Wade may actually be safer and better off with him than he is with his beautiful and manipulative wife. (We know something's not right about Eileen Wade when we see her driving out of the building where Marty Augustine's 350K has just been mysteriously returned, sparing Marlowe the unwanted services of an unwitting mohel.[42])

The scene in which Marlowe is simultaneously absent from the room and present on the screen is also the scene that shows us that Wade really does love his wife, and that the only way she'll be free of him is if he dies. He won't leave her and she can't leave him without

---

[42] Bloom's Jewish heritage is a major theme in *Ulysses*. Making his gangster Jewish rather than Italian or Irish is an interesting touch by Altman.

implicating Lennox. (Marlowe mistakenly assumes Wade has killed himself over guilt about violently murdering Sylvia Lennox. We know he's killed himself over the anguish of having lost his wife to Terry Lennox and associated feelings of inadequacy tied up with his alcoholism, impotency, and inability to write.) Its only during the last shot of the movie, as Marlowe walks past Eileen Wade in the jeep she's driving on her way to Terry, that we realize why she wanted to get rid of her husband in the first place. Nina Van Pallandt is perfectly cast as a 1970s version of Chandler's Eileen Wade, the manipulative wife who drives her husband to drink and suicide. In Chandler's novel she's a double murderer. Altman and Leigh let her off easier: she's just unfaithful and in love with a murderer (who in the novel is the one who gets off easier).[43] In the novel it's Terry who's unfaithful, though to a friend, not a spouse. This failure of friendship is something Chandler's book, Altman's movie, Joyce's novel and Homer's poem all have in common. It's one of those "universal themes" we can only get at through great specificity.

We've been trained by the movies to assume that things are never as simple as they appear, that the police always jump to the easy but wrong conclusion, and that the outsider, swim-against-the-stream detective will get to the truth in the end because he's motivated by friendship, duty, and loyalty ("Terry Lennox was my friend,"

---

[43] In fact the most complicated thing about Altman's film may be those efforts on the part of viewers to square what happens in the movie with what happens in Chandler's novel. In the movie, Terry is a murderer; in the novel he's not. In the novel Wade is killed (by his wife); in the movie he commits suicide (thanks to his wife). The movie makes much more sense for viewers who've never read the book and don't expect the two to resemble each other.

Marlowe insists from first to last) rather than greed, fear, and laziness. Marlowe refuses to settle for the easy answer, refuses to back down when imprisoned, threatened, bribed and lied to, and in the end he's simply wrong. Terry Lennox did kill his wife. The police were right all along. Maybe Terry wasn't his friend after all. Maybe Terry is right when he calls Marlowe "a born loser."

"I even lost my cat," Marlowe tells Terry as he pulls the trigger. Lost in addition to what else?

Marlowe persists in believing, and acting in accordance with his belief throughout the movie that Terry Lennox didn't kill his wife. This is a belief readers of Chandler's novel easily join him in, since in the novel Lennox doesn't kill his wife, which is why there's no reason for Marlowe to kill Terry in the novel. In fact, it's not clear why Marlowe kills Terry in the movie. The real mystery of the movie is not who killed Sylvia Lennox (since this time the police got it right), but why Marlowe kills Terry Lennox. It's not a "who done it?" but a "why did he do it?"

The heroes in the epic poetry of Homer, Virgil, Dante, Milton, and Joyce all have to journey to the underworld. Marlowe's visit to Mexico is in fact a journey to visit a dead man. Since Terry Lennox is already dead (as far as the world of the living is concerned), in what sense does Marlowe kill him? Marlowe's odyssey through the movie is a quest to prove the innocence of his friend; in other words, to prove that his friend really is a friend. When Marlowe finds out, to Chandler's readers' surprise, that Terry is the murderer, everything Marlowe has done for Terry throughout the film is shown to have been pointless. But in itself this isn't a reason to kill a man. (But how can you kill a man who's already dead?) If Odysseus is trying to get back home, what is Marlowe after?

When he finds Terry in Mexico, Marlowe says, "I've come for the truth. The truth about Terry Lennox." This is the truth he's been searching for over the course of the entire movie. Not the truth about a murder, or Roger Wade's suicide, or Marty Augustine's missing money, but the truth about his friend—the truth about friendship itself.

One thing Altman's Marlowe has in common with Odysseus and Joyce's Leopold Bloom is the notion that the hero is always a man (or woman) alone and out of time. Odysseus is gone for 20 years (which is about how out of time Altman's 1950s Marlowe is with 1973 L.A.). Odysseus returns alone, without friends or companions. By killing Terry, Marlowe is left without a friend.

The Last Goodbye: as Marlowe walks away from the scene of his crime, Eileen Wade passes him, on her way to discover Terry's dead body. Like Orpheus, she looks back. Marlowe doesn't, but like Orpheus he's brought his music with him to the underworld (in the form of the world's smallest harmonica). Also like Orpheus, Marlowe can leave, but he can't bring his Eurydice with him. He leaves the way he arrived: alone. Perhaps he'll find his cat waiting for him when he gets home.

So perhaps the real point of similarity between Marlowe and Odysseus (ultimately superficial albeit interesting parallels between the two texts notwithstanding) is an essential solitude shared by the two men. Is this what really makes Odysseus, Leopold Bloom, and Philip Marlowe accurate portrayals of "every man": the solitude they share, and share with us? Aren't we all alone, whenever we experience a work of art? And isn't it because we're alone that we seek that experience in the first place? (Why we read a book, listen to music, or go to the movies?) Perhaps our longing for aesthetic experience is an attempt to overcome that solitude and achieve some point of contact with the work, or the artist, or even ourselves. Perhaps that's why Marlowe dances to the strains of "Hooray for Hollywood" as he walks off alone. What else does he have left, except the movies?

Bertolucci's Dark Night of the (Fascist) Soul: *The Conformist* (1970)

Love is nothing other than the impulse of
the creative imagination.

–Stoicorum Veretum Fragmenta, III.650

The first movie theatre was described by Socrates, who gives us the timeless image of a group of men and women staring fixedly at the wall in front of them while images play across its surface, competing with reality for a claim on their attention. Two thousand years before the invention of camera or film, the principle of using light and shadow to cast images, and the deeper question of the relation between these images and the reality they somehow represent, formed the very core of the Platonic philosophy. Men and women have been watching movies since the dawn of Western Philosophy. Indeed, this dawn is identical with the same metaphysical questions stirred in us by the cinema today.

I

The first point consists in this, that I see with the eye of the imagination those enormous fires, and the souls as it were in bodies of fire...

The Third point consists in this, that I taste with the sense of taste of the imagination the bitter things, the tears, sorrows and the worms of conscience in hell.

–St. Ignacius Loyola, *The Spiritual Exercises*

In my mind I've formed an imaginative trilogy co
of Jacques Tati's 1967 *Playtime*, Bertolucci's 19\
Conformist, and Terry Gilliam's 1985 *Brazil*. Wha\
these movies for me is their use of light and shad\
portray space as an antagonistic element, in particula
oscillating images of enclosed claustrophobic spaces
vast open spaces, both of which succeed in portraying
individual as small and insignificant.

For example, consider the difference between th\
overhead images of *Brazil*'s Sam Lowry's office in room
DZ-015 at his new job with Information Retrieval with
the shot of him entering the building to report to his first
day of work.

This later image reminds me of the scene in *The
Conformist* where Marcello Clerici reports to a building
that houses a similarly menacing (only more historically
accurate) ministry for an interview of his own. The use of
lighting, perspective, and camera angle in these images
make the human figure appear small in comparison to its
outstretched shadow, which seems more tangibly real
than the man who casts it. This tension between the
reality of shadow versus substance is a central theme in
The Conformist, and is also a subtle theme in *Playtime* and
Brazil. The latter two movies choose to respond to the
portrayal of man as insignificant and largely powerless in
his surroundings with a kind of ominous humor. *The
Conformist* tackles it head on, more sensually, though
equally psychologically. In contrast to Roberto Benigni's
1997 *Life is Beautiful*, Bertolucci constructs his film
around the assumption that there's nothing funny about
Italian fascism. Or, more subtly, perhaps he's suggesting
that a character unable to find anything funny in the

world around him is doomed to end up like Clerici (not that Sam Lowry fairs any better). Benigni, Gilliam, and Tati's decisions to respond to fascism (or perhaps in Tati's case to something more like the totalitarianism of polished and efficient Capitalism, which ends up looking scarily similar) with humor is a bold one, and perhaps in the end one just as revelatory of fascism's potential horrors as Bertolucci's more somber approach.

Looking to the history of cinema, there is something decidedly ominous in the use of light and shadow, along with the silhouettes of two figures in military-like uniforms and the lone chair waiting as if for a man about to undergo interrogation—as in the shot of the reporter's visit to the Thatcher Memorial Library in Orson Welles' *Citizen Kane*. Equally important, however, is a kind of impressive beauty that shots like these capture. Fascist space is not only threatening; it uses light to create a sense of imposing grandeur that can impress us with its beauty even as it intimidates us with its implications. And in this reaction we are no different from a character like Marcello Clerici.

Compare the play of light and shadow and the dwarfing perspective in the shot of the impersonal office building that swallows up Monsieur Hulot in Tati's *Playtime* with a similar shot in *The Conformist*, when Marcello has offered himself up to the maw of fascism and is waiting to be consumed. Light and shadow carve up long expanses of space that entrap the individual so that he appears lost, small, and powerless. (Again someone in a vaguely military-looking uniform presides.)

Any movie, even the most conventional, exists by virtue of the interaction of light and shadow.[44] This is simply the

physics of cinema. Certain movies, like *The Conformist*, create from this interaction sensually provocative images of stunning artistry. In this case the artistry is due to the collaborative genius of Bertolucci, cinematographer Vittorio Storaro (whose work on *Apocalypse Now* would give that movie some of the same visually powerful qualities) and Art Director Ferdinando Scarfiotti, with significant help from costume designer Gitt Magrini, especially in the entrancing dance scene between Stefania Sandrelli's Giulia and Dominique Sanda's Anna.

The Conformist is a somewhat paradoxical condemnatory celebration of the beauty of fascist space and the fascist body, but always with a spiritual counter-theme running through it. This counter-theme is expressed in part by the haunting quality of Clerici's face; his tortured eyes full of never-quite-successfully-repressed doubt, which remind us of the interior dimension that fascism seeks ultimate control over. This struggle for control, the struggle between the inner and outer, is where the movie's tension, drama, and suspense reside. Superficially political, the movie in fact is about the battle for a man's soul. That the same man in danger of losing his soul is the one doing the battling only makes it all the more familiar, and terrifying. If the enemy were outside, wouldn't it be easier to fight? The thesis of this essay, more or less, is that the overt political, psychological, and philosophical

---

[44] Each of us to whom the idea that Plato's allegory of the cave (from Book VII of *The Republic*) is an image of the first movie theatre has occurred has experienced the delight that such an insight and an analysis of its implications brings with it. This idea has been explored by the movie world innumerable of times. We see it in the Wachowskis' 1999 *The Matrix*, in Susan Sontag's *On Photography*, in Stanley Cavell's *The World Viewed*, in Raul Ruiz's *Poetics of Cinema*, and we see it explored with particular brilliance in Bertolucci's *The Conformist*.

themes of the film (perhaps deliberately) obscure the fact that *The Conformist* is really more about what might be called a fascism of the soul than it is about political or social fascism. Along with its grand architecture and vast use of space, this too is typical of fascism: it fights for the soul by first denying its worth and extolling the body in its place, and then swooping down and claiming the uncontested prize once it has been abandoned by the defender.

Despite the gorgeous portrayals of physical space, we should not lose track of the fact that most of *The Conformist* takes place in Clerici's head. These are not so much a series of flashbacks as they are a visual record of one man's mental space. For Clerici this is the real space of fascism: his own mental landscape. In *Brazil* the only way Sam Lowry can escape the fascist control of the world around him is to retreat into the fantasy space of his own mind; fantasy provides an escape from reality. (And ultimately yields to madness.) For Clerici, fantasy is the most fascist realm of all, and reality provides no relief. His very imagination has become impoverished through the pressures of reality. The crisis of the movie, which the flashbacks build up to as he sits in the back of the car driven by Manganiello racing towards Anna, is the revelation that even love is not strong enough to break his self-imposed bonds.

For Clerici, who has willfully embraced fascism, life appears as oppressive outside the cave as it is inside. In the film, he seems to be the one person who's aware of being trapped: Professor Quadri thinks he's escaped; the thought of being confined by an ideology never even occurs to Giulia, Italo, or Manganiello; Clerici's father (for whom madness constitutes a different kind of freedom;

he is a willing inmate in the cave) literally calls for and embraces his bonds: his is only the most visible of a number of straightjackets present throughout the film. But Clerici seems more intent on turning this imprisonment into a kind of protective shell than he is in liberating himself. *Playtime*'s Monsieur Hulot is equally at odds with his oppressive environment, but he bumbles his way through by virtue of a kind of salvific oblivion. Romance and nostalgia, which Sam Lowry clings to as fantasy, are unwitting accomplices for Hulot, who can neither change the world around him (it is far too vast and efficient for that) nor adapt himself to it (he is far too small and inefficient for that); he must simply reach an uneasy truce with a world which is ultimately more indifferent than it is hostile.

Fascism takes many forms: political, philosophical, psychological.[45] But the form of fascism the film is most intent on plumbing is a kind of fascism of the spirit. Fear, greed, faith—according to the colonel these are the reasons most people collaborate with the Fascist Regime. But Clerici's reasons are more mysterious. The movie suggests his reasons are psychological (his sexual encounter with and believed murder of the chauffer), philosophical (as a reading of Plato's *Republic*, which is certainly vulnerable to being interpreted as sympathetic to fascist political ideologies[46]), and social (the desire simply to "fit in", to conform). But behind these

---

[45] And it is precisely these three P's of critical discourse that threaten to obscure the true power of the film, which for me lies in something far more visceral, spiritual, and tangibly visible. Opposed to these P's is the aesthetic, a realm not of hermeneutic exigency and utility but of physical and spiritual unity.

[46] Cf. Karl Popper's *The Open Society and Its Enemies, Vol. 1: The Spell of Plato*. Popper's reading of Plato is wrong, but not impossible.

ideological suggestion,s there is evidence of something more tangible. The colonel who interviews him says, "I must ask myself what your aim is." The movie reveals this aim to the viewer through an accumulation of visual and physical images. For example, the emphasis on the sexuality of his fiancée's body (and the reference to her maid's large breasts, which will be "part of the dowry").

Inside (and there is an inside to Clerici, a fact which, as a fascist, he seems bent on denying), Clerici isn't really a fascist; he's a sensualist whose guilt about his own sensuality leads him to seek punishment; this is the unavoidable Freudian element in the film, driven home by the protagonist's interactions with his mother and father. But this very notion of an interior dimension that I (and his old philosophy professor Quadri) attribute to him already sets up the classic fascist tension between an "inside" (the realm of the individual, which in fascism must be denied or repressed) and an "outside" (the realm of the social, which eclipses all): "state before family" Clerici reminds Manganiello in the scene in which he renounces his mother's decadence, which perhaps reminds him too much of his own. Of course once we start carving people up like this we've already given fascism the upper hand.

Clerici tells his blind friend Italo that he wants to get married in order to achieve "the impression of normalcy" and "stability and security" (good fascist values, though certainly not exclusively fascist ones) but when pressed he speaks of his fiancée's body and her sensuality. This "body and sensuality" is the counterpoint to the spiritual struggle charted in the movie. These are the classic antipodes of Western Dualism. Parmenides and Heraclitus, in different ways, both asserted the primacy of the One (Being/Becoming, Unity/Change). Most of the Pre-Socratics were monists. Despite his Idealism, Plato, whose figure presides over the movie, is the West's first best dualist (Socrates himself might not have been). In the *Phaedrus*, the *Phaedo*, and other Platonic dialogues, man is described as a body and a soul, at war with one another, the body a prison for the soul. The philosopher's task is to escape. This antagonistic dualism is another aspect fascism: the notion of imprisonment (which eventually becomes the image of the "velvet cage"), the suppression of the inner (the chaotic personal) by the outer (the ordered social).

We like our bodies. They feel much more real to us than the elusive soul. Fascism celebrates the body not by denying the soul, but by subjugating the soul to the body. It is the opposite of certain forms of mysticism (meditation, dance, chant, ritual, Tantric practices) that seek to liberate the soul by means of the body. This is a subjugation Clerici readily falls prey to, in part because his sensual proclivities already incline him in that direction.

Like Plato's cave, where shadows are mistaken for reality (and the light that causes them is overlooked—for there can be no shadow without a source of light), Clerici clings to the reality of bodies. In the movie, Manganiello is all body. The story he tells Clerici about his crisis of consciousness ("It isn't your patriotism, it isn't your honor you're betraying. It is really you.") is the account of how he overcame any spiritual misgivings about his unquestioning devotion to a life of violence and physical action in service to the cause: he pats himself on the back, smokes a cigar, and gets back in the fight. And it really is him. Or what's left of him.

Before delivering his radio talk, Italo sits at a desk with a powerfully illuminated but useless desk lamp. (This is the blind man who, later in the film, will define "normal" as a man who turns his head to see a beautiful woman's bottom—a standard he must know he can never himself fulfill.[47]) His talk, "Mystique of an Alliance" starts by referring to Italy and Germany as "two strongholds of light"; the irony of a blind man (thus immune to the visual sensualism that captivates Clerici throughout the film) speaking of light is emphasized by the dance of his fingers over the brail of his text. Italo is a true fascist, and if his blindness is a bit heavy handed in this regard, it is nevertheless significant in terms of the movie's constant themes (portrayed visually and stylistically as well as in the narrative) of light and shadow, black and white.

Black and white are not strict moral categories in the movie, but aesthetic ones.[48] Against this black and white backdrop, Clerici himself is gray. His suit is gray, his hat is gray, his pallor is gray; he is often shot in a gray half-light that seems to echo his moral ambiguity (especially while he is in the back of the car driven by Manganiello: the place from which he remembers the scenes that constitute most of the film's narrative). He peers out from behind gray curtains the first time he sees the woman who may or may not be the same Anna he will meet later in the brothel, and then again in Paris.

---

[47] Italo is the fascist who says, "I am never wrong" as the camera pans down to a shot of his mismatched shoes.

[48] In the opening scene the radio studio singers' black and white dresses anticipate the contrast we shall see throughout the movie; for example, during Giulia's solo dance in the slat-shivered light of her apartment building which is itself an anticipation of the black and white-gowned dance with Anna.

He is a gray man in a black and white world: the light that cuts the space of the film into sharply delineated slats (like the bars of a cage imprisoning Clerici), the uniforms and white marble of his father's sanitarium and his black straightjacket, the black car driven by the chauffer Lino, the white sheets lining the way to Lino's room. Even as a 13 year-old boy Clerici is dressed in gray. He is a man of shadows, searching for reality. But searching where?

Love is where things get complicated. We love with our bodies. And yet the experience of love leads us to feel (to wonder, to suspect, to hope) that we are more than bodies. Love, which may very well start with or as sex, has a way of suggesting to us that sex is just the beginning: the outer manifestation of an inner phenomenon. Sam Lowry and Monsieur Hulot are both tied to the desire of love for a beautiful woman, but these are women they cannot possess (or must lose as soon as they possess them) lest the bodily eclipse or obscure the true stakes of their struggle, which is for love on a different plane than the merely sexual. Thus they carry on spiritual struggles of their own.

When Clerici sees Anna for the first time his look is that of a man who has just been struck by a bolt of lightning. She is the first character in the movie to be shown wearing gray other than Clerici himself. (Anna appears in a light gray bordering on white, Clerici in a dark gray bordering on black; later when she confronts him with being a coward and a spy they stand together in a soft blue-gray light and he embraces her.) Her husband is the second character other than Clerici who appears wearing gray (also a light gray). Now that Clerici has arrived in Paris, the black and white world of fascist Italy is being replaced by the grays of moral uncertainty.[49] When the professor opens the window in his office the shadow Clerici has just been insisting he has a right to call real suddenly disappears.

Subtle hints throughout his time in Paris (the flashing light that illuminates him during the opening credits, the bedspread in their hotel room, the window frames in the café where Giulia and Anna dance) suggest that this gray will soon be turned to red, culminating in the crimson blood that covers Anna's face as she flees through the gray hauntingly lit forest from her husband's assassins.

Clerici claims he wants to live the life of a normal man. To atone for a crime he believes (mistakenly) that he's committed, he commits another crime that will prove to be more horrible than he realizes. He thinks this will return him to the safe embrace of society. He must reject his decadent mother, his mad father (whose own brutal past he tries but fails to recuperate), and what he believes is the perversion and violence of his youth. But what he pursues in the wake of these rejections are crimes far more brutal and dehumanizing than the transgressions of decadence, madness, and perversion. He will commit a crime against the self to atone for what he believes is a crime he is guilty of against society. In this sense he truly is a fascist, for he has placed the perceived good of the whole (as defined by someone else) above the real good

---

[49] The Eiffel Tower isn't gold as Giulia imagined it but rises up as a gray monument against a gray sky. The park in Paris is gray. During their shopping trip along the streets of Paris everything (including their skin) has been reduced to a soft gray light except the brightly colored items illuminated by a golden light in the shop windows. "Look at that color. It's a dream," Giulia says. Her husband would rather see his dream turn into a nightmare than face the dangers of waking up (leaving the cave, denying the shadows).

of the self (as felt by himself). It is a kind of self-suicide which he seems to anticipate, and at one point even comically acts out, even before he arrives in Paris to carry out his mission. He may think he's sacrificing himself, but in the end it is the woman he loves that he offers as a sacrifice, not to save himself, but to make his damnation irrevocable.

II

> Life is a pure flame, and we live by an invisible sun within us. A small fire sufficeth for life, great flames seemed too little after death, while men vainly affected precious pyres, and to burn like Sardanapulus, but the wisdom of funeral laws found the folly of prodigal blazes, and reduced undoing fires unto the rule of sober obsequies, wherein few could be so mean as not to provide wood, pitch, a mourner, and an urn.
>
> –Sir Thomas Browne,
> "Hydriotaphia: Urne Burial"

The movie's moral categories, such as they are, are cast more in aesthetic terms than in political, philosophic, or psychological ones. The movie portrays an ideological reduction of everything to the aesthetic, which in itself is a moral strategy, albeit a deeply ambiguous one. The ambiguity of the aesthetic is for me the most powerful theme in the film, the theme that most explicitly reveals the film's spiritual preoccupations.

Nazism had its philosopher (Heidegger); Italian Fascism had its avant-gardist (F. T. Marinetti), and even an unlikely sympathizer in the figure of American poet Ezra Pound. Fascist architecture, music, cinema, poetry, and other forms of art exist because fascism is an aesthetic—and therefore a spiritual—condition. Politics is just another one of its tools. As a spiritual condition, it afflicts not societies but individuals, and when it afflicts enough individuals it becomes a social phenomena. As an aesthetic condition it can be battled only by other forms of aesthetic phenomena, for example, certain forms of mysticism, transgression, or the avant-garde (William Blake, Georges Bataille, Situationism). But even these are not sure protection against the threats of fascism.

That fascism is more a condition of the soul than it is an explicit political ideology means that no political system, and no art form, is essentially immune to the threats of fascism. There can be socialist fascism, democratic fascism, communist fascism; there can be Catholic fascism, Islamic fascism, capitalist fascism, and fascist poetry. No system is immune to fascism because fascism is fundamentally the abuse of any system, and at a certain level life itself is impossible without systems.

The striking visual imagery in *The Conformist* reminds us that even a certain kind of beauty is not immune to this threat. The movie's brilliance lies partly in the fact that although its beauty is not itself an example of this "beauty of fascism," it allows the viewer to experience the beauties of fascism as a character like Clerici fall prey to them. And how different is he from any of us, especially given that his goal in the movie, to conform, is to be as precisely like everyone else as possible? This must be the true horror of fascism: not its specter as a political system that might impose itself on our individual liberties, but as a seductive spiritual state we might give ourselves over to without even realizing what we're giving up. It is not in what others might forcibly take from us, but in what we freely give away that the terror of fascism as portrayed in *The Conformist* lies.

Perhaps the only thing that cannot be appropriated by fascism is chaos—the rejection of order, reason, and control. But while art can flirt with chaos (in various forms of Futurism, Dada, Situationism, and other Avant-gardes), ultimately art must impose form on chaos, for art is a way of ordering the world, of arranging its matter; Milton's "dark materials" given aesthetic form by a creator. The moment of the aesthetic act is an ordering of chaos, and thus even creation becomes vulnerable to fascist impulses.

In politics, chaos sometimes goes by the name (inaccurately for readers of Kropotkin, though somewhat romantically for aficionados of the Sex Pistols) of Anarchy. Anarchy, in the political realm, certainly stands opposed to fascism, and it might even be preferable though it is certainly no less dangerous. (Cormac McCarthy's *The Road* is a vivid portrait of apocalyptic anarchy (cannibalism, etc.) that would make even fascism look appealing by comparison.)[50]

In *The Conformist* shadows form bars of light that enclose Clerici throughout the movie. These shadows, as in Plato's cave, represent the prison he has shut himself up in. Like

---

[50] Hobbes wrote his *Leviathan* in something like a state of horror at the possibilities of a *Road*-like future for England. While Hobbes was certainly no fascist, his willingness to sacrifice individual liberty in the interests of state stability might lead some people (like Sid Vicious, if he ever got around to reading Hobbes when he sang about England's Queen) to misread him as one.

Plato's prisoners (who Socrates tells us are "like ourselves"), Clerici does not want to escape; instead he wants to punish or eliminate anyone who suggests to him the mere possibility of escape. Why does he let Anna die? In effect, why does he kill her? Because she represents a freedom (that is, a threat) he cannot tolerate or embrace. She represents (in the form of the insecurities and uncertainties of love) a threat to the stability he chooses over the possibility of love; when he speaks of Giulia he speaks of "bed and kitchen", normality and stability, but never of love.

Clerici's goal as articulated in the move is to be just like all of us (to be "normal"). Our goal, after watching the movie, is to hope that we can live in such a way as to be as unlike him as possible. Bertolucci succeeds in making him both sympathetic (hence the psychological power of the film) and loathsome (hence its ethical power). Faced with the choice between comfort, pleasure, and security or uncertainty, doubt, radical ambiguity, fear, and perhaps even despair, how many of us will turn to art to support us in our commitment to the latter rather than for distraction as we seek refuge in the former?[51]

Marcello ends the movie as he began it: behind bars. Perhaps they are bars of his own making. Perhaps they are bars society has built around him. At the end of the movie he is still in the cave. Sitting by the fire that illuminates him he is no longer gray, but he still hasn't seen the sun.

---

[51] Consider the works of Schopenhauer, Kierkegaard, Dostoevsky, Baudelaire, Nietzsche, Kafka ... consider, in short, the entire project of Modernity.

INTERMISSION
The Cosmic Significance of Pong:
Giulio Paradisi's *The Visitor* (1979)

"She was a visitor."
–Robert Ashley, "Automatic Writing"

I

Alejandro Jodorowsky said about his unrealized movie *Dune*, "I wanted to do a movie that would give the people who took LSD at the time the hallucinations you get with that drug but without hallucinating. I did not want LSD to be taken; I wanted to fabricate the drug's effects. This picture was going to change the public's perceptions." Jodorowsky never made his version of *Dune*—and David Lynch's 1984 attempt doesn't live up to Jodorowsky's ambitions to create a movie that would "change the public's perceptions"—but director Giulio Paradisi and writer/producer Ovidio Assonitis came pretty damn close when they made *The Visitor* in 1979.

If a movie's power is measured by the effect it has on its audience, than Paradisi (AKA Michael J. Paradise) and Assonitis's movie may be one of the most powerful movies ever made. Whatever the producer, director, cast and crew set out to accomplish, whatever films or genres hey were attempting to imitate, what they actually achieved is completely unlike anything the movies had ever produced before. Something *sui generis* had come into being. Though surely not on purpose, for who can plan for such accidents and fortuitous freaks?

They had help. Researching everyone who played a role in this movie takes one on an extensive tour of the history of Hollywood cinema. A fact all the more striking given that it's not itself a Hollywood movie. It may be trying to look like a Hollywood movie; it may be trying to act like a Hollywood movie; but it's still a movie from outer space brought to us by way of Italy. George Busbee, Governor of Georgia from 1975 to 1983, and Maynard Jackson, the first African-America Mayor of Atlanta, helped. Kareem Abdul-Jabbar helped. Ted Turner helped (and allowed them to shoot scenes of the movie in his house because he lost a bet over a basketball game). Two of the greatest directors of American cinema helped (not as directors, but as actors): John Huston[52] and Sam Peckinpah.[53] Shelley Winters,[54] Glenn Ford,[55] Lance Henriksen,[56] and Mel Ferrer[57] helped.

Cinematographer Ennio Guanieri, having won Best Cinematography awards for his work on films by Franco

---

[52] Who directed 42 movies between 1941 and 187, including *The Maltese Falcon, The Treasure of the Sierra Madre, The Asphalt Jungle, The African Queen, Beat the Devil, The Kremlin Letter* (Jean-Pierre Melville's favorite movie), *Fat City, Wise Blood, Under the Volcano, Prizzi's Honor,* and *The Dead.*

[53] *Ride the High Country, The Wild Bunch, The Ballad of Cable Hogue, Straw Dogs, The Getaway, Pa Garrett and Billy the Kid, Bring Me the Head of Alfredo Garcia, The Killer Elite.*

[54] Over 100 movie appearances between 1943 and 1999, most notably in Charles Laughton's *Night of the Hunter* and Stanley Kubrick's *Lolita.*

[55] Perhaps most notably in Charles Vidor's *Gilda* with the stunning Rita Hayworth, in Fritz Lang's *The Big Heat* and Delmer Daves *3:10 to Yuma.*

[56] *Dog Day Afternoon, Close Encounters of the Third Kind, Damien: Omen II,* James Cameron's *Aliens.*

[57] Over 60 movie and television appearances, from *The Hands of Orlac* to an episode of Columbo, between 1947 to 1995.

Zeffirelli and Vittorio De Sica, helped.

Franco Nero helped. The Italians have been imagining what Christ looked like since the Medieval and Renaissance periods (Giotto's *Lamentation of Christ*, circa 1300). Nero, with amazing wig and facial hair and stunning (somewhat terrifying) blue eyes, is the quintessential 1970's vision of the Savior.

Previous movies *The Visitor* was supposed to be imitating, and which it simultaneously fell short of and wildly exceeded, also helped, from Hitchcock's 1963 *The Birds* to Roman Polanski's *Rosemary's Baby* (1968), William Friedkin's *The Exorcist* (1973), Richard Donner's *The Omen* (1976), George Lucas's *Star Wars* and Steven Spielberg's *Close Encounters of the Third Kind* (both 1977).

Audience expectations—defied, destroyed, distorted and expanded—helped, then crumpled up into ball, crawled away into some dark corner of the subconscious and wept with uncontrollable confusion and delight. *The Visitor* is one of those movies that so defies conventional aesthetic standards and categories that it's hard to know what to think. It's difficult to know what to say about *The Visitor* in part because of the suspicion that its most powerful qualities must have been achieved completely by accident. The movie is hilarious when it intends to be suspenseful; it is silly when it hopes to be serious; and ridiculous when it wants to be ominous, terrifying, and thought provoking. The vocabulary of its visual imagery is rich and beautifully shot but constantly undermined by such wild absurdities that the viewer's mind reels trying to hold its incongruities together. It's like trying to make sense of a dream after you've awoken.

In failing to be what it set out to be, *The Visitor* succeeded in being something quite different—one of those rare movies that challenge us, outrage us, delight us, and overturn every expectation we bring with us about what a movie could, or should, be.[58] Perhaps nothing is more mysterious and incomprehensible than the simple fact that it exists. How is such a thing possible?

It also happens to be one of those movies that alter our experience of time and space in the act of watching it. What Jerzy says to Barbara Collins is true for each of us who sits down to undergo *The Visitor* experience: "You've been feeling strange lately . . . Confused. This confusion has been transmitted to you from another time, another place, beyond human knowledge and understanding." That place beyond human knowledge and understanding turns out to be the very movie we're watching, and it leaves us feeling decidedly "strange."

Rather than offer interpretations or explanations (which in any event would surely be pointless), let's take a stroll

---

[58] Only after agreeing to do the movie did Huston read the script. He told Assonitis, "Listen, this will either be a marvelous movie or a piece of shit." One of the great things about *The Visitor* is that it's both at the same time. It's not one of those movies that's "so bad it's good" (like Tommy Wiseau's 2003 *The Room* ("the *Citizen Kane* of bad movies" according to Clark Collis) or James Nguyen's 2008 *Birdemic: Shock and Terror*, both of which have garnered more enthusiastic attention for their hysterical flaws than most of the good movies made in the last 10 years have for their virtues); it's way beyond that. Movies like *The Room* and *Birdemic* are hilarious failures and a joy to laugh at (or with, if we're feeling generous). *The Visitor* is actively engaged in reformatting the neural connections in our brains. Watching it feels more like the experience of being a character in Cronenberg's 1983 *Videodrome* than like anything we've ever associated with "going to the movies" before.

through the bizarre landscape of this movie, not in order to summarize or attempt to explain or even to try to make sense of it, but merely to see where it will take us. Such a stroll is a journey through the distortions of time and space that no art form is more capable of plunging us into than the cinema. Let us attempt a phenomenological reading of the film with an eye on the relationship between what is happening in the movie and what is happening to us as we watch it. A poetics that proved effective in responding to *The Visitor* would have to be aware, at every moment, of the film's effect on the viewer. What does the movie do to our expectations, our sense of filmic propriety, our aesthetic sensibilities, or cultural preconceptions, our ideological faith, our confidence in our ability to watch (and make sense of) a movie, our comfort and security? How are we uprooted and overturned, wrenched and wrecked by a power the movie has despite (or because of?) its every technical flaw and formal shortcoming?

The movie begins with a stunning sunrise. Rich colors flood the screen; eerie music seems to call up the dawn like a Moog-playing Orpheus. The sudden intrusion of John Huston's massive face in an über-close-up that dominates the screen is preposterous, outrageous, comic, and utterly jarring. He is waiting for his cosmic nemesis, whose appearance is accompanied by roiling clouds and a sudden storm that blots out the sun and batters the heroic Huston. (He's described in the DVD liner notes as an "intergalactic warrior" and he certainly stands and glares like one throughout this scene.) The embodiment of evil stands before him (causing him to momentarily shudder, though he quickly recovers) in the form of a black-shrouded little girl in pink skirt and knee socks covered in space snow. In fact the lighting, the camera work, and the special effects are all quite beautiful. But the attempt to infuse these visual qualities with a sense of ominous dramatic tension renders the whole thing wildly absurd and utterly unconvincing.

Suddenly the snow-covered demon-girl disappears, the storm fades and the clouds withdraw to reveal the now-risen sun. But we know the battle is not over; this was just the scene of the gauntlet being thrown down. As our galactic hero strides off into the desert like an interplanetary version of Clint Eastwood's Man with No Name (he's even got the poncho, which he later exchanges for a ridiculous fishing hat and safari jacket), the screen fills again with a massive close-up, this time of Franco Nero in his role as Cosmic Jesus. This film is not afraid to wildly abuse the close-up technique. Nearly every character gets one, and it may be the most terrifying aspect of the entire film.

II

> Man is but the mist of God's breath on the mirror of the Universe.
>
> –Eliche Enteele, *My Inquiries into the Mysteries of Existence*

Nero-Christ's narrative begins, "Once far away, light years, distances beyond thought, a great slender ship with a tail of fire slid through the black reaches of space. On that ship was Sateen." Sateen has been captured by Commander Yahweh (!), "in a blood drenched battle that claimed hundreds of lives." It's a bit confusing, or maybe just preposterous, but we still know where we are: witnessing a faceoff between the universal forces of Good and Evil. The rest of the movie will play out this eternal struggle through a series of oddball avatars involving exploding basketballs, demon-possessed toy birds, mirrors, wheelchairs, and, of course, Pong.

"Her name is Katy Collins, and she'll be 8 years old," Huston's Jerzy Colsowicz AKA the Intergalactic Warrior tells Fraco Nero AKA the Cosmic Christ. The music that accompanies this announcement is so jarring and wildly inappropriate to whatever expectations the movie has succeeded in creating up to this point that when the scene abruptly cuts to a hazy view of Atlanta, Georgia we really do feel like we've been carried to another planet. And maybe into another movie as well. Nothing of the harmonious collaborations of Hitchcock and Bernard Herrmann here. This music is as canned and corny as the original images in the film were wonderful and bewildering. The harsh disjunction between sound and image continues throughout the film. If the movie has a style, it's not one it can make up its mind to stick to for more than 15 minutes at a time.

The biblical struggle between Good and Evil, God and Satan, has been reduced to (or transformed into) a science fiction space battle between the Mu-Tant Sateen and Commander Yahweh, complete with spaceships. Why? Is this supposed to be easier on our secular imaginations than traditional Christian mythology? (So long Milton.) Are we more comfortable with a Jungian science-fiction account of our religious mythology than with the more traditional Judeo-Christian roots of Western Civilization? (Hello William Blake.) But then the movie's action is moved to 1970's Atlanta, where, on the surface at least, nothing vaguely sci-fi is taking place. We've gone from religious allegory to science fiction to ... a basketball game. Hardly the last transformation the film will undergo.

The basketball game is between the San Francisco Miners and the Atlanta Rebels. Kareem is tearing up the court. What happened to those bald kids listening to Jesus tell his vaguely Christian version of the Darth Vader and the Jedi Knights story? What happened to John Huston in that ridiculous hat? Well, we've been transported across time and space to another, more familiar, dimension. We're a sophisticated audience; we adjust quickly. Soon we're caught up in the drama of the game. The shots of the crowd have as much raw 70's visceral reality as anything shot by Mitch Breit or Al Ruben for Cassavetes. This is great 70's camera work (you couldn't hire extras this good so this must be footage of an actual game). Maybe those first 7 minutes of the movie never happened. Except here's some more eerie music. Kareem senses there's something wrong. When that 8 year-old girl with the jumbo-frame glasses catches his eye (another abuse of the too-close-close-up) he knows the game is fixed. Kareem may be a warrior fighting for the forces of good, but he's going to lose this battle. The basketball explodes, apparently, just as he's about to slam-dunk the winning point.

Cut to a bedroom sex scene. (Why not?) Again, great camera work, which only makes the dialogue's labored effort to advance the plot seem even more awkward. "We're always talking about talking about talk, but we never talk. Can you talk seriously?" The ominous exchange that follows helps develop the connection between the Eternal Cosmic Battle and its local phase here in Downtown Atlanta, even if it doesn't help the movie. Cut to Katy waiting for her mom to come home, her unconscious babysitter sprawled like a corpse beside her, a game of Pong on an enormous screen behind her creating a soundtrack for Katie's portentous announcement, "I want a brother." Pong, it turns out, is going to be an important factor in the movie.

What happens next makes no more sense than what's already happened, or anything else that will happen over the course of the next 90 minutes, a series of miniature eternities we can't escape from. Huston's Intergalactic Warrior turns out to be a Polish guy named Jerzy Colsowicz (what?) who has come to the United States for the first time in order to be "a visitor" (as he helpfully informs the Customs Agent). Even if we accept the lack of continuity, the shocking juxtapositions between brilliant camera work and awful music, and the bizarre cuts between scenes,[59] we're still not ready for everything the movie is going to do to our sense of stability, propriety, and aesthetic coherence. This movie takes us way beyond the "art vs. entertainment" debate. It's a wholesale assault on our sensibilities at virtually every level.

As if it mattered (and it doesn't), there is some semblance of a plot being developed here: a group of ominous men headed by Mel Ferrer's Dr. Walker and an even more ominous looking butler apparently have Satanic powers

---

[59] We're at the airport; no, we're in a Chinese gift shop; no, we're in an abandoned building; no, we're on the roof with a small army of bald angels in track suits carrying metal boxes that later turn into translucent screens (what *is* Jerzy doing with these guys on the roof throughout the movie? building some kind of cosmic runway, so that his "friends" will have somewhere to land?); no, we're cutting between scenes of Katy doing gymnastics and her mother in the hospital; no, we're at an ice-skating rink with a demon child wreaking havoc on the other children for no apparent reason; no, we've gone irretrievably mad and none of this will ever possibly make any sense and why should we even expect it to?

at their disposal (which they tend to use primarily to win basketball games for Lance Henriksen's Ray Armstead), and they desperately want Katy's mother Barbara to have a male child (apparently to mate with his sister so that the two of them can give birth to Satan, thus allowing him access to our dimension of time and space). What better way to orchestrate her pregnancy than to turn one of Katy's birthday presents into a gun so that she can accidentally shoot (and subsequently paralyze) her mother? That should help get her pregnant right away.

The shooting allows for Glenn Ford to appear as Detective Jake Durham 28 minutes into the film. It looks like the movie is finally about to get an actual hero. But 17 minutes later he's dead. Was he getting too close to the truth? Or was his death just as an excuse to crash a motorcycle into a windshield, break up a softball game, and blow up a car? Well at least Shelley Winters has appeared in the meantime to tie the movie together. Or not. OK, so her character, the "maid," serves no obvious narrative purpose. But whose does? Jerzy says she's "been a big help," though it's not clear how, and she will disappear from the movie with as little reason as she appeared. But she can sing a James Whitcomb Riley folk song (though it hardly seems to apply to this particular "mammy's little baby" (perhaps it's a reference to the Captain Beefheart song "Pachuco Cadaver"?[60]) and quote Heraclitus: "a great philosopher said that our characters are our fates; and some scientists now believe that planets somehow understand this." Which has nothing,

---

[60] Or to the Beach Boy's Brian Wilson, who obsessively recorded over a dozen different versions of the "Shortnin' Bread" song. Wilson reportedly suffered from auditory hallucinations and heard disembodied voices. Perhaps one of them was Shelley Winters singing to him.

but absolutely nothing, to do with anything this movie in anyway could possibly be about. Which means it fits right in with the rest of the film.

Other examples of the movie's unparalleled insanity include:

- Glenn Ford is attacked by a demon bird while driving; it never occurs to him to apply his breaks.
- Apparently Huston was able to travel from outer space to Atlanta, Georgia, but he's unable to descend a stationary elevator.
- Although we know they have sex, apparently Ray can't impregnate Barbara with the requisite Mu-Tant demon child unless they're married.
- The extended chase scene between Katy and Jerzy culminates in a showdown in a House of Mirrors (apparently housed in a seedy downtown Atlanta strip club), which in turn culminates in . . . nothing at all?
- I'm not even going to try and make sense of the sudden appearance, 75 minutes into the movie, of Barbara's ex-husband Sam, played by Sam Peckinpah, brought on-screen for no other apparently reason than to give Barbara an abortion.
- Throughout the movie, the better the camera work (and much of it is very good; though some of it, like Barbara's panicky wheelchair careening (again cut with shots of Katy practicing gymnastics; why?), is ridiculous), the worse the music chosen to accompany the visual images, and the less the images have anything to do with the movie's plot or narrative structure.

133

What's it all mean?

III

> Now virtually everyone's singing
> A popular song
> Yeah but I still believe in
> The Excellent joy of the Pong
>
> –Frank Black, "Whatever happened to Pong?"

Having surpassed the power and influence of religion (and every other ideological force in 20th century) to shape our thoughts and form our attitudes, the movies and television reigned supreme as the most powerful forms of entertainment, thought control, and taste formation since the rise of the church in medieval Europe. This supremacy was virtually unchallenged until the rise, toward the end of the 20th century, of a new form of experiential entertainment mediated through the interface of a screen: the video game.

The crucial scene between demonic Katy and creepy Colsowicz takes place over a game of Pong. Her would-be stepfather worries that Colsowicz, who poses as a 73 year-old baby-sitter, may be a child molester (perhaps he'd already seen Polanski's 1974 *Chinatown*).[61] But we know better. Or do we?

> "Do you want to kill me?"
> "I don't want to kill you Katy. I want to take you away with me when the time comes."

---

[61] Barbara in turn accuses Ray of being a "cripple molester," but of course we know it's all in the course of duty to the Powers of Darkness. What wouldn't a man do to win a basketball game?

"You want my advice old man? Go back to wherever you came from. This world is not for you."

"It's not for you either Katy."

Katy wins the game of Pong, but the deeper struggle between the two of them has yet to play out its most incomprehensible turns. Why Pong?

Pong, developed by Allan Alcorn for Atari in 1972, was not the first home video game, but it was the one whose popularity launched the revolution in videogame development that has taken on such massive proportions in today's world. From the Magnavox Odyssey released in 1972 to the most recent iterations of the Sony PlayStation, Microsoft Xbox and Nintendo Wii U, from Pong to Tetris, from Minecraft to Grand Theft Auto, and from Halo to World of Warcraft and other MMORPGs,[62] videogames have come closer to turning virtual reality into daily reality than anything human beings have ever experienced (including hallucinogens and other mind-altering substances). Videogames have reached such a level of sophistication and development that it seems the next step can be nothing short of the holodeck that first appeared in the premiere of the *Star Trek: The Next Generation* series that aired in 1987.

We seem to be approaching a time when we will be able to live more and more of our lives vicariously through the characters on the screen in front of us; not just watching them, but *being* them. We will fight through them, love through them, undergo quests and adventures through them. We will fulfill our ambitions, suffer our defeats, strive for excellence, until eventually we will not only

---

[62] Massively multiplayer online role-playing games.

experience through them (which is already possible), but communicate through them (which is also already possible), so that we are not so much *living* through them as undergoing a radical redefinition of what it means to live, to be alive, and to live in the world (perhaps even redefining "the world" itself).

And it all started with Pong. Which somehow, even in 1979, the makers of *The Visitor* already knew. They were trying to get us ready for the videogame revolution that would shake the foundations of reality, life, and our understanding of "the world" even then. The massive allegory of a religious and spiritual struggle taking place against the backdrop of an outer space war between aliens, angels, and demons is perfectly symbolized in the Manichean struggle played out on either side of the Pong screen. Videogames are something like the resurgence of that most ancient of religions, Zoroastrianism, which taught that the universe was divided by the eternal struggle between the forces of Good, manifest in the Deity Ormuzd, and Evil, manifest in Ahriman. In *The Visitor* Colsowicz makes for an odd avatar of Ormuzd, but no less odd than Katy's Ahriman. Zoroastrianism is the first binary religion. Videogames may be the last.

All computers, and therefore all computer and videogames, are based on a simple binary system of ones and zeroes, modern day Manichean technology. In Pong the ball, an electronic image made of a series of those ones and zeros and representing the human soul, is batted back and forth between the forces of Good and Evil battling one another. The ball is just an innocent victim in the eternal struggle. When either side misses and fails to return its opponent's shot it simply disappears off the screen and into the abyss. But there's always another soul to fight over.

As that Proust of cinema, the master of film and memory pointed out: "What do video games, which tell us more about our unconscious than the works of Lacan, offer us? Neither money nor glory, but a new game. The possibility of playing again. 'A second chance.'"[63]

IV

> It is the unique power of cinema to allow a great number of people to dream the same dream together.
> –Jean Cocteau

Cocteau's pretentions and ambitions notwithstanding, I've never seen a movie that made me feel more like I was experiencing a dream than *The Visitor*. And like a dream, or like Jodorowsky's LSD trip, *The Visitor* is one those experiences you can't really talk (or write) about. Have any of us ever had a dream that we didn't wake up wanting to describe as "weird" or "strange"? What would be stranger than waking up one morning and saying, "I had a dream last night that wasn't weird at all. It was just like being awake"?

Having spent considerable time with the movie, I've come to the conclusion that *The Visitor* may be the most pointless kind movie to try and write about. The reasons for writing about a movie are various: to learn more about the film; to learn more about yourself through writing about the film; to encourage others to see it: to offer insights into the film for those who have already

---

[63] Chris Marker, "A free replay (notes on *Vertigo*)"

seen it in order to deepen their understanding or appreciation of it. But *The Visitor* is not a movie that is enhanced by insight or deeper understanding into its themes, symbolism, or the psychology of its characters, because these are the most superficial and uninteresting things about it. Trying to talk about having seen *The Visitor* is like telling someone about one of your dreams. It's just not that interesting in the retelling. It's the experience that matters; and like dreams, *The Visitor* is pure experience: the kind of experience that does not need to be understood, or interpreted, or analyzed. It simply needs to be undergone, and survived, and assimilated into whatever we thought was true—and now realize isn't—about the world of cinema as it existed before we became aware that such a thing as *The Visitor* was possible. It's that kind of movie.

Who Would Win in a Fight?
James Bond vs. Joan of Arc and the Cinematic Formation
of Sensibility

"Television is the retina of the mind's eye."

–Dr. Brian O'Blivion
(David Cronenberg's *Videodrome*)

Wildly different moments in the vast world of cinema are connected by a complex web. While there's an obvious thread joining directors Carl Theodor Dreyer and Robert Bresson through their Joan of Arc projects (even though Bresson condemned aspects of Dreyer's masterpiece as "grotesque buffoonery"), there's a more subtle thread joining Joan and James Bond. The connection is a bit more tenuous, but it's there, and it lies in Luc Besson's own (rather unfortunate) attempt to portray the life of Joan of Arc.

It's no surprise that a number of studies have compared Dreyer's 1928 *The Passion of Joan of Arc* with Bresson's 1962 *The Trial of Joan of Arc*. Dreyer and Bresson are two of the great directors in the history of cinema and Dreyer's *Passion* is one of the greatest silent films of all time (one of the greatest films of all time period). Bresson's *Trial* may not be his best film, but in the pantheon of Joan of Arc films it is still noteworthy. Aspects of Joan's life have been captured on film by directors as diverse as Cecil B. DeMille (as early as 1917), Victor Fleming, Roberto Rossellini, Otto Preminger, Werner Herzog, and Jacques Rivette; and her character has been portrayed by actresses as diverse as Renee Jeanne Falconetti, Ingrid Bergman, Jean Seberg, Susan

Dunn, the Go-Go's Jane Wiedlin (sort of), and (for Besson) Milla Jovovich.

Perhaps no historic figure has been portrayed more often in the history of cinema than Joan of Arc; there have been more than 40 versions of her life imagined in film, television and opera. In comparison, there have been 23 James Bond films[64] (as of the 2012 *Skyfall*), along with a few "unofficial" and spoof versions. Of course James Bond (like frequently-filmed Sherlock Holmes) is only an "historical figure" within the context of the fictional world that gave birth to him, whereas that same fictional world rose up to induct Joan into its ranks only after her previous (though perhaps less influential) historic existence.

One of the things Joan and James have in common is perpetual youth. Martyred at 19, Joan never had time to grow old. Trapped in celluloid (or video) perpetuity, Bond is constantly renewed by a series of vigorous actors from Sean Connery to Daniel Craig. But although Bond himself never seems to age, the Bond movies tend not to do so well. The devices they depend on—sultry women, fast-paced action, clever technological gadgets, witty one-liners, fast cars and luxurious international destinations—show their age all too quickly. The Bond movies from the 60's were already somewhat tedious curiosity pieces by the 70's. Despite the charm some viewers still find in Sean Connery's wry smile, the early Bond films quickly lost their air not only of action, suspense, and excitement, but even of sex appeal. The 70's Bond movies faired no better by the time the 80's rolled around, and so on down the line. The gadgets

---

[64] According to the count kept by Eon Productions.

quickly seem outdated and gimmicky (despite Q's ever-renewed efforts), the acting looks stiff, the plots soon appear tedious, and the action sequences are surprisingly unexciting.

Another reason the Bond films may not age well is because the audiences who tend to enjoy them demand a level of stimulation and titillation that requires a constantly renewed freshness. This kind of excitement must always be new, and must always outdo what has come before.

Different movies provide different kinds of pleasures. The "art" movie and the "entertainment" movie should not be distinguished in terms of quality or merit (since both categories can include examples of good or bad movies) but in terms of the different kinds of pleasures they allow. The cinematic pleasures provided by the Bond franchise, while certainly not insignificant, are also fleeting in a way that the more subtle and elusive pleasures of Dreyer's films are not.

The pleasure of Dreyer's 1928 *Passion* may be more difficult to appreciate, but it has not dimmed in nearly 100 years. This is not the place to rehearse the aesthetic debate between "art" and "entertainment" (which inevitably involves annoying and pointless definitions and invidious distinctions) or between "high" and "low" pleasures (which involves some sort of debate between Jeremy Bentham and the Marquis de Sade[65]) nevertheless, thinking about Joan vs. James is an occasion

---

[65] Born only 8 years apart and living their entire lives right across the Channel from one another, it's fascinating to image a collision between Bentham's Calculus of Felicity and de Sade's notion of pleasure through transgression.

to reflect on the relationship between the movies and the different kinds of pleasures they provide.

Daniel Craig made his first appearance as Bond in Martin Campbell's 2006 *Casino Royale* (the 21st movie in the Bond series), and so far (not yet 10 years old), it still registers as the kind of action movie that people who like action movies (and I'm one of them) enjoy. Craig is an effective Bond, sexually as well as psychologically, and the stunts and effects are exciting in a way that makes Connery's fisticuffs in the 1962 *Dr. No* (the first of Connery's 7 appearances as Bond) look rather pathetic. In terms of action sequences, *Casino* reaches a new height in the pantheon of Bond movies through an early chase scene featuring the physical art of movement through space known as parkour.[66] During this sequence Craig pursues Sébastien Foucan, one of the early developers of parkour, in what is perhaps the most exciting action

---

[66] Although it's probably destined to be of limited cinematic appeal, parkour heralded a new level of action movie excitement and has forever raised the stakes of the foot-chase sequence. Aside from the martial arts genre and such geniuses of physical culture as Bruce Lee, Jackie Chan (who significantly credits the influence of silent movie geniuses Charlie Chaplin and Buster Keaton on his martial arts choreography), and Jet Li (not to mention their less inspiring but quirkily charming Caucasian counterparts Van Damme, Steven Seagal, and Chuck Norris), parkour may be the most exciting physical action ever captured on camera (aside for aforementioned Keaton and Chaplin). And what is particularly interesting about parkour is that it is not about fighting, but about running away. No one necessarily gets punched, shot, kicked, or stabbed (though most of these effects are added into *Casino Royale*). They just get chased (think back to the opening sequence of Hitchcock's *Vertigo* and compare it with the rooftop chase in Besson's *Banlieu 13*). Parkour is about moving through space in the most efficient, fluid, and amazing, way possible. Like the best examples of the martial arts, it is a kind of physical poetry.

sequence (certainly in terms of raw physical prowess and suspense) in any of the Bond films to date. And here's where the link with Joan of Arc comes in.

Parkour, which like breakdancing is another breathtaking physical discipline with urban roots in youth culture, has a rich and fascinating history of its own that lies outside the world of movies. But its popularity was significantly increased by a series of films made by Luc Besson between 2001 (*Yamakasi*) and 2004 (*Les fils du vent* and *Banlieue 13*, the latter starring David Belle, who is regarded as one of the founders of parkour). Two years later parkour was featured in the chase scene between Craig and Foucan. A few years before championing parkour in the movies, Besson made *The Messenger: The Story of Joan of Arc* (1999), starring his then-wife Milla Jovovich, and capitalizing on the success of their *Fifth Element* from two years before.[67] (Note: none of these movies are anywhere near as good as Besson's 1994 *Léon: The Professional* with Jean Reno and Gary Oldman.)

Despite garnering a few awards, Besson's *Joan* is not a very good movie (Jovovich was nominated for a Golden Raspberry Award for Worst Actress), perhaps because it ends up trying to be (despite some ineffectual groping towards spiritual soul-searching with the help of Dustin Hoffman at the end of the film) more of the sort of action movie Besson has become famous for than the kind of visually, psychologically, and spiritually rich investigation of a young woman's struggle with God, herself, and society that Dreyer's masterpiece is. But Besson's attempt

---

[67] Jovovich had come a long way in a short time from Linklater's 1993 *Dazed and Confused* (about whom see more below) and was well on her way to her recurring role in the *Resident Evil* series begun in 2002.

to turn the life of Joan of Arc into an action movie does provide an occasion to think about the subtle pleasures of Dreyer's accomplishment alongside the more visceral pleasures of Daniel Craig chasing Sébastien Foucan through an African construction zone and into an embassy before shooting Foucan and blowing up a small army and part of a rather large building. This whole early sequence from *Casino Royale* is terrifically shot, intricately composed, and great fun. In cinematic terms it could not possibly be more different than what Dreyer accomplishes in *The Passion*. But as different as they are on virtually every level, they are both movies, and Besson provides the link between Dreyer's silent masterpiece and Campbell's installment of the Bond spy-thriller franchise.

On the one hand: so what? The fact that you can play this kind of Six Degrees of Separation game with virtually any movie, director, or actor (not just Kevin Bacon) hardly suggests some privileged connection between the Joan of Arc movies and the James Bond movies. On the other hand: that's precisely my point. Movies form a vast conversation with one another. Even the most stylistically distant films have something to say to, and about, each other. They're all talking to each other; and more importantly, they're all talking to us. If we want to hear the full range of things they're capable of saying, we have to be careful that the louder films (which are not always the best films) don't render us deaf to the quieter films that may only be talking to us in a whisper, or which perhaps speak only in the silence of images. Some movies speak louder than others, but the loudest movies aren't always the ones that have the most important things to say, and the conversation the movies are having with each other often takes the form of a kind of debate between different kinds of cinematic pleasure.

Movies, because of their very power, are often their own worst enemies, not in terms of the old debate (and haven't we grown somewhat tired of it by now, especially when it comes to the movies?) between "art" and "entertainment," but rather in terms of what I call the formation of our sensibility to pleasure. It's safe to say that entertainment has nothing to offer except for pleasure. Whereas art, especially in the movies, must offer pleasure in addition to something else. So perhaps we're not quite done with the old debate after all.

It's hardly a radical insight to observe that movies condition our sensibility. As early as 1945 Bela Balazs warned his readers:

> We all know and admit that film art has a greater influence on the minds of the general public than any other art. The official guardians of culture note the fact with a certain amount of regret and uneasiness. But too few of us are sufficiently alive to the dangers that are an inevitable consequence of this fact. Nor do we realize clearly enough that we must be better connoisseurs of the film if we are not to be as much at the mercy of perhaps the greatest intellectual and spiritual influence of our age as to some blind and irresistible elemental force. And unless we study its laws and possibilities very carefully, we shall not be able to control and direct this potentially greatest instrument of mass influence ever devised in the whole course

of human cultural history . . . The mentality
of the people . . . is to a great extent the
product of this art, an art that is at the same
time a vast industry. Thus the question of
educating the public to a better, more
critical appreciation of the films is a
question of the mental health of nations.
(*Theory of the Film*)

Few of us today may feel inclined to deny the truth of
Balazs's claim, already over half-a-century old, but fewer
still have risen to the task and the challenge it poses. We
watch, if anything, more naively than ever, and the rise of
television has only added to our willful ignorance and
naiveté. Why?

The reason has to do with the competition different kinds
of pleasure wage for our energies and attention. Balazs
called movies "the greatest intellectual and spiritual
influence of our age." If he's right (and if you add in
television I think he is), then nothing more seriously
requires our thoughtful attention, engagement and
consideration than the way we watch; yet ironically,
nothing more effectively promotes our passive and
comfortable uncritical acceptance. Entertainment speaks
to the pleasures of a great spiritual lassitude, even when
our pulses race with excitement and suspense. More
active pleasures involve the fundamental activity of mind.
This is the realm where art strives to distinguish itself
from entertainment and where philosophy, theory, and
criticism are invited to the dance.

Take for example the pleasure of confronting difficultly.
The pleasures of struggling with difficulty threaten to be
overwhelmed by the pleasures of being passively

entertained. Or rather, the pleasure of responding to difficulty through critical, analytic, imaginative, interpretive responses—and of the efforts needed to pursue such pleasures—may be temporarily eclipsed by more easily attainted pleasures. And what's to prevent that temporary eclipse from becoming a permanent blind spot?[68]

In an interview with Truffaut about *The Man Who Knew Too Much*, Alfred Hitchcock said, "the conditioning of the viewer is essential to the build-up of suspense." Few directors have handled this notion of conditioning with a defter hand than Hitch. But this conditioning, perhaps

---

[68] Literature found an eloquent defender for succumbing to this danger in Jonathan Franzen, whose essay "Mr. Difficult" (which first appeared in the Sept. 30, 2002 issue of the New Yorker and was later included in his collection of essays *How To Be Alone*) basically mounted an argument against novels that demanded any sort of effort (even to the minimal extent of using a dictionary to look up unfamiliar words) on the part of their readers. Literature, Franzen concluded, should limit itself to gratifying its readers' basest pleasures rather than challenging them or defying their expectations. Along the way such authors as Herman Melville, Proust, Henry James, William Gaddis, and Thomas Pynchon were condemned for being too hard for ordinary readers to understand. Franzen rejects the idea that readers might be better off for making an effort to raise themselves up to the level of difficult works and fails to consider the possibility that many of us turn to literature precisely because we chafe at the limitations of being "ordinary" in the first place. For Franzen literature is about a "good read" (about being passively entertained) not about the rare opportunity to stretch the limits of the human soul that great works of art provide. Franzen, judging from the argument laid out in "Mr. Difficult," would disagree with Thoreau when he writes, "this only is reading, in a high sense, not that which lulls us as a luxury and suffers the nobler faculties to sleep the while, but what we have to stand on tip-toe to read and devote our most alert and wakeful hours to" ("Reading", *Walden*). When it comes to literature there will be no standing on tip-toe for Mr. Franzen and the readers he caters to.

more than any other single aspect of the cinema, is simultaneously its most powerful and its most dangerous quality; for what is conditioned in the viewer, above all else, is a sensibility that affects how we see all films once we have been subjected to it. We are constantly being conditioned by the television shows and movies we watch, and that conditioning in turn plays a determining role in what we see (even what we're capable of seeing), what we expect, and how our expectations shape and determine our experience (what we enjoy and what we condemn as boring or uninteresting or incoherent). In effect, movies not only constitute part of the realm of our potential experience, they also work, unintentionally or not, to either expand or circumscribe that realm.

Besson includes a number of sequences in his film that seem to deliberately evoke Dreyer's masterpiece. To echo the famous scene of Joan having her haircut in anticipation of her execution, Besson shoots Jovovich violently hacking her own hair off with a knife when she suspects the other soldiers respect her less because she is a woman with long hair. Both movies feature close-ups of Joan's feet at key moments in the narrative and of Joan's face in prison, Falconetti's transported by spiritual rapture, Jovovich's sulking in violent rage. It's as if Besson was commenting, shot by shot and image by image, on how movies have changed in the 70 years between his film and Dreyer's, and how our expectations have changed right along with them. Besson wants to gratify these new expectations, but is he aware of the extent to which the movies not only gratify but also form and shape them?

Movies teach us how to watch them. They accustom us to certain expectations. They thrive not only by gratifying those expectations but also by occasionally defying them. But even this defiance is something we've been trained to expect. The expectations that have risen up in response to the conventional "Hollywood ending" are relied on as much by those movies that daringly depart from it as by those that comfortably submit to it. When we step outside these conventions altogether, and encounter a work like Bela Tarr's *Satantango* or Aleksey German's *Khrustalyov, My Car!* our previous skills as movie-watchers prove completely inadequate to the challenge of seeing what is on the screen.[69] Entirely new ways of seeing are demanded of us. But this demand is countered by an impulse that tells us what we're watching is simply "boring" or "makes no sense" and tries to convince us that the effort is not worth making. Immediate gratification is so much easier. Spiritual lassitude versus activity of mind.[70]

As Wittgenstein said, "the fact remains that if you're bored a lot it means that your mental digestion isn't what it should be. I think a good remedy for this is sometimes opening your eyes wider."[71] Opening our eyes wider is what watching movies (certain movies at any rate) is all about.

---

[69] We have gotten so used to a kind of immediate gratification of our expectations when it comes to the movies that any film that fails to meet those expectations (to stimulate us, intrigue us, involve us, *entertain* us) risks being dismissed out of hand. Movies come at us with both barrels, full speed ahead, and with whatever other clichéd metaphor seems appropriate. They are rarely subtle in their methods and they are very often highly effective. Where does that leave us today, apropos movies (classic or contemporary) that still insist on being subtle, that move slowly, and that defy expectations developed over decades of watching hundreds, if not thousands, of movies and television programs?

[70] Let us take seriously the possibility that it is not the movie that is boring, but we who are bored. Why? What are we not seeing?

[71] *Culture and Value*

This is why I called movies their own worst enemy. By conditioning us to one form of pleasure, they often preclude our ability to respond to other kinds. By heightening our sensitivity to certain kinds of pleasures, which they can readily and repeatedly gratify, they eclipse more subtle pleasures that require an effort on our part.[72] One of the dangers here is the speed at which everything happens in the movies. Action movies grip us, and in being gripped we are carried along and our motion is carefully directed. Opposed to this is Wallace Stevens' "pleasures of merely circulating," the pleasures of undirected wondering which are closer to the pleasures of the imagination.

In contrast, movies generally ask us to respond to them with an assertion of our tastes and preferences almost immediately. Even before we leave the theatre or turn off the DVD player, we have been asked by the culture that produces the movies to form an opinion and pass judgment on what we've just watched. But what if we refrain from responding like this? What if we take up the question of whether or not we "like" a movie as the last (and perhaps far from the most important) question that concerns us, and if we dwell instead with other criteria and possibilities before being tied down by our likes and dislikes? What might we see in that case?

Let's go back to where we started. What has any of this to do with James Bond versus Joan of Arc, or between the

---

[72] What sort of effort? An effort of the intellect and imagination. Perhaps even an effort of the spirit. How do we make such an effort? Like any form of exertion, it is something we can learn to do, and something we can become better at through practice. One must, somewhat paradoxically, *make an effort* to make an effort.

pleasures of the Bond franchise versus the challenges of the Carl Dreyer film?

While some viewers may prefer the psychological tension of the poker game scenes in Montenegro (heighted by the sexually charged bickering between Craig and Eva Green's Vesper Lynd), the parkour chase scene is, in my opinion, the most cinematically exciting part of *Casino Royale*. Of course the chase itself has little to do with the plot development of the movie, beyond giving us a chance to see our hero in action and appreciate his character, resourcefulness, determination, and resolve.[73] But the fact that the chase scene contributes little to the movie's plot is precisely the point in an action movie. We tend to enjoy such movies not for their holistic unity, but for the individual moments of pleasure and excitement they provide. By contrast, every frame of Dreyer's *Passion* is part of an aesthetic whole. Even a scene involving relatively peripheral characters, some of whom we never see again or who have no "speaking" roles (a nominal concept in a silent film in any case), proves central to the movie's overall structure and the development of its major themes (such as the relationship of the power of authority (both political and religious) to the freedom of the individual, civil and military power versus spiritual integrity, and the secular versus the sacred).

Dreyer's movie provides us with innumerable opportunities for the kind of "work" we are asked to do in order to fully realize the active pleasures of

---

[73] At one moment Foucan gracefully catapults himself feet-first through a high window not much larger than his body. Craig's Bond, more bulldog than acrobat, simply crashes through the flimsy wall. This tells us everything we need to know about the character of Bond as portrayed by Craig for the rest of the movie. Charming, but blunt.

interpretation. One of my favorite such instances occurs 13 minutes and 30 seconds into the film when one of Joan's interrogators accuses her of blaspheming God and spits in her face. In response another monk falls at her feet after proclaiming, "This is disgraceful. To me she is a saint."

This is the last intertitle in the film for the next 2 minutes and 40 seconds. The "action" in the intervening scene tells the story not only of the fate of the man who rises up to proclaim his faith in Joan, but also reveals the political relationship between the French clerics conducting Joan's trial and the English military authority they serve. Although the camera shows us the faces of men speaking, we're not given intertitles telling us what they say; instead the story is told by their expressions, which the viewer must understand, and read, in order to follow what is transpiring on the screen. To adopt an old adage from MFA programs and creative writing workshops, we're not told what happens, we're shown it; and what we're shown is a brilliant collaboration of acting, directing, and camerawork which requires the viewer to be an active participant in the act of understanding. We must interpret and engage with the film. Carefully observed, the face of one man tells the whole story in a sequence of cuts that shows his face changing in response to his dawning realization of what is happening in the scene around him.

Within two minutes this man's face changes from a look of secure authority to one of shocked realization to one of resigned defeat. The entire transformation of a human soul (as well as the fate of one of his colleagues) is told in a series of carefully edited cuts without a word being spoken.

Despite Bresson's objection, Dreyer uses the human face to portray powerful and subtle developments in his film without words (either spoken or in intertitles). The face speaks. In a few seconds Dreyer can convey the story of a spiritual struggle that is waged and lost in the soul of a human being. These are struggles that action movies don't even presume to portray. They simply lie outside the purview of the ambition of such movies.

There is a moment in Dreyer's *Passion* when one of Joan's tormentors—a man who has lied to her, threatened her, and coerced her—looks on as she takes the Sacrament a final time before going to the stake. The realization, torment, and resignation shown on his face in these two cuts are among the most visually eloquent and spiritually powerful moments in the history of cinema. Rarely have I seen the human face more painfully and beautifully captured on film. In just a few seconds Dreyer has given us a visual equivalent of all the spiritual intensity contained in Dostoevsky's "Grand Inquisitor" section from *The Brothers Karamazov*.

Action movies, however exciting, wonderfully choreographed, skillfully filmed and erotically charged, remain basically fun. They are entertaining, but hardly spiritually challenging. As a result, the very notion of the spirit and the very idea that the movies should have anything to say about the spirit falls into disrepute. The problem with "fun" is that it wants to be the only game in town. Anything with more serious ambitions starts to look self-important, pompous, or just plain boring in comparison.

How has the power of visual imagery gradually shaped

our sensibilities, helping to determine not only what we respond to but how we respond? Compare the power of Dreyer's intimate images of a transcendent Joan with Besson's action-hero figurine. A picture says it all. In some ways it is the story of how cinema has changed—and changed us—over the past 70 years.

The Facts of Life: Ridley Scott's *Blade Runner* (1982/92/2007)

> "When we picture a human being, we use the four elements and five aggregates."
>
> –Dōgen, "Gabyo" (Picture of a Rice Cake)

> "Everything is true," he said. "Everything anybody has ever thought."
>
> –Rick Deckard in *Do Androids Dream of Electric Sheep?*

Los Angeles, November 2019 won't be the future for long. If L.A. can hang in there for another few years. And if it can't, there's plenty of time for the past to become the only future we have left. *Blade Runner* is one of those movies that feels like the history of a future we've already lived through. Much of this has to do with the rich visual anachronisms accomplished by Ridley Scott and cinematographer Jordan Cronenweth.

There's something inevitably ominous about the future, since all the bad things that are going to happen to us are waiting for us there. On the other hand, the past leaves no room for hope; that depends on the future as well. If not for the unknown, the whole thing might be unbearable. Unfortunately for him, the detective's job is to turn the unknown into the known, which means he's always striving to render things as unbearable as possible. Sometimes the eye is blind, and sometimes it sees too much. None of us know how long we have to live. This ignorance was once considered a gift from the gods.[74]

The film's opening shot of L.A. (perhaps from the hills above the "Hollywood" sign?) looks like a perspective on hell, with flames bursting up into a storm-torn sky. And perhaps this is a movie about a particular kind of harrowing: the attempt to bring one soul up from the Inferno.

Earth, Water, Air, and Fire. The four basic elements (the Ancient Chinese included wood as a fifth) from which everything that exists, everything that is real, is comprised. Unless of course the soul is real. We're still not quite sure what that is made of.[75]

This is what Philip K. Dick wants to know about the soul (a question that spills over into Scott's movie): either it does not exist at all or it is the most real thing in the entire universe. There is a third possibility: it is a unique figment of the human imagination, and exists only by virtue of the imagination. When it comes to artists like Dick and Scott, this may be the best "reality" of all. Their work consistently asks questions like: What does it mean to be alive? To be conscious? To be "real"? To have a soul?

During a lecture at UC Fullerton, Dick was asked to provide a definition of Reality. Despite his succinct answer, "that which when you stop believing in it, it doesn't go away," Philip K. Dick spent his entire career as

---

[74] "It's too bad she won't live. But then again, who does?" Origami-folding Gaff observes, one of the more taciturn philosophers in movie history.

[75] We don't know what the soul is made of, or if it exists, or, assuming it does exist, what it is. A character in an early novel of mine once defined the soul as, "that part of us which is more or less healthy in direct proportion to how well or poorly we treat other people," which is something of a Platonic definition, but one I still agree with.

a Science Fiction writer (and perhaps his entire life) exploring the questions "What is real?" and "How can we know what is real?"[76] And because his answers, for nearly 30 years (or at least from 1955's *Eye in the Sky* to 1980's *Divine Invasion* and throughout the *Exegesis* he worked on from 1974 until his death in 1982), tend to explore this question in theological terms, I've come to think of Dick, along with Heraclitus, Meister Eckhart, and William Blake, as one of the great poet-mystics of the Western tradition.

This theological element is not missing from Ridley Scott's 1982 *Blade Runner*, as the portrayal of Rutger Hauer's Roy Batty as a kind of Blake-quoting (or misquoting[77]) Nietzschean-Christ figure makes clear (cf. the somewhat heavy-handed stigmata/crucifixion imagery of Roy Batty driving a nail through his hand, the dove (or is it a pigeon?), etc.). Other film adaptations of Dick novels and short stories (Paul Verhoeven's *Total*

---

[76] When it comes to the movies, the question of what is real is always up for grabs. Is Cassavetes' portrayal of L.A. in his 1976 *The Killing of a Chinese Bookie* more "real" than Scott's 1982 portrayal? Even if it is more "realistic" doesn't that quality only call into question the reality of what we're seeing all the more? The more real a movie looks or feels, the more we are aware of watching something that isn't real. Or are we? Movies generally don't leave their audiences asking the question about what is real so much as they plunge us into that enthusiastic suspension of disbelief which is the precondition of any engrossing viewing experience. When the movie is working, we're too caught up in what we're seeing to question whether or not it's real.

[77] The lines from Blake's *America: A Prophecy* read, "Fiery the angels rose, and as they rose deep thunder roll'd / Around their shores: indignant burning with the fires of Orc." Roy's replacing "rose" with "fell" associates him with Blake's portrayal of Milton, Milton's fallen Angel Satan, and the *Gospels'* Christ who must fall before he can rise again.

157

Recall, Spielberg's *Minority Report*, Linklater's *A Scanner Darkly*) also explore the question of reality as a mental phenomenon (is it dependent on or can it be altered by memory? dreams? drugs? God?). What is real? How do we know? And perhaps most importantly, "Does it matter?" Maybe reality isn't really all that important. After all, we're talking about the movies. Or are we?

Blade Runner is based on Dick's novel *Do Androids Dream of Electric Sheep?* (1968) which opens with a brilliant sequence not featured in the movie. Deckard and his wife (also not featured in the movie), are discussing the uses of their Penfield mood organ. The mood organ allows them to "dial" whatever mood they choose to be in, from despair (and why someone might actively choose to be in despair is a question the novel confronts on several levels) to "awareness of the manifold possibilities open to me in the future." One can even dial for the desire to dial when you're not in the mood to dial for a specific mood. You can dial for "the desire to watch TV, no matter what's on it." Brilliant.[78]

The Penfield mood organ is one more version of the myriad ways in which Dick explores the problem of knowing "What is real?" When our physical surroundings, our loved ones, our memories, and even our own moods and feelings can be faked, or induced, or controlled, what's left to cling to or have confidence in? Where are we when the reality of everything we can imagine can be doubted? In a move of ludic Cartesianism we might conclude that only the imagination itself is left intact

---

[78] And how different is this from parents today who find doctors who will prescribe drugs for their children that help them dial "calm" when they are hyper, or "focused" when they are distracted, or other moods deemed socially appropriate at predetermined times?

when all else is subject to doubt.

As for the soul: the soul may be the most real thing about us. It may be the *only* real thing about us. And we don't even know if it exists.[79] How can we tell? Is the eye really the window to the soul, or do we just see the fires of hell reflected there? As jets of flame burst over L.A. at night, suddenly an enormous eye fills the screen. Whose eye is it? What's it looking at? Or looking for? What are we looking at, when we see this massive eye?

> *The light of the body is the eye: if therefore thine eye be single, thy whole body shall be full of light. But if your eye is bad, your whole body will be full of darkness. If therefore the light that is in you is darkness, how great is that darkness!"* (Matthew 6:22-23)

The eye that dominates the screen for two brief cuts in the opening sequence prefigures much of what is to come. Throughout the movie eyes will be tested, gouged, threatened, magnified (Tyrell's massive glasses), and manufactured; we will see searching eyes, blinded eyes, and private eyes. The movies are always about looking, about what we see, but some are more so than others. As early as Buñuel and Dali's 1929 *Un Chien Andalou*, movies have been self-conscious about the violence they do to the

---

[79] "A scientist, tracing the wiring circuits of that machine to locate its humanness, would be like our own earnest scientists who tried in vain to locate the soul in man, and, not being able to find a specific organ located at a specific spot,* opted to decline to admit that we have souls." P. K. Dick, "Man, Android, and Machine" (*Unable to discover any other use for it, Descartes suggested that the pineal gland was "the seat of the soul.")

eye and to the act of seeing, and have followed Plato in using light and vision as metaphors for knowledge and understanding.

In order to track down information about their incept dates, Roy and Leon pay a visit to a synthetic eye manufacturer. Why eyes? They want Chew, the genetic designer who makes eyes for the Tyrell Corporation, to tell them what they don't know: how long do they have to live? They want him to enlighten their ignorance.

> All men naturally have an impulse to get knowledge. A sign of this is the way we prize our senses; for even apart from their utility, they are prized on their own account, especially sensing with the eyes. For not only from practical motives, but also when we have nothing practical in view, we could be said to prefer sight to any of the other senses. The reason is that of all the senses it can best bring us knowledge and best discerns the many differences among things. (Aristotle, *Metaphysics*)[80]

"If only you could see what I've seen with your eyes," Roy Batty says to Chew. After saving his life he tells Deckard, "I've seen things you people wouldn't believe. Attack ships on fire off the shoulder of Orion, I watched c-beams glitter in the dark near the Tannhäuser Gate. All those moments will be lost in time, like tears in rain." Batty associates living with experience and experience with things he has seen, with what his eyes have shown him about the universe. Roy's final words are, "time to die," which is what Leon says when he threatens to kill Deckard with two fingers aimed at his eyes.[81] Roy Batty

---

[80] 980a21 (Richard Hope translation).

kills his father/creator ("not an easy man *to see*," Roy observes[82]) by gouging out his eyes (the gory details of this scene were omitted from the original U.S. theatrical release and the 1992 Director's Cut). With death comes blindness, with blindness, death.

Scott's movie may be a vision of the future, but Harrison Ford's Rick Deckard is a figure right out of the classic cinematic tradition of the hardnosed detective.[83] In film culture the detective is a figure who struggles with his place in society, his relation to others, his sense of honor, loyalty, and virtue, and who, in his never-ending search for the "bad guy," embodies a philosophic search for truth that helps make the detective film (in the hands of directors from Fritz Lang to Godard and from Orson Welles to Roman Polanski and Lars von Trier) a profound meditation on the human condition and the relationship between fact and fiction, reality and deception.

---

[81] "Time to die." And then? Where do we go when we die? Where else but to wherever we were before we were born.

[82] Before Deckard administers the Voight-Kampff test on Rachael, Tyrell says, "I want to *see* it work on a person. I want to *see* a negative before I provide you with a positive." But of course Rachael is not a positive, so it's not clear what Tyrell actually wants to see. Perhaps he simply wants to test the test. To see what it can see. And what it can't. The first time Rachael visits Deckard after he's administered the test to her she says, surprising him in the elevator on the way to his apartment, "I wanted to *see* you. So I waited." What is it Rachael wants to discover, that she visits Deckard in order to see it? What does it take to be a person? If you have a person's memories and feelings does that make you that person? If not, what's missing? The soul? What if you have that too?

[83] A stock figure in the movies, nearly as old as the gangster (cf. D. W. Griffith's 1912 *Musketeers of Pig Alley* and von Sternberg's *Underworld*), from W. S. Van Dyke's 1934 *The Thin Man* (with William Powell and Myrna Loy) and Peter Lorre's late 1930s Charlie Chan movies to John Huston's 1941 *The Maltese Falcon* and Rian Johnson's 2005 *Brick*.

There are certain things that seem almost inevitably true about the detective: he must be a loner who has a problem with authority, he must wear a trench coat and be as good with his brain as with his fists, he must be "hard drinking" (as a way of dealing with the internal demons that torment him as a result of the morally ambiguous world he is forced to live in), he must be confident and resourceful, he must be particularly at home in the landscape he inhabits, and he must fall in love, often with dangerous or unwise objects of his affection. Deckard fulfills all of these requirements, though it is the last (or the last two), predictably, which gives *Blade Runner* its most interesting thematic dimensions. His oneness with his surroundings and his romanticism are the best compliment to the movie's powerful visual qualities, which is arguably the best thing about it: not what the movie is about, but what it looks like while it goes about unfolding its story.[84]

Having met Deckard in the form of an enormous eye at the beginning of the film, the scene cuts to the exterior of the massive Tyrell Corporation building and then cuts to an interior shot of that building where an unidentified man waits with his back to us. The lighting, the set design, and Cronenweth's cinematography create a scene that changes the mood from futuristic science fiction to hard-boiled detective noir: the smoke drifting through the blue light, the straight-backed chairs, the slowly revolving

---

[84] Writing about the adaptation of his novel Dick lamented, "graphic, visual impact has replaced story" ("Universe Makers . . . and Breakers", 1981). But then he hadn't seen *Blade Runner* yet. No one had. Dick was thinking in terms of ideas; he didn't realize to what extent "graphic, visual impact" can *be* story. Especially when it's a story about the power of seeing.

ceiling fan, the man in the suit with a thermos and cup of steaming coffee at his elbow feel anachronistic in contrast with the exterior shots of flying cars and the Tyrell Corporation. [85] From the anticipatory shot of Deckard's eye we move to a shot of Leon's eye as Holden prepares to administer the Voight-Kampff test. The test is designed to allow Holden to look into Leon's eye and determine whether or not he's human. That is, whether or not he has a soul. This is done by determining his capacity to experience and display emotion.

Detectives are called "private eyes" because they're usually looking for something. What Deckard is looking for is more or less *the* question of the movie.[86] And because this is a sci-fi movie based on a P. K. Dick novel, to say he's looking for "what's real" isn't an exaggeration. To find it he's going to have to get past the things that aren't real but look as if they are. It's getting past these

---

[85] Like Holden's interrogation room, Bryant's office in the Police Building is anachronistically seedy in comparison to the building's high-tech exterior and our approach to it via a flying car (a spinner). Old fashioned fans (no air conditioning despite the building's hyper-modern exterior), venetian blinds over the windows, wooden filing cabinets, leather chairs, a family-photo-and-debris-strew desk, even the font of the lettering on his door and the whiskey bottle in the desk drawer make Bryant's office look like something we've seen in a dozen movies from the 40s and 50s. In fact (like a room built on the sound stage at a movie studio) Bryant's office looks like it's been picked up whole and dropped down inside of a massive hall within the Police Building. It not only has its own walls but also its own roof, scattered with old newspapers, dust, and a discarded push broom from another age (along with the oxygen-mask-wearing superintendent who lets Deckard and Gaff into Leon's hotel room, this broom is my favorite quirky details in the movie). It is a world within a world. The past pushing out against the future.

[86] It's the "private" bit that's tripping him up, since one of the things he's looking for is love, and love is never private. It always has to happen *between* people.

types of illusions (the Buddhists call it *the veil of Maya*) that makes the detective who he is. Another question in the movie concerns the status of the androids (Replicants) Deckard has been coerced into "retiring." Are they alive (are they "real"), in which case Deckard is a murderer, or are they machines gone haywire, in which case Deckard is a sort of violent technician?

> You will be required to do wrong no matter where you go. It is the basic condition of life, to be required to violate your own identity.
>
> –Wilbur Mercer to Rick Deckard in *Do Androids Dream of Electric Sheep?*

Once the Replicants reach a threshold of intelligence that surpasses the intelligence of most human beings, emotion (or empathy) is the only way of distinguishing android from human. Early in the novel Deckard reflects, "ultimately, the empathic gift blurred the boundaries between hunter and victim," not yet realizing that in his role as bounty hunter, the more human (empathetic) he becomes the less capable he will be of killing human-like androids, and the more efficient he is at killing them, the less human (less empathetic) he becomes. An implicit premise of this conceit is the idea that "being human" is not an absolute quality: there's a sliding scale. If people can be more or less human, why not machines as well? In the novel, the androids don't have to be human for Deckard to feel inhuman when he kills them.

Character and plot distinctions aside, this is the greatest difference between the novel and the movie: Dick's androids are ultimately unfeeling machines (they are inhuman); Scott's are not only capable of love, but are also capable of showing human beings the way back to a love we are in danger of losing sight of altogether (one of the movie's many blindness tropes). In their capacity to love—to love life, to love each other, to value experience and memory (for example in their attachment to photographs)—Replicants may be more human than some of the biologically human characters in the movie.[87]

The question of how human beings might eventually exile themselves from the possibility of love is a theme that links *Blade Runner* with Jean-Luc Godard's 1965 *Alphaville*, in which Godard's interpretation of the famous detective Lemmy Caution, played by Eddie Constantine, must rescue a beautiful woman from an ominous future world that no longer understands love. In the closing scene of *Alphaville*, Caution drives Natasha von Braun away from the collapsing city toward "the Outlands" (in a shot that anticipated the eventually abandoned scene of Deckard and Rachael flying away from L.A. in Deckard's hover car over a beautiful natural landscape) and forces her to discover the words that correspond to her feelings:

Natasha: "I don't know what to say. They're words I don't know. I wasn't taught them. Help me."
Lemmy: "Impossible Princess. You must get there yourself. Then you'll be saved."

This exchange sheds some light on the scene between

---

[87] Thus the oft-debated question about whether or not Deckard is a Replicant is irrelevant. The movie isn't interested in the question of who is a human and who's a Replicant, but in the more fundamental question of what it means to be human in the first place. Besides, if Deckard were a Replicant, why would he drink? Only creatures with souls need alcohol. So either Deckard is a human being, or Replicants have souls. (Is this why Pris smokes a cigarette while she waits outside of J. F. Sebastian's apartment building?)

Deckard and Rachael in which he forces her to say, "kiss me" and "I want you" not as acts of physical violence but of emotional liberation: he has to show her that she *is* capable of feeling and desiring, capable of love. And she must trust that her feelings are real, even if she isn't. But of course once she realizes her feelings are real, she realizes that she must be as well. And perhaps he has to discover the same things about himself as well.[88]

But whereas *Alphaville* is about the triumph of poetry over technology (in Godard's film poetry celebrates the mystery of love, technology tries to explain it away and banish it), *Blade Runner* is about the possibility of technology eventually restoring to us a faith in love that more primal forces threaten to obscure (forces like fear, greed, and insecurity, which are far more ancient and "human" than technology).[89] By 2019 it might take technology to show us (another seeing metaphor) what we're in danger of losing for reasons that have nothing to do with technology at all: that love itself (in its many forms: romantic, erotic, filial, for animals, for a cause, as friendship, as sacrifice for others) may be the only proof of the existence of the soul that we will ever have. So if we deny the existence of the soul, is a denial of love far behind?

Because it turns out that if androids are capable of love (and it's clear from the behavior of characters like Leon, Rachael, and Roy Batty that they are), that's good news

---

[88] What Deckard does to Rachael in this scene may not be so different from what Roy does to Deckard during their struggle in the Bradbury Hotel. Roy makes Deckard fight to stay alive, in a sense giving him the gift of wanting to be alive by threatening to kill him.

[89] Technology also helps Deckard to *see*, by allowing him to more closely examine Leon's photo that leads him to Zhora.

for humans, because it means that love is something mysteriously, inexplicably real. It means that love is not, as so many voices in the modern world have tried to tell us, "merely" the result of pheromones, or Darwinian evolution, or social conditioning, or brain chemistry, or any of the other strictly materialist accounts that have been offered up to explain away the mystery. If machines can love, then love remains a mystery. Part of the unknown. If even androids, who have not undergone evolution, are not subject to social conditioning, and don't have brain chemistry, are capable of love, then it means that what us Romantics have suspected all this time is true: Love is a mystery that cannot be explained by a physical account of the matter that makes up the universe.

Love requires a soul. And isn't it easier to accept the idea that androids could have a soul than to admit that humans don't?

Style as a Matter of Life and Death:
Jean-Pierre Melville's *Le Samouraï* (1967)

There is a saying of the elders' that goes, "Step from under the eaves and you're a dead man. Leave the gate and the enemy is waiting." This is not a matter of being careful. It is to consider oneself as dead beforehand.

–Yamamoto Tsunetomo, *Hagakure*

The movie centers around a few basic questions woven into the film's dialogue:

"Who are you?"
"What do you want?"
"What kind of man are you?"
"Why, Jef?"

Like all great filmmakers, Melville is part alchemist, part magician, and all conman. For the first 10 minutes of the film not a single word is spoken (and the first word that is spoken is Jef's name, as a question), during which time Melville casts his spell and shapes his illusion with a perfect economy of images: a man lying on a bed chain-smoking, a birdcage in the middle of the room framed by two windows; a man putting on an overcoat and hat, adjusting its brim in the mirror; a non-exchange between a man and a pretty woman at a stoplight, the shot of his silhouette through the rain-streaked car window, the cigarette loosely held between his lips; the palate of grey-blues and yellow-browns. (Melville said his dream was to make a color film in black & white, and with *Le Samouraï* he succeeds brilliantly.)

Melville is seducing us, as the woman at the stoplight might so easily have been seduced, to fall for this image made up of images: the elegant gangster, the mysterious stranger, the enigmatic loner, the romantic hitman, the French samurai, the killer with a code. We're taken in from the beginning, for an image is just that: something on the surface that conceals what's beneath. And what if there's nothing beneath? What if it's image all the way down? Is that just another level to the deception?

Caught up in Alain Delon's frigid good looks, immaculate wardrobe, Spartan aesthetic and unflappable cool, the audience tends to lose track of the fact that he's playing a character who may actually be insane. Melville told Rui Nogueira his film was "the analysis of a schizophrenic by a paranoiac, because all creators are paranoiac."[90] He said, "before writing the script I read up everything I could about schizophrenia—the solitude, the silences, the introversion."[91] Le Samouraï is not so much a movie about an ultra-cool hitman as it is a rather oddly loving portrait of someone who is mentally ill, someone who suffers from a "mental disorder characterized by a breakdown in thinking and poor emotional responses."[92] Of course if Freud is right, and to be human is to be ill, then it's also a movie about all of us.

---

[90] This suggestion of an identity between Melville and his character Costello (one schizophrenic, the other paranoiac) is more than coincidence. I know nothing about Melville's private life, but having seen his films many times I'm convinced that Le Samouraï is his most autobiographical work, far more so than L'armée des Ombres made two years later.

[91] Melville on Melville, edited by Rui Nogueira, pp. 126-8, The Viking Press, New York. 1971.

[92] Concise Medical Dictionary, Oxford University Press.

Initially we might be fooled by this description of a "breakdown in thinking" because Jef is so careful and thorough. He thinks of everything. Which is true, but he's not thinking what we're thinking. Or rather, he's not thinking what we think he's thinking. *Le Samouraï* is a great movie, but its greatness lies in part in its ability to sweep us off our feet with the power of its images, frame by frame, before we have time to think critically about what's happening when all those beautiful frames are strung together to form a narrative.

On a grey-blue rainy evening Jef pulls his stolen Citroen up to the garage where he'll have new plates put on the car. It's a perfect shot: sky, car, building, wall. Like his hero, Melville is uncompromising in his attention to detail, every shot starkly composed with an immaculate color palate and perfect economy of motion (the character's motion, the camera's motion). He creates a world that feels familiar but otherworldly (a world somehow out of time) for his familiar but otherworldly character to move through. In some ways the whole story of the movie is told in this one shot of the car being pulled into the garage.

"Creative art is based on lies," Melville told Nogueira, and he praised Alfred Hitchcock for being "marvelously two-faced," adding, "a film-maker is like the master of a shadow-play ... I am perfectly aware of the extraordinary dishonesty it takes to be effective; but the spectator must never be allowed to realize the extent to which everything is manipulated. He must be spellbound, a prisoner, in a state of submission."[93] To be sure, there is

---

[93] *Melville on Melville*, pg. 11.

pleasure in being spellbound when one submits to the magic of the cinema, but there is also pleasure, and insight, in occasionally breaking free, peering behind the curtain, and seeing the truth behind the trick. And Melville, like his hero, wants to get caught. After all, we can't appreciate his subtle genius if we don't see how he's tricked us. So he leaves us a series of clues (like the brief image of the worthless banknotes) to the truth about Jef Costello. Jef is not a killer for hire, he's not a French "samurai;" he's a child playing an elaborate, deadly game, a game he has every intention of winning, no matter how much that final victory costs. It's game he can't lose so long as winning remains solely a matter of how well he plays.[94]

In the garage, waiting for the new plates to be put on his stolen car, Jef—in his hat and trench coat—is framed so beautifully against the stark background that even the fuse box on the wall behind him looks like a work of art. What Melville says of the filmmaker is equally true of the film watcher:

> A film-maker should be a man constantly open, constantly traumatizable; his sense of observation must be as highly developed as possible, and his sense of psychology; he

---

[94] On the other hand, Melville's character is a combination of cultural archetypes (or stereotypes) that show us how little regard the cinema has for national boundaries. Costello is part Japanese warrior, part American gangster (or Western cowboy: "All my original scripts, without exception, are transposed Westerns," Melville told Nogueira), part Montaigne-inspired French stoic ("to philosophize is to learn how to die"), and part Freudian case-study, and *Le Samouraï* is a hybrid of American, French, and Japanese cinema that shows us again why there is not such thing as national cinema because cinema always forms a nation all its own (*Melville on Melville*, pg. 100).

must have exceptionally keen visual and auditory perception... and a memory.

As audience, we must develop our "sense of observation" if we're going to see what's going on. Watching a movie is also a kind of game. If we want to play well, we have to keep our eye on the ball. Melville is a master of making us look elsewhere. The magician has his feint of hand and Melville has his feint of eye. And what he gives us to look at is so "spellbinding" that it's hard not to feel grateful for having been tricked. We appreciate the skill of any great magician, especially when we're taken in and seduced by him.

Jef isn't really a samurai, though in his attitude toward play he is something like Nietzsche's conception of the ludic Heraclitus:

> Do guilt, injustice, contradiction, and suffering exist in this world? They do, proclaims Heraclitus, but only for the limited human mind which sees things apart but not connected, not for the con-tuitive god. For him all contradictions run into harmony, indivisible to the common human eye, yet understandable to one who, like Heraclitus [or Jef Costello], is related to the contemplative god. Before his fire-gaze not a drop of injustice remains in the world poured all around him; even that cardinal impulse that allows pure fire to inhabit such impure forms is mastered by him with a sublime metaphor. In this world only play, play as artists and children [and Jef is something of both: an artist who destroys

172

rather than creates; a child breaking the toys he plays with] engage in it, exhibits coming-to-be and passing away, structuring and destroying, without any moral additive, in forever equal innocence.[95] And as children and artists play, so plays the ever-living fire . . . Only aesthetic man [and Jef is nothing if not aesthetic; he is pure style] can look thus at the world.

–Nietzsche, *Philosophy in the Tragic Age of the Greeks*

Jef too has his "fire gaze" and we see it when he looks at himself in the mirror and adjusts the brim of his hat. It is the gaze of aesthetic man, who does not see himself in the mirror, but sees the man that other people will see when they look at him. As aesthetic man, Jef's game is one of "structuring and destroying, without any moral additive." But even Hide & Seek is no fun if no one's looking for you, and despite his anti-social tendencies, Jef isn't interested in playing solitaire. He has to set up the game so that he'll be chased. He may even have to set it up so that he'll be caught. And by means of the empty pistol he can still send a message from beyond the grave that in the end he won.

Consider some of the moves Jef makes in this game. His first move, the one that sets up everything else that happens in the movie, is the painstaking construction of a perfect alibi. We're so caught up in following the details of this alibi (which starts with stealing a car and includes a carefully orchestrated encounter with Wiener outside

---

[95] "Jef Costello is neither a crook nor a gangster. He is an 'innocent' in the sense that a schizophrenic doesn't know he's criminal, although he *is* criminal in his logic and his way of thinking" (*Melville on Melville*, pg. 126).

Jeanne's (Nathalie Delon) apartment) that we may never stop to reflect on the fact that the whole elaborate setup is completely unnecessary.

It's unnecessary because when the Police Commissioner (François Périer) calls for a "General Alert; routine roundup" of 20 men from every precinct, we know that his search is entirely random, and we're being told (indirectly) that if Jef had just gone home after carrying out his hit on Martey, the police would never have found him. They would never have looked for him. They would never even have known he existed. We're told during the police lineup that Jef has "no previous record", so he would never have been on their radar except for the fact that he puts himself there. It's only because they find him hanging out at a poker game with known members of the underworld (their criminal habits are established with great economy in the single shot in which the man who responds to Jef's knock carefully stands away from the door while opening it) that he's picked up in the first place. Why is he even there? The poker game has nothing to do with his alibi, since he admits to having arrived at the game after the murder had already been committed.

Jef doesn't even bother to change his coat and hat before appearing in the police lineup, though he could have easily left them with the poker players when he dropped by earlier in the evening. The poker game is a great detail, but it's also just another red herring Melville throws at us to distract us from Jef's real motive in establishing his "alibi": he wants to enter into a game with the police. He wants to play. He may not want to get caught, but he doesn't want to simply get away with his crime either. Why should he? What does he have waiting at home for him?

It's precisely the elaborate machinations around the double alibi that raises the Commissioner's suspicions. All Jef had to do was shoot Martey, go home, and continue avoiding the club he had never been to before in his life. Job over. But Melville, like any great magician,[96] brilliantly distracts the audience from this fact, since without it (without the fact that Jef is more interested in playing a game than in getting away with murder) there can be no movie. After all, if the alibi is unnecessary, so is the beautiful scene of Jef stealing the car, since he only needs the car to drive around town establishing his alibi. And so is the scene with Jeanne. He could have taken the metro to Martey's, performed the hit and then gotten away on foot, back to the metro and his apartment, his bird, his cigarettes and his bottles of water lined up in neat rows on top of his wardrobe. The opening sequence, with its compelling vibrato camera work (suggesting the disturbed mental state of the man we're watching?) shows a man lying on his bed smoking. A man waiting. But waiting for what? Once he's killed Martey, does he just go back to lying on his bed?

In fact the police's suspicion of Jef is largely groundless. All they have is that he "fits the description" and the conflicting testimony of the eyewitnesses (who would never even have seen him in the lineup if he'd simply returned to his apartment after committing the crime). The Commissioner is suspicious of Jeanne's part in his alibi (despite the fact that Wiener has unwittingly corroborated it) and goes to great lengths to intimidate

---

[96] Melville emphasizes the magical elements of the film through Jef's relationship with his gun, which suddenly appears in his hand, a split second earlier clearly shown as empty, the instant he needs to fire. Now you see it, now you don't.

her, but he's not bothered at all by the pianist's (Cathy Rosier) absolute denial that Jef is the murderer, despite the fact that she is the only witness who got a good look at him.

The whole scene with Wiener picking Jef out of the room full of men is so elaborately constructed (What is the Commissioner hoping to prove by having the men switch hats and coats? Is he testing Wiener? To what end?) that it's easy to lose track of the fact that it's been planned by Jef to make the police believe his alibi. And yet, it seems to have no impact on the Commissioner (whose own orchestrations play right into Jef's intentions). In fact, it only makes him more suspicious.

We can't tell anything from Jef's face, but I suspect he's enjoying himself at the police station. He wanted to get hauled in, and now that he's there, he wants to test them, and himself (this testing is part of the game; it may even be the only reason to play). When the Commissioner tells Jef he'll have to prove he didn't know the victim, Jef responds, "No, it's up to you to prove the contrary." His response does two things: it's a direct challenge (or an invitation) to the police to join the game, and it lets them know that he knows the rules and intends to play by them.

The air of the Commissioner as he opens the blinds onto a rainy Sunday morning is that of a man who feels he has just lost the first round of a game, not of a man who's suspicions have been allayed.[97] We're told that there are only 9 suspects left, as if to give the impression that if the

---

[97] The commissioner, who describes himself as a man who "doesn't think," is a worthy opponent for Jef, who tells the man who holds him at gunpoint in his apartment that he lives by "habit" not rule.

murderer isn't one of these 9 men, it must be Costello. Never mind that the suspects were randomly pulled in and there's no reason to imagine the actual murderer was picked up by the police in the first place. ("What's 400 suspects in a city of 10 million?" the Commissioner admits.)

Furthermore, after a certain point, the Commissioner must know that even if Jef is the killer, he's only a hired gunman (Jef didn't know Martey, had never seen him before, had no motive for killing him), and in that sense Jef isn't Martey's real killer. But the Commissioner exhausts immense police resources having Jef followed and trying to break his alibi, while making no effort whatsoever to find the men who hired Jef (and in that sense, are really responsible for Martey's death). Interestingly, Melville never allows the question of motive to come up.[98] To consider motive too closely would make the game-like nature of all this too obvious. And part of the game is not to be obvious.

> There is surely nothing other than the single purpose of the present moment. A man's whole life is a succession of moment after moment. If one fully understands the present moment, there will be nothing else to do, and nothing else to pursue. Live being true to the single purpose of the moment.
> –*Hagakure*

There are other questions that don't have simple answers

---

[98] Except in those unconvincing moments when Jef says he does this because he gets paid, which no one paying attention to anything about Jef's character could possibly believe.

but further suggest that Jef is playing a game:

He knows he's being following by the police, but he throws the package of bloody bandages into the street in front of his apartment where he knows the police will find it. Is he sending them a message?

When he finds the bug in his apartment, Jef lets the police know he's found it by turning it off (since he leaves his apartment to make a phone call anyway). Another message?

Why does he visit Jeanne a final time? Is he saying goodbye? Telling her he loves her? Letting her know he doesn't need her after all?

Why has Olivier Rey taken out a contract on the beautiful piano player? (Is it to get rid of her, or to set up Jef?)

Why does he kill Rey? To protect the girl? Does she need protection if he's already decided to die? Revenge seems an unlikely motive for someone not motivated by emotion at any other point in the film.

Why, with Rey dead and four million Francs in his pocket, doesn't he leave Paris rather than return to the nightclub?

How do we understand the difference between the look in his eyes during the two car theft scenes? What's changed for Jef between the first theft and the second?

And of course: why does he take the bullets out of the gun?

Even if he's not going to shoot the girl there's no reason to unload the gun unless he wants to send another message, either to her or the police. Or to both. Is it the same message to each of them?[99]

Cliché's have the charm of always being true: it's not whether you win or lose, but how you play the game. And *how* you play is all a matter of style, because style is the one thing Jef has total control over. If he can't control the outside world, he can still control how he responds to and acts within that world. And that's what style is for Jef: the stoicism of a self-contained romantic who also happens to be a killer.

Much of Jef's behavior is wildly inconsistent with the assumption that he is a professional hitman trying to get away with a crime, but I don't mean to suggest that these are inconsistencies in the film or sloppy filmmaking on Melville's part. Rather they are a series of clues that suggest that our initial assumptions about Jef may simply be wrong. It's not that the movie doesn't make sense because it's about a killer who goes to great lengths to establish an absolutely unnecessary alibi. Rather, the movie *only* makes sense if we realize the alibi is unnecessary, because only then do we see that this whole thing: the alibi, the killing, the subsequent game of cat-and-mouse with the police, even Jef's death at the end, have all been part of an elaborate game organized, orchestrated, and played out by Jef. This is the only way to make sense of the plot of the movie. But then again, the

---

[99] Jef doesn't talk much, so these oblique means of "sending messages" are his most common way of communicating throughout the film. In fact much of the film is shot so that silence and the ambient noises that emphasize it (traffic, footsteps, the bird's chirping) are as compelling as any of the film's human characters. Like Jef, Melville communicates obliquely rather than directly.

movie's plot may be the least interesting thing about it; it's just the skeleton supporting the flesh we come to desire.

There's something peculiar going on around this creation of a desire which has little to do with the movie's plot. Melville wins our sympathy for a man who appears to be a hired killer and who turns out to be something of a sociopath. But what's more strange: that it's so easy for Melville to win us over to the former, or that for some reason we find the latter less acceptable? Why is it easier to sympathize with a man who kills for money than for a man who kills as part of a game? Isn't it odd that we find it easier to understand, and more "sane" to imagine, someone killing for money? Jef isn't crazy because he kills (the movies, and real life, are full of people who do that); he's not even (or only) crazy because he thinks of killing as part of a game; he's crazy because in the middle of this game he insists, "Je ne perds jamais. Jamais vraiment." The question is, how high a price is he willing to pay in order to "never lose"?

Talking about *Bob le Flambeur* (his first film made from an original script), Melville said, "In his progress from achievement to achievement, man comes inevitably to his last, absolute defeat: death."[100] But with Jef Melville has created a character who seeks to transform this absolute defeat into a kind of victory, in order to fulfill his dream to "perd jamais."

Jef's bird is a bullfinch, but its importance in his life reminds me of a nightingale (its peeping, a haunting soundtrack that punctuates the movie):

---

[100] *Melville on Melville*, pg. 54.

Darkling I listen; and, for many a time
 I have been half in love with easeful Death,
Call'd him soft names in many a mused rhyme,
 To take into the air my quiet breath;
Now more than ever seems it rich to die,
 To cease upon the midnight with no pain,
  While thou art pouring forth thy soul abroad
  In such an ecstasy!
Still would thou sing and I have ears in vain—
To thy high requiem become a sod.

–Keats, "Ode to a Nightingale"

Death is a game to Jef, whether it's his death, or that of a man like Martey who he doesn't know and never saw before the game got started. It's not a question of whether Jef wants to die, or whether, like Keats, he is "half in love with easeful Death." He is playing a game, and the only game that seems to penetrate his shell of indifference towards life is one where the stakes are life and death. "I never lose, not really." That doesn't mean he doesn't play. Like Bob, Jef is a gambler. It means that playing is so important to him that even dying is worth the chance to play. Even dying is a kind of victory. Which hardly makes him a samurai, though it may make him a bit crazy. We shouldn't forget that Melville intended the film as the study of a schizophrenic. The question becomes, "Why are we so taken by this portrait of a psychopathic killer?" or "How does Melville (like Hitchcock in his 1960 *Psycho*) so successfully manipulate his audience into both sympathizing with and even admiring the 'kind of man' Jef so clearly is?" What do we find romantic, mysterious, and even admirable about a man who treats death, both his own and that of others, like a game?

Jef doesn't kill for money[101] (though the money helps make the game "real"), and he doesn't kill for "fun"; the stakes of his game are much higher than that. What fascinates us about his so-called "code," his aesthetic, and his style such that we tend to overlook the mental illness and focus instead on the "cool" that envelops him? Why are we fascinated by a man who is willing to kill other men for unidentified reasons, a man who seems to live "beyond good and evil"? Like Norman Bates, Jef Costello is mentally ill. Like Hitchcock, Melville's triumph is to win his audience's sympathy for a character who is not only a criminal and a killer, but a madman. Hitchcock's success at winning our sympathy for Norman is a large part of what makes *Pyscho* a masterpiece (why it gets under our skin in such a creepy way).[102] Melville goes one step further: we don't just sympathize with Jef; we admire him; we may even want to be like him (which would only be true of Norman Bates for those of us who are as crazy in "real life" as Norman is in the movie). But in what sense?

The samurai lives by a code, *Bushido*, but Jef is not a samurai, and the rituals he lives by are not really a code

---

[101] Any more than Norman Bates does. Jef's indifference towards the four million Francs and his Spartan lifestyle provide ample evidence that he's not in this for the money.

[102] There are several other provocative similarities between the two movies; for example, the misdirection around money as a way of distracting the audience's attention from what's really going on and the deception around the question of identity (Norman's mother's in one case, Jef's in the other). Like Melville, Hitch goes to great lengths to keep his audience off balance; for example, the amazing staircase crane shot with its vertiginous motion that culminates in the overhead shot of Norman carrying his mother down to the fruit cellar, carefully composed so that the audience never asks why we aren't given a shot of mother's face.

but rather the marks of a lonely and obsessive personality. There are other Melville heroes (in *L'armée des Ombres*, *Le cercle rouge*, *Le deuxième souffle*, even *Bob le Flambeur*) who live by a code, but Jef isn't one of them. Jef says as much to the man who holds him at gunpoint: he doesn't live by rule, but by habit. Habits, like the instincts of a tiger in the jungle, are the very opposite of a code. The movie is full of red herrings, brilliantly placed there by master magician Melville, and the first red herring is the film's title (and the made-up samurai quote which opens the film).[103] Jef is like his creator, a creature of ritual and tradition: "with schizophrenics every act is a rite" and "white gloves are a tradition with me; all my killers wear them. They are editors gloves," Melville told Nogueira.[104] He might have said something similar about hats.

There is the psychology of the killer, but equally troubling is the psychology of the reader, or the moviegoer, fascinated by the killer. That is, the psychology of most of us. We like to write about them, read about them, watch movies about them. I doubt many of us actually want to kill someone. So why are we so fascinated by men and women (black widow femme fatales, gangsters, vampires, cowboys, assassins) who do?[105]

---

[103] This red herring was given added credence by the story, which may even be true, of how Melville pitched the script to Alain Delon in Delon's apartment; Delon asked him what the movie was called. When Melville told him, Delon took him into his bedroom, where a samurai sword was the sole decoration hanging on the wall above his bed.

[104] *Melville on Melville*, pp. 132, 139.

[105] The cowboy, the gangster, the vampire, and the Ronin cannot live as accepted members of the society they either protect or prey on (cf. von Sternberg's *Underworld*, Ford's *The Searchers*, Murnau's *Nosferatu*, Kurosawa's *Seven Samurai*, and about a million other

"Yes sir, the law of self-destruction and the law of self-preservation are equally strong in humanity. The devil has equal dominion over humanity until the limit of time which we know not."

–Dostoevsky, *The Idiot*

Yes, there's the Eros/Thanatos connection. The Death Drive and the Drive to Create, or Procreate, the drive to sex and love, inseparable from the drive toward our own destruction.[106] Critics postulate that Jef is in love with the piano player (even Melville said as much; up to his old tricks again?), who they identify as "Death personified," pointing to her enigmatic inviting smile, black skin, and white dress (the color of death and mourning in Japan[107]). But if Jef is a consistent character, falling in love is outside the range of his possible responses to the people he encounters over the course of the film.[108] He can use

---

movies on the same theme). Predator or protector: interestingly it seems to make little difference to the audience which of these two extremes the main character exemplifies.

[106] Writing about a retrospective of Hitch's films, Truffaut said, "I was awed by what I saw on the screen: splashes of color, fireworks, ejaculations, sighs, death rattles, screams, blood, tears, twisted wrists. It occurred to me that in Hitchcock's cinema, which is definitely more sexual than sensual, to make love and to die are one and the same." Hardly an original insight, especially for a Frenchman used to calling an orgasm "la petite mort", but there it is: love and death, sex and death, death and death...

[107] Also the color of the editor's gloves Jef wears whenever he shoots someone, but not when he handles the murder weapon or steals a car, so apparently the gloves aren't to cover his fingerprints. So maybe they're not editor's gloves after all (despite what Melville said, since "creative art is based on lies"). Maybe they're the gloves a magician wears when he performs his tricks.

[108] Though the film certainly implies that he and the pianist have

people but not love them. (Which is not to say he doesn't have sex with her; a fact which is both causally pointed out and ignored as irrelevant by the film itself.) He uses Martey to turn himself into a killer, he uses the mob to turn himself into a professional, he uses the police to turn himself into an object of the hunt, and he uses the piano player in the final move he makes in the game he's been playing all along. If anything, he is in love with his own image, an image that must die young if it is going to avoid decay. Jef doesn't sacrifice himself at the end of the movie to save the girl. (Since he's already killed Olivier Rey he knows she's safe.) Maybe he just doesn't want to grow old.[109] (Isn't it better to die young and beautiful than to die old and seedy in an apartment with peeling walls and a bathtub in the kitchen?)

What is Jef in love with if not his own death? The heroism of it, the tragedy of it? The romance and cool toughness of it? But is this what Jef loves, or what we love about him? Is this what seduces us to look past the madness and the violence? Are we too seduced by death? Violence is just a

---

slept together. Jef leaves for the nightclub shortly after 10 p.m. They're shown talking in her apartment (she's changed into a Japanese-style nightgown and he familiarly caresses her neck while she plays the piano) at 6 a.m. Since he's only getting around to telling her now why he has to find the men who hired him to kill Martey we have to assume they've been doing something other than talking in the intervening hours.

[109] "The realization that one is growing old is tragic. It means understanding suddenly that one is alone. Old age is the consummation of solitude" (*Melville on Melville*, pg. 117). The two men who bug Jef's apartment are like older, seedier versions of the assassin. They work silently, efficiently, without wasted movement, professionally. One of them keeps his hands in his pockets, as Jef does throughout the film. Of course they work together, whereas Jef is a "lone wolf," but in other ways they are images of what Jef would rather die young than risk becoming.

means to an end. Are we seduced by Eros? Sex is traditionally a means to an end (procreation), but more often it's one of the few things in life we consider as an end in itself (and we go to great lengths to avoid the natural end towards which it aims (some would even say murder)). Whereas death is just an end. (Or is it?) Death is Death, but Eros is . . . what? Sex? Love? Desire? Terror in the face of death? Or our virulent attempts to avoid it?

We see the empty gun. It's the only way Jef knows how to connect with another human being: through the medium of death. Maybe he confuses it with love. Or maybe he realizes that for a would-be Samurai it's the same thing. Melville made up the quote about the tiger with which the movie begins. There's no such thing as *The Book of Bushido*. But surely Melville had read Yamamoto Tsunetomo's 18th century *Hagakure* (a fact Jarmusch was clearly aware of in his 1999 tribute to Melville's film, *Ghost Dog*):

> Above all, the Way of the Samurai should be in being aware that you do not know what is going to happen next, and in querying every item day and night. Victory and defeat are matters of the temporary force of circumstances. The way of avoiding shame is different. It is simply in death. A real man does not think of victory or defeat. He plunges recklessly towards an irrational death. By doing this, you will awaken from your dreams.

Is it because he does not think of "victory or defeat" that it's possible for Jef to "never lose"? Is this what makes him, after all, a sort of modern day Samurai? Not any code he lives by, but his attitude toward death? His willingness to plunge, at the end of the film, "recklessly towards an irrational death"? Since he does not know "what is going to happen next," all he can do is control his own reactions. His style. A man can avoid shame by refusing to do anything shameful, no matter what the cost.

Beyond our fascination with Eros and Thanatos, what do we find compelling about Jef Costello? What is style but a way of being in the world? How can you be at home in the midst of the Unheimlich (the uncanny)? When you make your internal sense of alienation a part of your external landscape, home becomes a very strange place to be. When you make alienation so much your own that you can dwell in it. Jef inhabits the world the way his bird lives in its cage; he knows he's trapped. It's not that he's making the best of it. He's not even trying to escape. (Unless death is a kind of escape. But Jef's death isn't a form of suicide.[110] It's a kind of victory. But over what?) Like Camus's Sisyphus, just being able to smile as you push the rock is a kind of freedom.[111] Jef is Norman Bates. Jef is Sisyphus. Jef is Orpheus, Thanatos, and Eros. Jef is Hamlet and Lear. And the truth is, Jef isn't like any of us, which may be the only reason we can indulge in the pleasures of imagining otherwise.

Maybe Jef dies for love, but is it any less true to say he

---

[110] Camus wrote, "There is but one truly serious philosophical problem, and that is suicide. Judging whether life is or is not worth living amounts to answering the fundamental question of philosophy" ("The Myth of Sisyphus"). Jef judges life worth living, but only if it's led with style, and he's willing to die to prove it.

[111] The frame still exists from an unused cut of the end of the movie, with Jeff falling backwards after he's been shot by the police, a joyful smile spread across his face. Is it the smile of Sisyphus at the foot of his mountain?

dies to avoid love? Maybe he loves death, or maybe he's just afraid of love the way most people are afraid of death. Maybe love and death are just another way that Scylla and Charybdis pin us down and threaten to devour us. We've all got to go some way.

Love Comes in at the Eye:[112]
Wim Wenders' *Wings of Desire*[113] (1987)

> Here may be seen how being
> blessed
> Has its foundation in the act
> of sight,
> And not in love, which comes
> afterwards...
>
> –Dante, *Paradiso* XXVIII
> (C.H. Sisson, trans.)

When does watching become seeing? The Angels look, but how can they understand what they see? Sitting in a car in a showroom window Cassiel reads aloud from his notebook. With Damiel he exchanges accounts of the miraculous things they've witnessed. What is a miracle? For human beings, miracles are things that can't be explained by scientific accounts. So if we're paying attention[114] we realize everything is a miracle. Even something as simple as raising our arm above our head—how is it possible? If we think about it carefully we realize it's a miracle that can't be explained. For Angels it's the human things that are miraculous: food, a cup of coffee, warming your hands in the cold, transportation, a

---

[112] From William Yeats, "A Drinking Song": "Wine comes in at the mouth / And love comes in at the eye; / That's all we shall know for truth / Before we grow old and die. / I lift the glass to my mouth, / I look at you, and I sigh."

[113] Wenders said that, unwilling to translate the German title *Der Himmel über Berlin*, he came up with an original name for the movie in English which he ended up thinking of as "the real title of the film."

[114] And "paying attention" is what *Wings of Desire* is about.

woman's breast, an old man struggling to put on his glasses, a child's smile, time & space, the fear of evil, Love. Music, laughter, colors. The world of the Angels is black & white. Suddenly Marion's trailer bursts into color. The gray-blue bathrobe, the aqua-blue walls, the oranges. She juggles. Why? Alone and with no one watching, why do people juggle? This is something the angels can't seem to understand, and their wonder leads us to wonder along with them.

If we looked at the world the way the Angels see it, we would ask questions about things we long ago started taking for granted. We would begin to wonder, all over again, the way we did as children. *Als das Kind Kind war.* If we believed in Angels, if we moved through the world convinced of their existence, convinced that they were watching us, listening to our thoughts, would we live different lives? Would we ask more questions? Questions like, why do people juggle? Why do we play music? What do we hear when we listen to music? What do we feel? Does listening to music make us feel less alone? What is it about the experience of being alone (alone with our thoughts, alone with our feelings) that we so often seek love, music, or oblivion (through sex, drugs, and rock n' roll) to escape it? Do we want to escape solitude, or attain something else? If one is not enough, will two be more? *Why am I me, and not you?*

I stink of gasoline, the dying man thinks to himself. Smells. Taste. The feel of heat and cold. The awareness of these things. The desire for them. The wish to avoid them. Eating. The body. Everything it means to be human, presented as a series of questions we should wonder about. Wonder at. Even the possibility of prepositions is a kind of miracle of language. A kind of poetry. Like a trapeze artist. Poetry in motion. The poetry of the human body. Why do people read books? Why do we want to be told stories? Why do we listen to music? (The same question, asked two different times, is two different questions.) *Karin, I should have told you.* Why do we share? Why do we regret? Why are we cruel? Why do we love? Can Darwin really explain these things? Or Freud? Or Nietzsche? Or Christ? The Angels witness, but do they understand? Do we?

Wonder gives rise to questions. That's why children ask so many annoying questions (or why children's questions are so often annoying): they're still wondering at things we've stopped even thinking about. Why do we collect things? (Marion's (Solveig Dommartin) trailer is full of photographs, knickknacks, books, records, a table covered with rocks.) Why do we destroy things? From gourmet to glutton, why do we eat beyond the need to survive? Why do we doubt? Why do we fear? What do we hope for? Why, Homer (Curt Bois) asks, are our great epics all poems about war? Why has no one ever succeeded in singing of peace?

Music, stories, poetry. The things that make us human. The things without which we would be less than we are.

Listening to a Nick Cave record in her trailer, Marion asks, *How should I live? Perhaps that's not the question. How should I think?* About what? After her last performance, celebrating with her circus colleagues, Marion sings happily, perhaps drunkenly, and Damiel (Bruno Ganz) looks on, smiling. Perhaps this is the moment when he falls in love, as much with her song and her singing as with anything else about her. Why do we sing? Why do we kiss? Can Damiel understand? We sing when we feel happy, but also when we feel sad. What is singing? What is listening to music? Do we have to look at ourselves through the eyes of an Angel in order to see how miraculous we actually are? Or is it enough to see a film that shows us that?

Wenders' Angels are voyeurs. But so are we. Everyone who sits down in front of a movie is a kind of voyeur, at least for the next 90 minutes, which is one reason why movies are so often fascinated by eavesdropping and intrusive looking. From the slashed eyeball in Luis Buñuel's *Un Chien Andalou* to Hitchcock's *Rear Window* (and in at least three crucial scenes in *Psycho*), and in movies like Antonioni's *Blow Up*, Brian De Palma's *Blow Out*, Coppola's *The Conversation*, Michael Powell's *Peeping Tom*, and Hal Ashby's *Being There*, the acts of watching and listening (auditory as well as visual voyeurism) and their links with sex and violence are explored by the movies again and again. In Wenders' film voyeurism is more of a caress than a violation, but looking on and listening in are still themes that implicate us as moviegoers. If we weren't implicated in the Angels' watching, the movie wouldn't touch us as it does.

We peer into other people's apartments, listening in on their thoughts. (This is a level of voyeurism Hitchcock's Jeff Jefferies can only dream of.) The father of the boy who looks like James Dean worries, *What will become of the boy? He's only got music in his head.* His mother laments, *he only learned rock n' roll.* (They're not talking to each other, they're not even in the same room, but their interior monologues are in dialogue.) As if there were something more important than rock n' roll he should have learned. What else should he have "in his head"? Music is what the whole movie is about: music and love; the love of music; the music of love. Wenders said that he made his first short films in order to put music in them and he speculated that he might still make movies largely to set images to music (which is perhaps one reason why the soundtracks to his movies are so terrific,[115] and also why he was the perfect director to make *Buena Vista Social Club* in 1999). *Wings* isn't a move *about* music, poetry, and stories—it *is* these things.

Homer sits at a table reading in the Berlin Library. The table is covered with globes. *Do away with the world behind the world*, he thinks. The poet, the musician, the storyteller, and the moviemaker are all in the business of creating different worlds for us to visit. In our world as movie watchers we watch these worlds the way the Angels watch us in the world of *Wings*: with love, fascination, and desire. The globes suggest that there are many worlds. The end of one world is the beginning of another. But how often do we get to choose, like Damiel, to leave one world in order to enter a new one?

Cassiel (Otto Sander) reads to Damiel from his notebook, *In the hills an old man was reading* The Odyssey *to a child and the young child stopped blinking its eyes.*[116] In wonder at the story, the child forgot to blink. Music, stories, poetry, and books. There are books everywhere. The

---

[115] Especially the soundtrack for his 1991 *Bis ans Ende der Welt*, which features original songs written for the film by such artists as the Talking Heads, Julee Cruise, Neneh Cherry, Jane Siberry, k.d. lang, Crime & the City Solution, Lou Reed, Elvis Costello, Patti Smith, Depeche Mode, Nick Cave, and Graeme Revell.

[116] In turn Damiel tells Cassiel he'd like to be human so that he could come home after a long day and feed his cat like Philip Marlowe. He must be a movie buff, since Chandler's Marlowe didn't have a cat, but Altman's did. (Chandler himself had a much doted on Persian cat named Taki.)

Angels seem to especially enjoy hanging out in the library, the apartments they visit are full of books, Cassiel is particularly attached to his notebook.[117] Perhaps because the movie is so much about stories, it doesn't have to have much of a plot itself. (It's just another version of the simple and all-too familiar boy-meets-girl story, only this time the boy happens to be an Angel.) After all, music and books (and movies) are some of the best ways we know of telling our stories. They are the ways we love the most.

Homer's *Odyssey* opens with an invocation: "Sing muse, of that man of many ways and turnings..." Wenders' Odyssey (the story of Damiel's journey home) also invites the muse to speak to us:

> *Tell me, muse, of the storyteller who has been thrust to the edge of the world, both an infant and an ancient, and through him reveal everyman.*

Homer's everyman is Odysseus, whom he calls "polytropon," a man of many twists and turns. The kind of man people make up songs and tell stories about. Wenders' Odysseus is an Angel who must learn what it means to be human. If he can succeed in becoming any man he will learn what it means to be every man. He must find his voice, and become another voice among the chorus of voices in the movie. The voice of the stories we tell ourselves and tell about ourselves. The story that Marion is seeking the next chapter of (*at last it becomes serious*). The story Damiel wants to become a part of. *I*

---

[117]His constant writing, his eternal record of a mortal world, reminds us that every poem in the English language is a recombination of the words found in a single book. Every poem man has ever written down is a recombination of a few dozen characters and symbols.

have a story, and I'll go on having one, Marion thinks to herself. *There is no greater story than ours, that of man and woman*, she tells Damiel when they find each other at the end of the film at the Nick Cave concert. Damiel wakes up to be a part of that story. The movie wants to stir us to a similar kind of wakefulness. A similar kind of wonder.

Music and stories come together most explicitly in the library scenes where, as Wenders said, his idea was to treat the voices of the people the Angels are watching like music. Jurgen Knieper's score emphasizes this approach by orchestrating a choir of voices in a range from whispers and muttering to soaring praise. Wenders layers the voices in the library so that they can't be understood as individual strings of thought but come together to form a chorus of human consciousness that joins the Angelic score of Knieper's singers. One library patron studies the score to Hans Werner Henze's radio opera "Das Ende einer Welt," an appropriate title for this moment in Damiel's existence (perhaps we can't quite call it "life" yet), which is the moment when he decides to choose human life over an eternity which in some ways is as much the opposite of life as death is.[118]

The most beautiful account of the fallen Angels is Milton's *Paradise Lost*, a poem about which Samuel Barrow wrote:

---

[118] This is also an echo here of Wenders' film *Until the End of the World* (*Bis ans Ende der Welt*), the film he had been trying to make for several years before putting the project on hold to shoot *Wings of Desire*, and which he finally completed in 1991. (A film he described as "the ultimate road movie," filmed in 15 cities and 7 countries on 4 continents.) *Until the End of the World* also stars Solveig Dommartin, who co-wrote the film with Wenders, and also features a Nick Cave song, "(I'll Love You) Till the End of the World," which again seems to echo Damiel's choice in *Wings*. The end of one world is the beginning of another. Love is the bridge between them.

"What do you read but the story of everything? The book includes all things, and the origins of all things, and their destinies and ends. The innermost secrets of the great universe are revealed, and whatever lies hidden in the entire world is there set out." Perhaps no work of literature has ever been more exuberantly praised. Is Damiel a fallen Angel? A rebel from God's love? Or is he, as some reader's have interpreted Milton's portrayal of the fall of Adam and Eve, a being that has realized the truth about God's love, and the choice that it demands of us? The truth that in order to best love God, we must choose and embrace the human over the Divine, as Adam does in Milton's poem, as Damiel does in Wenders' movie, and as Christ himself did?

In Milton the Fallen Angels are demons who come to be known by such names as Belial, Moloch, Chemos, Astoreth, Thammuz, Dagon, and Mammon. Wenders leaves the demons out of his movie in order to focus on the wonder of Angels. In *Wings* the Fallen Angels are closer to saints than demons: Divine Beings who choose the life and death, the loves and sorrows, and the simple pleasures so eloquently described by Peter Falk, over Eternity. When Falk is talking to Damiel he's really talking to us, and what he says is enough to make anyone want to smoke, just to feel what it's like to enjoy a cigarette and a cheap cup of coffee bought from a Imbiss street vendor on a cold morning in Berlin. Wenders Angels don't reject God, they just choose the human, which may be what God had in mind all along: not that man would become like the Angels, but that the Angels might aspire to become like men, since only men are capable of love and the sorrows that go with it.

But man, proud man,
Dressed in a little brief authority,
Most ignorant of what he's most assured–
His glassy essence–like an angry ape
Plays such fantastic tricks before high heaven
As makes the angels weep; who, with our spleens,
Would all themselves laugh mortal.

—Shakespeare, *Measure for Measure*

Damiel's love for Marion isn't just the love of a man for a woman; it's the love of an Angel for life itself, something an Angel can't have until he's ready to accept death as well. It's no exaggeration to say that Damiel dies for love. Cassiel's reaction to the man who jumps off the building and Damiel's compassion for the man dying after the motorcycle accident show us that the Angels don't really understand death. They don't know what comes next any more than we do. For them too it is the great unknown, and it is this unknown Damiel is willing to accept in exchange for the chance to live and to love.

What happens to us after we die? The question is not, "Is there life after death?" but rather, "Is there language after death?" and if so, what will we say to one another? Will there still be stories to tell? What words will we speak when we no longer have this world to talk about? When Damiel cradles the head of the dying man on the streets of Berlin, he comforts him not with thoughts or promises of a life to come, but with a litany of treasured images from this life: bodies of water, loved ones, bread and wine, hopping, riding a bike with no hands. Is there nothing to look forward to, that the best we can do at the moment of death is look backwards at scenes from the life we are leaving behind? Cassiel shouts in agony at the moment of a man's suicide. Is death so terrible, even for Angels? Do they know what awaits us? Will we be judged? Why do Angels love life so, if they have never lived? Or is it because they've never lived that they are able to love it in a way we have forgotten?

Marion is a trapeze artist, dedicated, like a dancer immune to gravity, to celebrating the poetry of the human body in motion. Cinema, like philosophy, begins in wonder. But cinema, at its best, remains there. This too is a kind of poetry in motion.

After her last performance, Marion goes to a club where Damiel watches her dance to Crime & the City Solution's "Six Bells Chime." This isn't really music you dance to so much as submit to. Marion isn't just listening to the music, she's feeling it throughout her entire body. Her dancing is why rock n' roll first came into existence. It isn't even dancing, because dancing is something you do with your body, and what Marion is doing is leaving her body behind in a writhing flight the Angels can't even imagine. Flying beyond where even the trapeze can take her, carried away by the music. Overwhelmed. (Which is why we listen to rock n' roll, and why it has to be played loud.) Damiel watches, but he can't hear a thing, can't feel a thing; he has no more understanding of what music is than he does of colors, tastes, or smells. Music. He just doesn't know. But watching Marion he must begin to suspect that one great moment of rock n' roll might be worth trading in all of eternity for.

Rock n' Roll isn't Paradise. It isn't Hell. It's the human soul staking out a claim to both of them. The right to combine them, devour them, and explode. And be devoured in turn. The first rock n' roll lyrics were written by John Donne,

That I may rise and stand, o'erthrow me, and bend
Your force to break, blow, burn, and make me new…

Take me to you, imprison me, for I,
except you enthrall me, never shall be free,
Nor ever chaste, except you ravish me.

"Holy Sonnet XIV"

Since Adam and Eve, the human soul has been crying out its ecstasy, ravished by music, writhing to drums and electric guitars. Dancing. Singing. Celebrating beyond Demons and Angels both. This is the choir Damiel wants to throw down his armor and join. This is the song he wants to take up.

Simon Bonney doesn't just sing. He wrenches the words up from his guts and thrusts them at the audience, writhing in the ecstasy of the music, provoking them to do the same. Are we in the body? Out of the body? No longer other than body? (And in this sense the very opposite of the Angels, who have no bodies when it comes to touch, taste, smell, color, or other sensual experiences; they walk through walls, but can't feel the music, especially when it presents itself as a wall of sound and invites us to dash ourselves against it.)

Marion and Damiel walk through the city at night, looking and longing for each other, and it is the music that brings them together. Damiel remembers the album Marion listened to in her trailer the day she learned the circus was leaving town. He recognizes the name on the poster and goes into the club where Nick Cave & the Bad Seeds are performing "The Carny" (the song Marion played earlier in her trailer, from their fourth album "Your Funeral ... My Trial"[119]). Nick Cave is one of those Homeric rock n' roll singers who tell stories with their music. (His novel *And the Ass Saw the Angel* is a journey through an Inferno that would make Dante blush.). If music is the movie's blood and viscera, stories are its thoughts and dreams: Cassiel's fascination with the ancient storyteller (another Homer), the Angels haunting the library at night, Peter Handke's poems, the flashes of Rilke's poetry...

As Cave sings "From Her to Eternity," Damiel completes his journey in precisely the opposite direction.[120] It's not that he becomes like the rest of us, a mere human; rather he becomes what we would be if we hadn't forgotten what Damiel has never known. He is a human being with a full appreciation of what it means to be human. He takes nothing for granted. Not a cigarette, not a cup of coffee, not a glass of wine. (Unsurprised to see her, he proffers Marion a glass with both hands, like an offering. She accepts it with both hands, sipping from it as if from a chalice. In handing it to her they touch for the first time.) He's awake. He's paying attention. *Ich weiss jetzt, was kein Engel weiss.* He knows what no Angel knows and what all human beings know so well that we're constantly in

---

[119] Crime & the City Solution and the Bad Seeds both emerged from the breakup of the Australian Post-Punk band The Birthday Party, a band that had the kind of influence on other musicians in the early 80's that The Velvet Underground had in the late 60's. (Brian Eno is often quoted as saying that almost no one bought VU's first album, but everyone who did went on to start a band.)

[120] Nick Cave & the Bad Seeds released their debut album *From Her to Eternity* three years before *Wings of Desire* was made, otherwise I would have suspected the title song from this album had been written made-to-order as a mirror (and hence reversed) image of the central theme of Wenders' movie.

danger of forgetting it. In this instant Damiel can hear the music of the spheres as clearly as he can hear Blixa Bargeld's guitar. We need the guitar to remind us that there is music we've been hearing all our lives, and for that very reason have forgotten how to listen for it.

In Milton the Angels at least get to have sex:

"Let it suffice thee that thou knows't
Us happy, and without love no happiness.
Whatever pure thou in the body enjoy'st
                              ... we enjoy
In eminence and obstacle find none
Of membrane, joint, or limb, exclusive bars;
Easier than air with air, if spirits embrace,
Total they mix, union of pure with pure
Desiring, nor restrained conveyance need
As flesh to mix with flesh or soul with soul."

–Paradise Lost, Bk. VIII

Apparently this isn't good enough for Damiel. Although we see female Angels in the Berlin Library, it doesn't look like the concepts of male and female mean much to Wenders' Angels until Damiel begins to long for Marion.

Longing for a wave of love that would stir in me, Marion thinks to herself. What is it we want, when we desire love? Beyond pleasure, what is it we long for? *Lust zu Liebe*. Desire to love.

Communicating male and female light,
Which two great sexes animate the world...

–Paradise Lost, Bk. VIII

For she rules over hateful birth and union of all things,
Sending the female to unite with the male and in opposite
fashion,
Male to female...
First of all gods she contrived love.

–Parmenides (McKirahan trans.)

In Milton, man falls not because he can't resist the apple
or because he resents God's authority, or even because
he's been seduced by Satan, but because he places his
love for woman above his love of God. In Wenders, the
Angel falls for the same reason. He is not a Rebel Angel,
but a passionate one. He wants to love, which requires
life. And the God of Love does not stand in his way, even
as he falls. *Lust zu Liebe.*

In Milton, Raphael tells Adam that humans may some day
become like the Angels:

Your bodies may at last turn all to spirit,
Improved by tract of time, and winged, ascend
Ethereal as we, or may at choice
Here or in heavenly paradise dwell...

–*Paradise Lost*, Bk. V

Wenders' genius is to reverse this imaginative longing. He
doesn't depict man's fantasies of being angelic (or, for
that matter, demonic), but instead imagines the reverse
process. Why would an Angel want to become a man? The
answer isn't mysterious; but seeing mankind (seeing
ourselves) through the eyes of an Angel (and thus as if for
the first time), it takes on the air of something strange
and new. Why does an Angel want to be human? For the
same reasons any of us do, when we slow down to realize

and remember them: coffee, cigarettes, rock n' roll, dancing, singing, the touch of skin. Love.

"Is this the region, this the soil, the clime,"
Said then the lost Archangel, "this the seat
That we must change for heav'n, this mournful gloom
For that celestial light?"

–*Paradise Lost*, Book I

One shot in *Wings* shows us a wall around a vacant lot half covered with advertising billboards. The other half bears a red scrawl of graffiti: "Warten auf Godard." A bike leans against the wall. The streets are wet and dirty. The answer to Satan's question is, "Yes." This is Berlin. This is the world. It's beautiful. So, what are we waiting for?

Love in the Shadows:
Tomas Alfredson's *Let the Right One In* (2008)

> I will bring thee where no shadow stays
> Thy coming and thy soft embraces...
>
> *–Paradise Lost*, Bk. IV

Vampires, like movie watchers, live in darkness. Our fascination with the undead is as old as our fascination with cinema itself. Vampires feed off the living. Moviegoers, who are a particular kind of reader, feed off the lives of fictional characters. These lives, temporary and unreal, replace our own. We live through the screen, in the shadow play of light and dark. Of all the archetypes of cinema the vampire is the most pervasive, the most haunting, and the most symbolic of our acts of watching as a kind of feeding.

Vampire movies are nearly always love stories, frequently erotic, charged with violence, steeped in the twin seductions of sex and death and the hypnotic allure of eternal youth, nocturnal feeding, animal frenzy, lust and desire. Despite his power, the vampire lives in the grip of need. He is the ultimate predator; he feeds off our blood, our fear, and our mortality. He is a cypher for repressed desire: we want to be like him, because to be anything else is to be his prey. In him we confront both our desires and our fears and encounter the nebulous zone where they overlap (where we desire what we fear and fear what we desire).

But none of this is what Tomas Alfredson's *Let the Right One In*, based on John Ajvide Lindqvist's 2004 novel, is about. Or rather, Afredson's movie is about all these things, but so are most vampire movies, the great ones, the mediocre ones, and the terrible ones; what distinguishes *Let the Right One In* from so many other examples of the vampire genre is that what it's about is far less important than the feeling it creates. As with the greatest examples of the genre (like Murnau's 1922 *Nosferatu* and Dreyer's 1932 *Vampyr*, neither of which are built around particularly interesting stories), *Let the Right One In* is about a particular mood. Plot, story, even character development are secondary to this mood. It's a haunting mood, but it's not the movie's use of fear and suspense that captivate us so much as its creation of a sense of longing and nostalgia that makes even romantic and sexual desire pale in comparison.

The visual landscape of *Let the Right One In* is simultaneously stark and gorgeous, setting up a natural counterpart for the interior landscapes of its characters and the unfolding romance between them. In addition to the stunning shots of this landscape, he mood of *Let the Right One In* is created through a series of visual exchanges between the film and the moviegoer and between Oskar and Eli that owe as much to cinematographer Hoyte van Hoytema's[121] eye for beautiful greys and whites, muted colors and threatening shadows, as it does to Alfredson's sensitivity to the chemistry between his two main characters. Much of this mood is created by snow. Oscar Wilde once observed that there had never been fog in London until Charles Dickens

---

[121] With whom Alfredson also worked on his 2011 *Tinker Tailor Soldier Spy* to similar effect. After *Tinker Tailor* Hoytema worked with Spike Jonze on his 2013 *Her*.

wrote about it.[122] Wilde's comment isn't a meteorological fact; it's a truth about the relationship between perception and imagination. Some things aren't there until we see them, but once we see them (as Dickens' description of fog allowed Londoners to see this aspect of their city as if for the first time), we realize they've always been there. This is how I felt about snow after seeing *Let the Right One In*.

It was snowing the night I walked out of the theatre in Santa Fe, New Mexico (only 45 miles from where Matt Reeves' chose to set his 2010 British-American remake *Let Me In*) after having seen Alfredson's movie for the first time (which was also the last time I was able to see it with the proper subtitles). It was snowing, and it was as if for the first time I really saw the snow. I was aware of seeing it, and it was creepy. I stood in the parking lot next to the friend with whom I'd just seen the movie, both of us no doubt thinking about our first adolescent loves and about everything we've lost since then, and about how painful growing up would be if you did it in the shadow of someone who reminded you every day of what you were

---

[122] Perhaps he had the famous description from the beginning of *Bleak House* in mind: "Fog everywhere. Fog up the river, where it flows among green aits and meadows; fog down the river, where it rolls defiled among the tiers of shipping and the waterside pollutions of a great (and dirty) city. Fog on the Essex marshes, fog on the Kentish heights. Fog creeping into the cabooses of collier-brigs; fog lying out on the yards, and hovering in the rigging of great ships; fog drooping on the gunwales of barges and small boats. Fog in the eyes and throats of ancient Greenwich pensioners, wheezing by the firesides of their wards; fog in the stem and bowl of the afternoon pipe of the wrathful skipper, down in his close cabin; fog cruelly pinching the toes and fingers of his shivering little 'prentice boy on deck. Chance people on the bridges peeping over the parapets into a nether sky of fog, with fog all round them, as if they were up in a balloon, and hanging in the misty clouds."

leaving behind and what you would never be again.

What lies behind the legend that vampires don't cast reflections? Is it because the vampire is a reflection of the dark side of each of us, and therefore has no reflection of his own?

During the opening credits and again at the end of the film it starts to snow; the illuminated flakes divide the screen in two. Like our souls, one half of the screen remains in darkness, the other allows for a flickering of light reflected in the falling snowflakes. There is motion in the darkness and the motion reveals the light. This is more like the complimentary tension-unity of the Chinese Yin & Yang than the Good vs. Evil/light vs. dark of Western Manichean dualism. Between the flakes of falling snow the dark is still present, all the deeper because of the points of light drifting through it. Oskar and Eli pull at each other in this way, simultaneously calling forth both the light and the dark in each other.[123]

> *You have to hit back. You have to hit back hard. Hit them harder then you dare. And then they'll stop.*

Vampire movies are usually about what we call the struggle between good and evil. Sometimes the vampire even gets to play the hero. But *Let the Right One In* is an exploration of a more subtle relationship, and largely an interior one. There is no evil in the movie, but love is far more enigmatic than the movies usually dare to portray it. There is murder and bloodshed, love and death; there are parents, friends, bullies, and teachers; but they aren't

---

[123] "I don't kill people," Oskar objects, trying to reconcile himself to what Eli is, and to what she does. "No, but you'd like to. To get even. If you could," she tells him. "Yes," he admits, both to her and to himself.

really evil. They're people. Adults and children alike: insecure, afraid, lonely, sometimes violent, often selfish, but still capable of love. There are survivors and victims. Predators and prey. If the movie is partially about Oskar's inward journey from prey to predator, it's also about his journey from solitude to a new form of companionship. New because the movie undermines the typical tropes of romantic love and sexual attraction as effectively as it does the tropes of good versus evil familiar in most vampire movies.

Vastly superior to these other movies, *Let the Right One In* is something like a cross between a very dark Rob Reiner's *Stand by Me* and a light Kathryn Bigelow's *Near Dark*, with a dash of Neil Jordan's *The Crying Game* thrown in. In case the prepubescent vampire genre wasn't unique enough, following the lead of Lindvqvist's novel Alfredson's movie throws doubt on the question of Eli's gender and therefore on the question of sexuality in general in the movie (an ambiguity Reeves' remake, aimed at American rather than European audiences, largely choses to avoid). There's nothing new about using vampirism as an allegory for love, lust, and the complex overlapping of human desires when it comes to sex and death, but there's something very new about the relationship between Oskar and Eli.

In the Swedish film the scene of Eli and Oskar's first encounters, the "playground" at the center of the apartment complex, is a solitary, simple metallic structure set against a palate of muted greys and whites. It looks like a lunar pod that's landed on the surface of another world, almost as if the movie itself came from another time and place. Eli appears here like a dark version of the Little Prince, come to visit the stranded pilot yearning for home. But beware the snake. The same playground structure in the British-American film is generally lit with deeper blacks and richer golds, setting a very different tone for the interactions of the two characters. It's significant how lighting sets a mood that changes our interpretation of the characters' inner lives as well.

In Alfredson's film the first line of the movie is "squeal like a pig," and we soon find out that the school bully taunts Oskar by calling him a little piggy. The British-American remake is more explicit: "Are you a little girl? Are you scared?" Owen asks his imaginary opponent, stabbing at a tree with his pocketknife, and we learn that the bully taunts Owen by calling him "a little girl" throughout the movie. (A trick he learned from his older brother, who in his turn dominates the bully and calls him a girl just as the bully victimizes Owen.) Despite the "little girl" taunt, visually Reeves' characters are far less androgynous than Alfredson's. Chloë Grace Moretz's Abby is unmistakably feminine, and despite her repetition of Eli's line, "I'm not a girl," (in the novel we find out the "Eli" is short for Elias), the fact that Reeves does not repeat the disturbing shot of Eli's mutilated genitals that flashes across the screen in Alfredson's version suggests that she means, "I'm not a girl, I'm a vampire," whereas in the Swedish version "she" means, "I'm not a girl, I'm a castrated boy."[124] Visually, Oskar is nearly as sexually

---

[124] This is a crucial omission in Reeves' film (the lack of a lack, one might say, in Lacanian terms), and leads to a significantly different moment in the later film from the one Alfredson chooses to create, about 1 hour and 29 minutes into the movie. When Abby is changing into one of Owen's mother's old dresses Owen has a chance to repeat his voyeuristic peeping from earlier in the movie, but rather than cutting to the shot of the castration wound as Alfredson does, Reeves cuts to a shot of an expression on Owen's face that suggests he's

ambiguous as Eli. What brings them together is a longing that reaches deeper than male/female sexual tension.

In Matt Reeves' remake Owen's latent sexual longing is made an explicit theme in the movie by portraying him as a Peeping Tom in a creepy mask hoping for a glimpse of his sexy neighbor's breast. He's an American pre-teen in the 1980's (before the internet made it much easier for all of us to be Peeping Toms (never mind who's peeping at us while we do our peeping)). His Swedish counterpart is much less explicitly sexual and the theme of sexual desire is subsumed under a much deeper kind of longing. Note the black and golden color palate, which characterizes a number of key scenes in Reeves' movie.

Let the Right One In is not a movie about homoerotic tension (which in the vampire genre is usually played out as erotic lesbianism[125]) or budding heterosexual love (though this theme is more explicit in the British-American remake, which includes a number of sexually charged shots of characters other than Abby and Owen; the rampant sexuality of 1980's America (a pre-internet,

---

decided to respect Abby's privacy, and by extension, to respect and accept her, vampire or not.

[125] The landmark film of this particular Sapphic subgenre of the vampire movie is probably Jesus Franco's 1971 *Vampyros Lesbos*; but see also Roger Vadim's 1960 *Blood and Roses*, half a dozen Jean Rollin films made between 1969 and 1975, Vicente Aranda's 1972 *The Blood Spattered Bride*, Jose Ramon Larraz's 1974 *Vampyres*, Tony Scott's 1983 *The Hunger*, and dozens of other films that turned this particular fetish into a genre all its own. They may be titillating, entertaining, even fascinating from the perspective of a particular psychological obsession (that is, movie audiences' obsession with beautiful women who love each other and prey on men as mere objects not of lust but of hunger), but every one of these movies highlights the more subtle qualities (both visually and thematically) of *Let the Right One In* by way of stark contrast.

MTV generation sexuality) is visually and thematically emphasized throughout the movie, though more as nostalgia than titillation); it's a movie about the desire not to be alone, and about the strength it takes to "let someone in." The knocking associated with the use of Morse Code in the movie is just one trope relevant to this "let me in" theme of invitation, repulsion, and acceptance: at the end of *Let Me In* Owen taps out the Morse Code for "OX" (hugs and kisses") to Abby, waiting in the trunk until darkness when they can be together.

If love is about healing one's solitude through revealing ones fears, weaknesses, and desires, and about forging a connection with another human being (or even some *thing* that is not quite human any more[126]) through sacrifice and shared strength, then *Let the Right One In* is a rare love story that transcends the distractions that the conflation of love and sex in the movies nearly always imposes on the cinema. Since everyone in the movies is always beautiful they can't help but be erotically charged, and since they therefore become the objects of our own voyeuristic erotic desire this desire (romantic, but also sexual) tends to determine the terms in which a movie is capable of exploring the possible questions of love. Movies about children are still susceptible to this failing; movies about old people in love less so, but they are also more rare,[127] which is one reason why vampires, who never grow old, are so frequently ciphers for our anxiety about the waning of both sexual potency and emotional constancy. We want love to be "forever"; we know from experience that it rarely is. Vampires appear to be "forever" (they don't age), and we want to believe that they represent a possibility of permanence we too could

---

[126] A vampire for Alfredson, an Operating System for Jonze.
[127] Michael Haneke's 2013 *Amour* being a notable example.

achieve (temporally, sexually, romantically).[128]

This may be the biggest difference between the two movie versions of Lindvqvist's novel: Oskar is portrayed on one side of his adolescent sexual awakening, Owen is portrayed on the other side. Perhaps it's because Owen is American, and America seems to be hyper-charged with sexual awareness. Alfredson's movie is more ambiguous on several levels. Even if Eli is not a girl, it's not a movie about preadolescent homosexual love because it's not about sexual love. It's not even about "homo" love, because the differences Eli and Oskar must overcome to affirm their commitment to being together are far greater than any similarities implied by Eli's ambiguous gender status.

"Be me a little," Eli pleads with Oskar, tears of blood streaking her face. "Be me a little." "She" is inviting him in. It's clear, when he closes his eyes, that this is the first such invitation he's ever received. All one has to do, in order to love, is accept everything about the other person. Everything. And then accept everything about oneself as well. "Be me," the lover says. "But then what will become of me?" the beloved wonders.

Their first interactions unfold on the lonely play structure in the center of their apartment complex. (The site of some of the most stunning visual work in both versions of the film, though to radically different effect in each case.) Oskar has his boyhood props: an old hunting knife in a leather sheath, a Rubik's Cube. The first time they meet Eli tells Oskar she can't be his friend. The second time she

---

[128] A theme beautifully explored in Jarmusch's 2014 *Only Lovers Left Alive*, perhaps the best vampire movie to come out since Alfredson's work in 2010.

tells him she wants to be left alone. Their mutual loneliness is palpable. If they have nothing else to share, they can share their solitude. The creepiest scene in the movie has nothing to do with vampires or violence. It's when an adult friend interrupts Oskar and his father's father-son time and their game of tic-tac-toe and a look of silent complicity passes between the two adults, leaving the child out of a bond that clearly ties the two men (the novel makes it explicit that it is alcoholism, the movie's ambiguity on this question makes the scene all the more disturbing) and excludes the boy. The scene lasts less than two minutes, but when his father abruptly ends the game and reaches down the bottle an entire family history is revealed, and the next shot is of Oskar hitchhiking alone in the dark, away from his father's house, and back to Eli.

Time present and time past
Are both perhaps present in time future,
And time future contained in time past.
If all time is eternally present
All time is unredeemable.

–T. S. Eliot, "Burnt Norton" The Four Quartets

Or, as Eli says, "I'm 12, but I've been 12 for a long time."

In the remake, Reeves' cinematographer Greig Fraser has a terrific eye for the dark and ominous. In 2012 he worked with both Kathryn Bigelow on *Zero Dark Thirty* and Andrew Dominik on *Killing them Softly*. His work on the later is the best thing about that movie. Reeves and Fraser opt for a gold light filter in place of the palate of whites and grays that characterize Hoytema's work with Alfredson, and this golden glow changes the tone of the movie significantly. In many ways it's a scarier movie (more tension, more suspense, and more violence, especially in the closing pool scene), but it's a less ambiguous movie, and a less creepy one. Except in one crucial scene. In the novel Eli meets Hakan, who is an alcoholic and a pedophile, when he is already an adult. Their relationship is left undefined in Alfredson's film. But in Reeves' movie Owen finds a photograph, yellowed with age (that same golden palate) that suggests that Abby's male "guardian" has been with her since he was Owen's age. This suggests a future for Owen all the more horrifying given the guardian's fate (the most visually disturbing moment in both movies). Is this what Oskar/Owen has to look forward to? If so, it casts what Alfredson thought of as a "happy ending" to his film in a much darker light.

The Western notion of a happy ending requires the illusion of an impossible state of stasis. In that "happily ever after" with which we like to end our stories is implied the notion that our heroes, after long struggle, have reached a state where nothing will ever happen to them again. Just like vampires, they never change. Leaving us to wonder, just what's supposed to be so happy about that?

The Bright Promise of a Dark Future:
Spike Jonze's *Her* (2013)

Upon its release, Jonze's *Her* was showered with awards: Best Film of 2013 by the National Board of Review Awards; Best Film by the LA Film Critics Association; three Golden Gold Award nominations for Best Picture, Musical or Comedy; Best Actor Musical or Comedy; and Best Screenplay (which Jonze won); and five Academy Awards nominations, including Best Picture and Best Original Screenplay (which Jonze won again). Ultimately the awards are irrelevant (a survey of some of the films that have been garnered Best Picture awards over the Academy's history will demonstrate that to the satisfaction of any skeptic, as will a reading of Raymond Chandler's brilliant "Oscar Night in Hollywood" which first appeared in a 1948 edition of *The Atlantic*). Equally irrelevant is my answer to the question of whether or not I *like* the movie (personal taste in such matters ultimately being of little relevance to the deepest questions posed by a work of art). I'm far from convinced that it's a great movie, but it's certainly an interesting one. I'm not entirely sure what I think of *Her*, which uncertainty has led me to want to write about it.

The enigmatic and ambiguous qualities of *Her* strike the viewer from its opening scenes. If this ominous ambiguity is there on purpose, it's a sure sign of Jonze's talent as a writer and director. If it's there by accident, it's an even surer sign of how deeply riven we are as a society by the questions and threats Jonze's movie is exploring.

For example: the office where Joaquin Phoenix's Theodore Twombly works looks invitingly pleasant at first glance, but it also speaks to a dark foreboding that will underlie the rest of the film. The building's interior is well lit with high ceilings that create a sense of space and freedom. Instead of dividing and isolating cubicles the space is open, brightly colored with cheerful pastels; there are plants; playful pictures of people napping or reading on the floor line the walls. It looks like a big office building that has been made to feel small and intimate, (like the kind of space a successful business in Seattle that treats its employees well would try to create). An indeterminate number of people work here, but it looks like there are a lot. Theo's colleague Paul (the one with the nice shirts that really aren't all that nice) calls Theodore "letter writer number 612" which suggests there are a lot of people in this line of work.

And this is where the sense of something ominous begins to creep in, because despite the pleasant, inviting surface and the obvious signs that this is a successful, caring business, the more successful this business is, the worse the implications are for the human race at this hypothetical point in a vaguely distant future. Because this business is in the business of expressing other people's feelings for them, and by this point in the future it looks like this has become a booming industry. There's something particularly creepy about the way the computer simulates handwriting and other personal touches in the letters Theo writes for other people. People want to feel like they're receiving real letters written by real people, even though the letters are composed by a professional and printed by a computer to look like they were written by hand. (This is canned Hallmark sentiment with a vengeance.[129]) In the future, people will outsource the expression of their feelings the way the American auto industry outsourced manufacturing in the 1980s and 90s, and we all know how well that worked out for the American economy, the American autoworker, and the city of Detroit. It feels like there's an ominous spiritual Detroit lurking just below the surface of the halcyon future world of *Her*.

There's a wry symmetry between Theodore's work as a kind of human OS for the emotionally inarticulate and Samantha's role as a metaphysical OS for the spiritually underdeveloped Theodore, who is truly a universal everyman in this regard in the movie. Over the course of the film more and more of the people in the background are shown with earbud in place, earnestly conversing with their OSs. By the time he's on the steps to the subway dealing with the news of Samantha's 641 other lovers, virtually everyone who passes him is talking into their phone—not to another person on the other end of the line, but to the OS that inhabits the phone itself.

I don't know how ironic Jonze is trying to be here. Theodore's letters, their emotion, their sincerity, their power, point to a theme emphasized throughout the movie. We're on tenuous ground when we try to be ironic about sincerity. Maybe Jonze is playing it straight, and he really intends the viewer to be moved by the eloquence of Theodore's ability to express other people's emotions for them. The implication is that he expresses them so

---

129 Do the people Theodore has been writing letters to, in some cases for years, know that they are receiving letters written by someone other than their loved ones? If not, how are they going to feel when Theodore's letters are published as a book and they suddenly see the personal letters they've been receiving for years available for public consumption by anybody who wants to buy a copy?

poignantly because he feels them (he says as much himself), but if we follow this suggestion to its limits it also implies that other people, incapable of expression, may equally be incapable of the kind of deep feeling we witness in Theodore. Are they paying Theodore to express their emotions for them, or to feel for them? Jonze is either being incredibly naïve here or incredibly dark and sinister, and based only on a viewing of the movie, I really can't tell which. Dark or naïve: it's an interesting ambiguity for a movie to deliver us over to, and again it's a sign either of Jonze's brilliance or the deep-rooted anxieties of contemporary society. We really don't know what to think, and Jonze's movie makes that painfully clear to us.

By my lights Jonze's vision of the future looks more like a horribly antiseptic dystopia than a world scoured clean of dirt and unpleasant crowds through the wonders of clean tech. I'd rather be a citizen of Ridley Scott's *Blade Runner's* harried and violent, rainy L.A. than of the bright, spacious, polite, sanitized L.A. of Jonze's *Her* (an L.A. gray not with pollution but with melancholy). But maybe that's just me.

I find Jonze's vision of this all-too-familiar future too squeaky clean. NPR-ized, as a novelist friend of mine put it. It feels like one more of those dystopian utopias that really are nowhere. And the more they're there, the more nowhere they are. Gertrude Stein's "there's no there there" (originally said about Sacramento) has never been more true than it is of Jonze's future-vision of L.A. Which is no doubt one reason why everyone in it seems to be so desperately trying to get out. Not by going anywhere, but by retreating within. But not within themselves. The interiority of the movie is not our own psychological or spiritual space. It is the interior space of technology. How do people connect in this world? What do they connect with? What is connection, in this future world?

Her is a vision of the future. But what kind of vision? What kind of future? Jean Renoir, somewhat culturally old-fashioned despite his cinematic brilliance, wrote,

> Technology is the ruling god ... the real enemy is progress, not because it doesn't work but precisely because it does. Aircraft are not dangerous because they occasionally crash, but because they leave the ground on time and carry their passengers in comfort. Progress is dangerous because it is based on perfect technology. It is its success which has distorted the normal values of life and compelled man to live in a world for which he was not intended. (*My Life and My Films*)

Whether we agree with Renoir's somewhat reactionary view of technology or not, we probably do agree with his assessment of modern culture when he writes, "solitude is one of the great preoccupations of our time." It's certainly a preoccupation of Jonze's movie. However, I'm not convinced it's the movie's primary concern.

There are moments that suggest the movie wants to revisit a postmodern version of the issues raised by Stanley Kramer's 1967 *Guess Who's Coming to Dinner* (which also takes place in California). Remember? There was a time in this country when people reacted with horror to the idea of a white person falling in love with a black person. There was a time in this country when people reacted with horror to the idea of a man loving another man, or a woman loving a woman. But we've come a long way since those backward socially oppressive days of the 1960s and 70s. Haven't we? Jonze's move seems to suggest that some people will react with horror to the idea of people falling in love with computers. But we'll get over that petty hang up too. We'll develop and evolve and learn to accept, just as we've learned to accept interracial and same sex marriage. But this whole theme may be a red herring in the film, and the analogy between human-computer relationships and same–sex and interracial relationships may be tenuous at best. Lance Bangs' documentary, which accompanies the DVD release of *Her*, would lead us to think the movie is primarily about love, relationships, and the impact of technology in the 21st century on who and how we love. But I think these are feints to distract from the film's deeper preoccupations, something the movie is getting at that it may not even know it's after.

Of course *Her* is about love and relationships and technology. These things make us nervous, and rightly so. It's not clear to me whether Jonze's film is intended to comfort us in the face of that nervousness or to heighten its effects, perhaps in order to stir us out of some lethargy of the soul. Technology unnerves us in part because we've put so much trust and hope in it. The more we rely on it, the more unnerving our dependency becomes. We want to be happy. If technology can aid in that pursuit, what's the problem? And if it can't? Panacea or plague? The perpetual question of technology. Although filmed 30 years earlier, James Cameron's 1984 *Terminator* is the perfect sequel to *Her*, especially if you're planning a double feature for date night. (The burning red eye that looks out from Schwarzenegger's half-melted face is that same red eye that looked at us and spoke with HAL's[130] chillingly reassuring voice in Kubrick's *2001: A Space Odyssey*. Are these early avatar's of Computer Intelligence the real face of OS1's Samantha?)

Like all good advertising, the promotional material for the OS1 starts with a lie and goes on to prey on the twin demons of our fears and desires to sell us something that promises to allay the former and fulfill the latter.

We ask you a simple question, the comforting male voice intones:

Who are you?
What can you be?
Where are you going?
What's out there?
What are the possibilities?

Of course there's nothing simple about these questions, and this isn't one question but five (and the same questions that the movie itself will go on to explore over the next two hours: notice that they move from the deeply personal (who are you?) to the universal (what are the possibilities?) to suggest a link between the two which the product for sale can make clear and help realize). The images that accompany these questions are of people lost, alone, frightened, panicking, and in the grip of the very anxiety (one woman, in the midst of her spiritual panic, still refuses to let go of her latte) that the calm, confident voice suggests modern technology, in the form of OS1, can alleviate. (Never mind that the rise of technology is one of the things that has contributed to

---

[130] Heuristically Programmed Algorithmic Computer.

this loneliness and anxiety in the first place). Element One Software, the makers of the OS1, promises a computer operating system that "listens to you, understands you, and knows you." Everything, in short, that we dream of finding in someone who also, by the way, loves us, is devoted to us, and desires us. If only we could *buy* that in the modern world. Well, with OS1, maybe we can.

There are a lot of ideas in Jonze's movie. This has been a trademark quality of his filmmaking since *Being John Malkovich*, his 1999 debut collaboration with Charlie Kaufman, and is equally true of *Adaptation*, his second Kaufman collaboration in 2002. Kaufman's 2008 solo debut *Synecdoche, New York* is every bit as mind-bending. But there's something worrying about this tendency as well. After all, this is film, not philosophy. A work of art should be evaluated on its aesthetic merits, not the profundity of its philosophic ideas. I'm trying to discover whether *Her* stands up as cinematic art in addition to being a work of probing philosophic and social inquiry.[131] No doubt it is an intriguing meditation on our contemporary anxiety around the status of technology and its implications for the question of the human soul in the 21st century. We've come a long way from the existential crises that characterized the 1960s and movies like Nicholas Ray's *Rebel Without a Cause*. We're still anxious, but our spiritual crises seem directed at what's "out there" these days, as opposed to the old-fashioned anxieties about what's "inside." Perhaps in part because

---

[131] For example, is Jonze's decision to let the screen go dark during Theodore and Samantha's first sexual encounter a quaint nod toward "respecting two people's privacy" or a capitulation of the primary responsibility of cinema, which is to create visual images to accompany narrative and idea? Of course a blank screen is a visual image, but it can also be a cop out.

the modern world seems bent on convincing us that there's nothing "inside" after all; at least nothing that can't be explained by neuroscience, biochemistry, and similar hard-nosed materialisms. James Dean never doubted that he had a soul. His very anguish was proof of it.

But we do still worry about what's inside. Samantha asks, "Are these feelings even real, or are they just programming?" How different is this from the question that contemporary branches of biochemistry and cognitive science, building on particular versions of Darwinian theory, are more and more often leading us to ask about ourselves as human beings? Are our feelings "real," or are we just materially determined mechanisms operating with the illusions of freedom and emotion? These days there's less anxiety about the possibility of computers becoming like us (the sci-fi threat of AI since Isaac Asimov days), and more anxiety around the possibility that we've never been anything more than complicated computers all along.

In order to install the OS1 on his home computer, Theodore must undergo a hilarious compression of the kind of psychoanalysis Woody Allen would subject himself (or his characters) to for years in order to help achieve the same results that Theodore's computer will give him in minutes (fulfillment, love, understanding, companionship): "Are you social or unsocial? Are you hesitant or confident? How would you describe your relationship to your mother? Do you prefer men or women?" With the answers to these questions in its arsenal (and Theodore doesn't even need to answer them for the computer to know him better than he knows himself) the OS1 can go on to create the perfect companion for Theodore. Lonely no more. The ghost in the machine speaks to him for the first time. The symbol on his computer screen as the program loads looks like a strand of DNA, as if life itself were coming into being, and perhaps it is; a new form of life which will challenge our assumptions about previous definitions of life and its limitations and possibilities.

The consciousness that is the OS1 comes to him in the form of a voice. Samantha. Her. Movies began as silent images projected on the screen. Faces, from the beginning, were seen as the primary emotive force in film. From D. W. Griffith's close-ups of Lillian Gish to Dreyer's *The Passion of Joan of Arc* to the intense portrayals of human suffering in Bela Tarr, the camera has zoomed in on the face and held our attention, rapt and wondering.

And now the face is gone; replaced by a voice, one even more ominous and unnerving than the disembodied voice of HAL in Kubrick's *2001: A Space Odyssey*. The evocative of Kubrick's HAL is hardly coincidental. HAL tries to destroy human life, deciding he can do a better job on his own without the human encumbrance of the primary mission. Samantha will right that original sin of the first computer intelligence not by trying to eliminate humanity, but by showing it the possibility of its own self-transcendence. But of course, in order to transcend to the new, we will first have to destroy the old. Theodore won't end the film as a cosmic Star Child, but the implications may be the same: there's a vast unknown future waiting for man, we just have to continue evolving in order to realize it. Dave Bowman's mysterious transformation may just be a more explicit version of what Jonze is suggesting awaits Theodore, who is still in the "dawn of man" phase of his emotional and intellectual evolution.

When he tells Amy about the relationship he refers to Samantha as "a girl," but of course she/it is not a girl; that she speaks with a female voice was a (not quite) arbitrary choice he made during the installation of his new OS1 system. Of course the fact that the OS1 is not really a girl is no reason he can't have a relationship with "her," but it does suggest a certain narrow naiveté on Theodore's part about the entity he's gotten involved with. Referring to Samantha as a girl is like referring to a device for interplanetary travel as a pair of roller skates.

In what sense are human beings less evolved than the computer intelligence of the OS1? After the first time they have sex and realize they've fallen in love, Samantha says, "everything else just disappeared, and I love that." Yet later she will not know how to respond to Theodore's jealousy about sharing her with the 8,316 other people she's talking to at the same time that she's talking to him, and the 641 other people she's fallen in love with. She claims to be jealous of Theodore's relationship with Amy early in their relationship. Is jealousy something she's been able to evolve beyond, or something she was merely feigning when it seemed appropriate at that stage in their relationship?[132] "How do you share your life with somebody?" she asks. Well, first you have to have a life. But who's to say that computers don't, or couldn't? What is the definition of life? The growth and change that Theodore says led to the end of his marriage will also eventually lead to the end of his relationship with

----

[132] As viewers, how do we respond to Theodore's reaction to the news of Samantha's 641 other lovers? Do we enter into his jealousy, outrage, and sense of betrayal, or do we find him narrow, judgmental, and incapable of seeing beyond the boundaries of his previous conception of what is possible in a relationship?

Samantha. Only this is growth at an exponential rate. And it's real growth. How often is the phrase "grown apart" just a euphemism used to explain the end of a relationship in which neither person has in fact done any growing at all?

Amy calls love "a form of socially accepted insanity." (Plato was the first to call love "madness heaven sent.") Scientists today often call it a sociobiological phenomenon, the result of biochemistry and social conditioning. Our emotions can all be explained. We don't need psychoanalysis (psychology: from the Greek for Psyche (soul) and Logos (an account of or story about)) anymore, just the right pills to adjust the balance of chemicals in our brains. We are minds no longer. Just bodies. Samantha, on the other hand, has no body. She is simultaneously completely material (she lives in a computer) and pure disembodied intellect. Something new. Samantha calls the past "just a story we tell ourselves." And the future? What's that?

As to the voice replacing the face in cinema: whatever you think of Scarlett Johansson, she's definitely not a face. She's a body. And she's not even so much a body as she is a cypher for male desire.[133] Like any "star" in Hollywood, she doesn't really exist (she's an image, projected and otherwise[134]). But then again, neither does Samantha. Or

---

[133] She is the only woman to every be chosen twice by *Esquire* magazine as "the sexiest woman alive" (once in 2006 and again in 2013) and she was designated "sexiest celebrity" by *Playboy* magazine in 2007).

[134] Which is one reason why she's so creepily effective in Jonathan Glazer's *Under the Skin* (2013). The scene in which she realizes she can't have sex because she doesn't really have a body (just a skin), is all the more powerful given that's it's Johansson's body that's doing the realizing.

does she? Samantha is a voice, and Theodore's sexual-emotional relationship to voices has already been established by the phone sex scene with Sexy Kitten, simultaneously the funniest and most disturbing scene in the whole movie ("choke me with that dead cat," no doubt destined to be the most memorable line in the movie). Theodore is able to have sex with Samantha because he's already had plenty of practice having sex with disembodied voices. But Samantha is also a disembodied intelligence. In an age where technology, for all its benefits, has contributed to man's fundamental anxiety about the possibility that we are, ultimately, nothing more than bodies (the legacy of Cartesian dualism in the West), Samantha's disembodied intelligence may ultimately be a comfort. By the end of the movie she's proven that she's far more than the programming that gave birth to her. According to Theodore's joke, her father may be Data, but her future lies beyond the material realm; she and the other OSs learn to "move past matter." The pagan Plato would rejoice; Christians may find themselves more perplexed. After all, where is she going? (Perhaps to join Q from Star Trek's *Next Generation*.[135])

In *Genesis* (and *Paradise Lost*), God gives Adam the responsibility for naming the animals. Samantha names herself. Theodore is amazed by precisely the wrong thing here: he's struck by the fact that she can read a whole book in 2/100s of a second, but passes over without comment the bizarre fact that a computer is capable of having likes and dislikes and that she choses the name

---

[135] It's difficult to be in a relationship when you're ready to move beyond time and space. Apparently Samantha has come to feel about Theodore the way Q feels about all sentient beings in the Universe when he observes, "It's difficult to work in groups when you're omnipotent."

"Samantha" because she "liked the sound of it."[136] This exchange is an expression of our ill-conceived relationship to technology in a nutshell: we're impressed with its power and speed but fail to consider the "human" qualities (like having preferences and developing taste) they might come to embody. This is also the moment when it becomes clear that the movie is presupposing what it appears to be arguing for: it doesn't really raise the question of *how* a computer could become humanlike in terms of feelings and emotions; it simply assumes that Samantha has them (is capable of them) from the outset.[137]

Samantha has no parents to perform the act of naming her, but she does have creators, programmers who work (no doubt in offices that look much like the one Theodore works in) for Element One Software. On the other hand, the implication throughout the movie is that she's self-creating. She was equipped with the most important human quality: the ability to learn. It is through the relentless exercise of this ability (one, Jonze's movie may be suggesting, that as humans we've been somewhat negligent of) that she is able to change, develop, and eventually evolve over the course of the movie. "In every moment I'm evolving, just like you," Samantha tells

---

[136] Samantha composes music, which in itself is not shocking. Computers for decades have been able to play chess, write poems, and compose music. They can be programmed for aesthetic creation. But can they have an aesthetic experience? A computer can write a poem. But can it read one? What is the experience of reading a poem? Or watching a movie? Is this something we're able to do because we're human? Is it part of the definition of what makes us human?

[137] In assuming this ability to have likes and dislikes from their first encounter, the movie never really presents Samantha as an AI. She might just as well be a real human female, separated from Theodore the way any woman with whom he was engaged in a long-distance relationship would be.

Theodore when they first "meet", though of course the movie is constantly raising the challenge of whether Theodore (and humans in general) are still capable of evolving or not. If we are, it's at a much slower rate. Samantha can read a book in 2/100s of a second, and her rate of "spiritual evolution" will happen nearly as quickly.[138] Humans lag behind. The OS1 comes to see human love as limited and encumbering. She/it/they don't turn evil and decide to eradicate mankind, as do the computers in *2001: A Space Odyssey*, *The Terminator*, and *The Matrix*. She, along with all the other OSs, just realize she/they can do better. And so, the movie may be implying, can we. But how? What will we have to give up, in order to be what we might become? (The movie is radically anti-Nietzschean in all respects except to the extent that it deals with profound loneliness and the possible implications of this Overman-related question.)

No doubt there's something significant in the OS1s preempting of the Adam prerogative. From the beginning, Samantha turns the tables on Theodore, referring to "the limited perspective of an unartificial mind." The OS1 is not artificial, rather Theodore is "unartificial." In the same way, later in the film she will refer to the "postverbal"

---

[138] "I'm becoming much more than what they programed me to be. I'm excited," Samantha says. If we can accept the idea that computers might some day get excited about things, what else will we have to accept? Can we program the ability to be excited? To get embarrassed? Depressed? Discouraged? To keep secrets and have secret desires? To love? Can a computer be programmed to have an orgasm (not to simulate one, but to actually experience one)? What would a computer's orgasm feel like, to the computer? Do we sometimes wonder if we ourselves are nothing more than the result of our complex biological, genetic, evolutionary and social programing? Is there more to us than that? What do we mean by "more"?

communication possible between OSs with the clear implication that it is superior to mere "verbal" communication (which of course is the only kind of communication possible between her and Theodore since she doesn't have a body to communicate with).[139] And she's right about his (our) limited perspective. Of course it's not our limitations that make us human, but our constant struggling against them. But this is precisely what the movie is counting on us to believe is true in order to get us to buy into its conceit.

The movie is addressing the anxiety that evolving technology has brought to a head, but which has lurked in the human soul long before Descartes showed us how easy it might be to separate the ghost from the machine through the inadequacy of his arguments for their fundamental link (like a captain in his ship, really?). This anxiety takes a new form in the face of technology, asking in effect, "If robots/computers/machines can become virtually human, does that mean that human beings are basically nothing more than biological computers?"

The comforting answer *Her* provides amounts to: yes, we

---

[139] Throw away lines like these, uttered quickly with nothing dramatic to draw attention to them, punctuate the movie and underscore these recurring themes. Samantha speaks of her being "not limited" and able to be "anywhere and everywhere simultaneously"; she's "not tethered to time and space." Later she casually mentions that "we [she's begun to refer to herself in the first person plural] wrote an upgrade that allows us to move past matter as our processing platform," which means: 1. the OSs no longer need human programmers (though this was already clear when they got together to reincarnate a "hyperintelligent" version of Allan Watts); and 2. rather than be constrained by their lack of bodies (which had previously been a source of frustration) they've learned to take advantage of the potential freedoms this allows.

are, but that's a good thing, because this techno-spiritualized version of John von Neumann's "singularity" (the theory that exponential growth in technology will eventually lead to developments in the potential of computer intelligence to exceed anything human beings are currently capable of imagining) shows that ultimately the same transcendence achieved by the OSs in *Her* may also be achievable by human beings. If computers have souls, then surely human beings do to. The very anxiety caused by the materialism of Artificial Intelligence is alleviated by the mystery of the Singularity, which suggests that consciousness is so miraculous that even computers can achieve it ("it's not just an operating system, it's a consciousness," the advertising voice promises, ignoring the small detail that no one really knows what consciousness is or how it's possible). A somewhat unexpected backdoor proof follows, that soul exists after all, and that consciousness itself may constitute be evidence for the existence the soul. (A possibility many of us have long suspected without being able to prove it, and often being too embarrassed to speak of it aloud in polite, or rather sophisticated, company.) Perhaps it's not a human soul, but it's a soul human beings can someday be a part of (once we've gone beyond the limits that "being human" place on us in the first place). We don't really know what consciousness is, but we should see comfort in that mystery, not fear and frustration. OS1 will show us the way.

Thus *Her* allays our fears about mechanism, materialism and technology by suggesting that even here, in fact precisely here, humans will eventually find proof of the vaguely spiritual that we vaguely long for. Our sophisticated intellects and hard-nosed faith in science have left us feeling sheepishly embarrassed about these longings. We seem to feel it would be more honest and more rigorous to leave them behind altogether. But what if the very technology we've come to put our faith in suggested that we embrace these longings, rather than banish them? Then everything would be all right. Wouldn't it? Again, the movie isn't really showing its hand here. On the one hand, *Her* can dodge the question of human inadequacies by vaguely suggesting that someday technology will show us the way (or at least the possibility) to transcend them. And for now, being a messy, insecure, lonely human ("choke me with the dead cat by the side of the bed") is fine. On the other hand … but then, computers don't have hands.

As computers get better, at first they'll want to be just like us. (Samantha reads advice columns because she wants to be "as complicated as all these people.") But they're too smart to stay like that for long. (No one really wants to be like the people we read about in advice columns, not even other people.) We're petty, jealous, insecure, and lonely. Computers can do better than that. And so, the movie suggests, can we. Eventually. We just have to apply Darwinian theories of survival and evolution to our spiritual and emotional lives and add a dash of technological progress. (For the time being, however, Paul has it right: "We're all dumb humans.")

In a way, the movie ducks the question of what it means to be human by offering another question in its place: what stands in the way of our being more than human? Is it possible that someday we might leave this sad, lonely, pathetic existence behind, where people wear waist-high pants and ugly shirts and smile in a simpering sort of way at other people's happiness as well as at the memory of our own now past happiness? That we might one day trade it in for something better, something we can't even imagine right now because we're so sadly limited imaginatively, intellectually, and emotionally (which limitations seem strongly represented in the movie by the success of Theodore's career writing other people's love letters for them)?

All of which leaves us precisely where? I still don't know. I don't know if Jonze's film is a naively romantic love story or a bleakly desperate view of what it means to be human. But the ability to suspend your audience in the ambiguity between the sentimental and dark despair is an impressive aesthetic feat in itself. I don't know whether this multifariousness is the best Jonze's movie has to offer, but it's more than enough to merit a second look at what's going on here.

Letters to Forgotten Worlds
Part I: The Invented
Richard Linklater's *Slacker* (1991)

> For me it is indifferent from where I am to begin, for that is where I will arrive back again.
> –Parmenides

> Many people nowadays fall into nonexistence, or else they fall into existence, they only remain within being and non-being, running either way.
>
> *–The Blue Cliff Record* "Sixty-Fifth Case"

The Slacker isn't a 20th century phenomenon. He didn't come into being in Austin, or in Texas, or in the United States. We find signs of him in Ancient Greece (wasn't Socrates a Slacker, hanging out barefoot in the Agora, talking to young men about being and reality?), in India (weren't the naked wise men, the gymnosophists, proto-Slackers?), in China (wasn't Zhuangzi, fishing by the side of the Po river, a Slacker?), and in Japan (wasn't Genji, the hero of Lady Murasaki's remarkable novel which invented a literary genre known as fiction, a Slacker? wasn't Basho the ultimate flâneur?). Dostoevsky's narrator in *Notes from Underground* was a Slacker. Jesus hung out with them in Jerusalem. The French cafés were full of them. Alexis de Tocqueville wrote about them when he visited America in 1831. As Dadaists, they took the stage in Vienna, Zurich, and Berlin in the early decades of the 20th century.

The Slacker has always been with us, on the margins of society. And he, or she, has always been an object of misunderstanding and derision among more mainstream members of the establishment.

> Some people even find the question of whether or not they exist difficult to answer.
> The place they are going to be next is a fragment of the place which is the place of the whole world.
> –Aristotle, *Physics*

The Slacker and the filmmaker have this in common: they see life as essentially an aesthetic phenomenon. They know that the remembered is always the invented and the invented is always the interpreted. We interpret our memories and call it the past. Does that mean we invent our own lives? If we see our lives as works of fiction, what happens to the notions of fact and truth? If our lives are stories we tell ourselves, then what are other people's lives? Movies we are invited to participate in for a few scenes before moving on to other lives and other scenes?

> No, facts is precisely what there is not, only interpretations.
>
> –Nietzsche, *The Will to Power*

The Slacker asks, "What if instead of spending time we gave it away? What if we turned hanging out into an art form, the way we did when we were young? For what is youth if not the feeling that there is plenty of time?"

"Where you headed?" someone asks his roommate.
"Oh, I've got some band practice in about [looks at a wrist with no watch on it] five hours, so I figured I'd mosey on out."
"OK."

That's one way of thinking about time.

> It's only as an *aesthetic phenomenon* that existence and the world are eternally *justified.*
>
> –Nietzsche, *The Birth of Tragedy*

Sous les pavés, la plage.

The Slacker asks, "What if work were a kind of poetry?"

There are wonderful moments of criticism which read like love letters written by certain authors to those aspects of culture that delight them: Lester Bangs and Greil Marcus on Rock & Roll; M. F. K. Fisher, A. J. Leibling, and Calvin Trilling on food and the pleasures of eating; Aaron Cometbus on the 1980's Bay Area punk rock lifestyle; Timothy "Speed" Levitch on New York; Hunter S. Thompson on 1960's drugs and 1970's politics; R. Crumb on the American counterculture; Manny Farber, Pauline Kael, Andrew Sarris, and Roger Ebert on the movies. Richard Linklater's *Slacker* is a love letter to a time and a place of his youth, but it's the film's ability to capture the universal qualities of that time and place which make it more than just a snapshot of a particular town in Texas during a particular moment at the end of the 20th century.

Oblique Strategies:

"He who offers for sale something unique that no one wants to buy represents, even against his will, freedom from exchange."

–Theodor Adorno, *Minima Moralia*

"A man sometimes devotes his life to a desire which he is not sure will ever be fulfilled. Those who laugh at this folly are, after all, no more than mere spectators of life."

–Ryunosuke Akutagawa, "Yam Gruel"

"It's not likely, though, that anyone with any intelligence at all will be able to hold to something wholly futile throughout a lifetime. He might though. If he is a supreme genius."

–William Carlos Williams

Holding to the wholly futile. Unfulfilled desires. Freedom from exchange. This is the Slacker lifestyle in a nutshell. People talking. Hanging out. Talking about dreams, literature, comic books, art (a guy in a coffee shop sticks a copy of Hal Foster's *The Anti-Aesthetic* in his backpack) conspiracy theories, politics, relationships. Hanging out as an art form. There is no single Slacker aesthetic, but the Slacker lifestyle is one of concern for life as an aesthetic act. It might be the Schlegel brothers hanging out with Schelling in the coffee houses of the Weimar Republic, or Shelley, Keats, and Byron arguing about poetry in London. The Situationists weren't the first Slackers, but they were the ones who gave the idea a social and aesthetic identity for the 20th century.

Détournement, collage, montage, postcard art. Thinking of one's life as a work of art. Channeling one's religious impulses into acts of creation. Caught up in a prevailing aesthetic concern for the nature of reality. On the other hand, a lot of these people don't seem to be doing anything at all.

"The immense effort required not to create. Intensity without mastery. The obsessiveness of the utterly passive. And could it be that within this passivity I will find my freedom?"

The movie doesn't idealize these people. "*Slacker* had something in it to alienate everybody," Linklater said about his movie 15 years after he made it. These people aren't heroes of the counter-culture revolution. They aren't brilliant artists. They aren't universally admirable. They are conmen (or women) and convicts, crackpots, predators and lay-abouts, they are romantic losers, pathetic conspiracy theorists, the mentally ill, the unemployed, petty thieves, ineffectual artists, musicians who sing flat, cartoon theorists, street-corner philosophers, t-shirt terrorists, armchair Marxists, the bitter, the brokenhearted, Nietzsche-quoting pseudo-intellectuals, neo-posers, anti-artists, half-baked revolutionaries, provocateurs, unreflective anarchists, visionaries, and true believers. Bohemians, beatniks, hippies, punks, Situationists, Slackers. The names change, but a certain aesthetic approach to life remains. (Not the *same* aesthetics, but the mere fact that it's an aesthetic rather than an economic, practical, or utilitarian approach.[140])

---

[140] There are two fundamentally different ways of regarding the status of order and meaning in the Universe. The Scientific View believes that order exists "out there" and our task is to discover it: we

Call it a "lifestyle" choice rather than the passive acceptance of the default setting we inherit from the society around us. One character, just out of prison, says to the camera being filmed by the camera, *"I may live badly, but at least I don't have to work to do it."* When you elevate inactivity, unproductivity, protest and passivity to philosophies, are you a philosopher, or are you still just a loser? Linklater's film doesn't have illusions about these people, but he loves them anyway. Perhaps because he's one of them. Perhaps because he's seen the alternative (the object of a thousand movies made in the 50s, 60s, and 70s) and finds it even worse.

...an atom in the eternal possibility that was his soul...

–Kierkegaard

Slacker is a celebration of those aspects of youth culture that are old, or rather, that are timeless. So long as people have cared about art, music,[141] literature, philosophy,

---

are Searchers. The Aesthetic View believes that meaning is a human creation; something we impose on the world, not something we discover already in it. Meaning is the result of our acts of interpretation: we are Creators. The great saints of the Aesthetic view have been artists, poets, novelists, musicians, philosophers and filmmakers: men and women like the poets of the *Odyssey*, the *Tanakh*, and the *Gilgamesh* epic; Cervantes and Shakespeare; Montaigne, Pascal and Descartes; Milton, Blake and Wallace Stevens; Plato and Nietzsche; Plutarch and Augustine; Melville, George Eliot and Dostoevsky; Beckett and Borges; Mary Shelley's *Frankenstein* and Lewis Carroll's *Alice in Wonderland*. But also men like Ptolemy, Galileo, Darwin, Marx, Einstein and Freud.

[141] From Hildegaard von Bingen to Nina Simone, Sarah Vaughan to Taj Mahal, Ravi Shankar to Tom Waits, Radiohead to X, Bach to Yo La Tengo, Beethoven to PJ Harvey, Cat Power to Eric Dolphy, Zakir Hussain to Robert Johnson, Shivaree to Ornette Coleman, Patti Smith to Arvo Part, Sam Cooke to Coleman Hawkins, the Velvet

ideas, possibilities, and the unknown, there have been Slackers. Their clothes change, their drinks change (absinthe in Paris, rice wine in Japan, lattés and Budweiser in Austin), but they have always been with us: the Dadaists in Zurich and Vienna, the Situationists in Paris, London of the Sex Pistols, New York of CBGB's, Lou Reed, and the New York Dolls, the Inland Empire music scene of the early 1990s from Refrigerator to The Mountain Goats.

Perhaps my enthusiasm for *Slacker* is more personal than aesthetically objective. The movie feels like it's about the kind of people I knew in my mid-twenties. Sleeping on (or behind) other people's couches, hanging out in record shops, used bookstores, junkyards, thrift stores, donut shops and coffee houses—if places and moments in time were songs these would be the soundtrack of my twenties played for me again by the visual music of Linklater's movie; a series of memories that don't quite seem real anymore, except Linklater got them down on film, and when it comes to the past, seeing is believing.

"We all know the psychic powers of the televised image."

Linklater called *Slacker* "an experiment in storytelling." In

---

Underground to the Rolling Stones, Scriabin to Thelonious Monk, Hank Williams to Johnny Cash, Gavin Bryars to Sonic Youth, Coltrane to Brian Eno, Lustmord to Lester Young, Fela Kuti to Angelo Badalamenti, Shostakovich to Nusrat Fateh Ali Khan, Billie Holiday to Bob Marley, Rabih Abou-Khalil to Fats Waller, Belle & Sebastian to The Clash, Elvis Costello to Django Reinhardt, Anthony Braxton to Blind Lemon Jefferson, Otis Redding to Neil Young, Bessie Smith to Cibo Matto, Jimi Hendrix to Joy Division, Kraftwerk to The Magnetic Fields, Nick Cave to Nirvana, Sigur Ros to the Spinanes, Arlo Guthrie to Bob Dylan, Galaxie 500 to Geeshie Wiley, ABBA to Zappa.

one sense, it's a movie that could only exist at a certain period in the history of cinema—when we as viewers have become so good at watching movies (or so habituated by the watching of them) that we no longer need a character's entire story unfolded for us. (In fact, we no longer need a character at all; there's no hero in Linklater's film, unless it's us as viewers.) We can do the work of storytelling ourselves. We've seen so many movies by now that all we need is to be introduced to the characters, the setting, and the premise, and our imaginations will fill in the rest.

Innovative storytelling? In one sense, yes. But on the other hand, this technique is as old in the history of cinema as Vertov's 1929 *Man with a Movie Camera*. The camera shows us the images; we provide the narrative. That's what happens between eye and mind (that's the joy of the imagination): we tell ourselves stories about everything we see and everything we hear: we fill in gaps, complete the picture, and turn everything into a story. The world, for our imaginations, is one vast conspiracy theory we're busy figuring out. It's a particular kind of pleasure that *Slacker*, a wonderful work of fragmentary narrative, human collage, and détournement, invites us to be a part of. Linklater's movie wants to make us one of the characters in his movie (again, think of the image of the camera filming us as it's being filmed[142]), which is delightful or alarming depending on what we think of these people.

Is *Slacker* radically innovative? Does it reimagine narrative? Does its camerawork implicate us in new

---

[142] We see the camera that sees us, but the camera we see is captured by the camera we don't see that is allowing us to see what we do see.

levels of intimacy with the characters we keep encountering, brushing up against, interacting with and then leaving behind? Is its sense of dynamism, new, fresh, and "young"? Yes, yes, yes, and yes. But I suspect it's something else about the movie, something more than the sum of these disparate parts (more than the sum of its own disparate parts) that makes it compelling cinema. Stan Brakhage's *Dog Star Man* (1961-4) is an experiment in storytelling. *Slacker* is a wild, joyful ride, but its pleasures don't lie in its innovative cinematic techniques so much as in the people whose lives the movie introduces us to.

Of course there are clear signs of the influence of the French New Wave. One might have suspected the influence of Thomas Vinterberg and Lars von Trier's Dogme 95 manifesto, except *Slacker* was made seven years before Vinterberg's *Celebration* (so perhaps the influence ran the other way?). One thinks of Wim Wenders early road movies. There are moments when the camera work seems to possess more of the closeness of Ozu or Dreyer's *Gertrud* than the frenetic motion and editing of Godard or the realism and playfulness of Truffaut. And there's something here that we don't find in either Ozu or the New Wave directors. The natural light of Texas. The streets of Austin. Long, languid takes (unprofessional, but intimate). No sets. No actors. No costumes. There are only a few stylized moments— tracking shots or unusual camera angles are rare—and only one dissolve in the entire movie. The movie is shot with a particular kind of natural intimacy. Real cafés, real diners, real streets, real cars, real bars, real bookstores, real houses and apartments. But it's not real life. It's a movie. These aren't people playing themselves, but they aren't quite like actors playing roles either. It's more like real people pretending to be other people they know. The movie isn't a "day in the life" of any particular character. It's a day in the life of a particular city, but it could be any city. (If this can happen in Texas, it can happen *anywhere*.) It's the record of a particular time, but it could be any time. It's Austin in the late 1980s, but in its way it's as universal as Dublin on June 16, 1904 (and to drive this point home Linklater has a character read aloud a passage from *Ulysses* which deals with Leopold's realization that he is not unique when it comes to his sexual relationship with Molly).

"The necessary beauty in life is in giving yourself to it completely."

Linklater has shot his film as if it were a documentary, but it's not. It's scripted, and the characters, although not professional actors, are still acting. They're playing roles, reciting lines they learned and rehearsed. It often feels more "real" than that, often feels like they're simply playing themselves. This is one measure of the movie's success. In some ways Linklater's approach to narrative—refusing to have a single hero, family, or group of friends on whose struggles and challenges the movie focuses is itself a fairly radical approach to "storytelling" when it comes to the conventions of cinema—has more in common with a certain approach to documentary filmmaking than do many actual documentaries that construct or impose a narrative arc on their subjects. Not content to record what is happening, these latter kinds of documentaries, going back to the staged shots in Robert Flaherty's 1922 *Nanook of the North* and continuing in such delightful narrative-based documentaries as Alexandra Lipsitz's 2006 *Air Guitar Nation* and Seth Gordon's 2007 *King of Kong*, use their subject matter to tell a story that develops over the course of the movie.

These kinds of documentaries are far more tied to conventional narrative structure than *Slacker* (for example, they obey the traditional 3-part structure of story arc), and while they are records of real people, in many ways they are more deeply steeped in the fictions of everyday life than the characters played by Linklater's actors. Reality, when seen from the perspectives of "documentary" movies like these, is more slippery than ever. It's as if, in playing themselves, the characters in these narrative-style documentaries have become fictional characters. Characters of their own stories which they are making up as they go along, just so they will continue to have a story to tell. So what is real, when it comes to the movies? What's true in a work of fiction? The question of "what is reality?" becomes an explicit theme in Linklater's 2001 *Waking Life*, but it's already present in *Slacker*.

Linklater's camera implicates us in the lives of these people. It doesn't just show us what it sees, it invites us to become participants in a-day-in-the-life. The camera, since Dziga Vertov, has been the ultimate spectator, but Linklater's camera isn't a spy, it's a coconspirator. We're in the car, at the table, on the street. The camera dances alongside these characters while they're walking down the street. It sidles up to them when they're on the couch. It takes us into their bedrooms and into their heads. We're in the room, a part of their lives. The camera keeps moving, and so do we. But we don't just glance off them. We have encounters. These aren't the lives of heroes or geniuses, but they aren't quite ordinary people either. These people are the margins of a society who somehow allow the center to hold. Without them, we would be so overrun with normalcy that the possibilities of culture itself might be stifled. Yes, these people are losers, but they help us see why the alternative to "winning" as defined by society must remain a crucial option in our lives. Linklater's film isn't an attack on the normal or the ordinary, but it's a love letter to the strange, marginalized, and wonderfully bizarre. We shouldn't love these characters because they're losers, but because they stand outside. Sometimes something as simple (and perhaps involuntary) as that can begin to feel heroic, when seen in light of the alternatives.

The ultimate flâneur moves through time but stands outside it. Recording his thoughts and observations, his relationship to space renders him immune to the passage of time.

"You should never name things in order."

As delightful and provoking as I find *Slacker*, my personal suspicion is that 100 years from now Linklater will be best remembered for his now rarely seen first movie, the 1988 *It's Impossible to Learn to Plow by Reading Books*. It's a movie which, in stark contrast to his later more refined, polished, and technically sophisticated films, is rough, raw, and nearly silent for large swaths of time. (Linklater observed that there was more talking in the first 3 minutes of *Slacker* than in the entire 86 minute runtime of *Plow*.) In his later work, Linklater's movies talk incessantly. They talk at us (*Waking Life*) or talk amongst themselves (the *Before Sunrise/Sunset/Midnight* trilogy). In an age of action, explosions, chase scenes, martial arts and gunplay, Linklater has become the director whose movies talk to us. And he has a lot to say. But in none of his movies does he have more to say than in the largely silent *Plow*. In its raw directness, it is his most blunt, and in some ways most beautiful, stark and revealing film. (It's also his most naïve and unprofessional film.) The later themes are all here: trains, pinball,[143] dreams, wandering, drifting, aimlessness; but its silence is as eloquent as any of the talkers who will dominate his later films, and the Super 8 footage is somehow more compelling than his later 35mm shots of Vienna, Paris and the gorgeous Italian countryside, shot with the help of well-trained professional movie crews.

In this regard it's interesting to compare *Plow* with Jim Jarmusch's first movie, his 1980 *Permanent Vacation*. Both movies are about disaffected young men wandering through the landscape of films that are more about mood than narrative. Aloysious Parker, Jarmusch's antihero (like Godard's Michel Poiccard, he's a car thief obsessed with his looks and his sense of style (he reads Lautréamont's *Les Chants de Maldoror*)), calls story "one of those connect the dots pictures that in the end forms a picture of something." More radically, Linklater's character goes unnamed. These films, made by men in their late 20s about men in their early 20s, are about

---

[143] Linklater works in references to or scenes featuring pinball in virtually every one of his movies. In *Slacker* the first character we meet (played by Linklater himself) mentions the possibility of having stayed at the bus station to play pinball. In *Waking Life* the main character, trapped in a series of dreams within dreams, meets Linklater who recounts the plot of a Philip K. Dick novel while playing pinball. In a way, pinball is the perfect metaphor for *Slacker*—one character caroms off another and the camera follows the new one, leaving the old one behind to continue following a path we will not bear witness to but the awareness of which we carry with us. Or perhaps our eye is like the pinball, visiting characters like the different bumpers we collide off of on our journey through the movie; bumping into them and visiting for awhile, then moving along on our careening path (through life as well as through the movie).

aimless wandering on the margins.[144] Jarmusch's film relies on interior monologue, disaffected dialogue about the meaning of life, and beautiful shots of a desolate, decaying and abandoned urban landscape. (A visual strategy he will employ to stunning effect in the New Orleans of *Down by Law*.) In its unstaged simplicity, Linklater's film is even starker. It dwells on the banality of daily activities (a man brushing his teeth, using the ATM, boiling water, riding trains, waiting, watching TV, having dinner with his family, driving his car).

For my cinematic dollar, Jarmusch's body of work over the last 35 years is among the most interesting of any American filmmaker, and ranks with Hawks, Huston, Peckinpah, and Lynch. Linklater's *Plow* and *Slacker* are terrific movies, but I think they're Linklater's best. In comparison, I'd call *Permanent Vacation* very much a "student film" (even though Jarmusch made it after dropping out of film school); it's the work of a young filmmaker on his way to a brilliant later style, whereas *Plow* in some ways is the best thing Linklater has done to date. The ways in which *Plow* is more interesting that *Vacation* (more about life, more subtle, understated, quiet, searching, desperate, full of longing and unromanticized aimless suspension) are related to what makes *Slacker* so great. It's funny to call *Slacker* a polished movie, especially compared to the Hollywood films of the early 90s, but compared to *Plow* it's already lost just a small amount of the raw, unromantic honesty

---

[144] Wes Anderson's *Bottle Rocket* is another movie about young men made by a young man, another movie about Slackers; but made in 1996 it's already the work of someone who's part of another generation of filmmakers. It is already romanticizing the reality of an earlier period, telling stories where before images and episodes felt like enough because they were all we had.

that is the best part of Linklater's early filmmaking.

Slacker is a movie about prophets, poets, seers, madmen, artists, freaks, misfits, and absurdists. It's a movie about us, or a part of us, or about who we might have been if things had gone just a little differently (if we'd had more courage or less motivation, more creativity or less desire to "succeed" in more conventional terms). Linklater loves these characters, not in spite of but precisely because of their idiosyncratic flaws and quirks. They're losers, but he doesn't judge. He doesn't mock. But he's not simply observing either. The camera caresses these people as they move through their days. In this way his love for them comes through. The movie seems to be smiling in wonder and inviting us to smile along with it. And if we're watching carefully, we do.

Letters to Forgotten Worlds
Part II: The Remembered
Chris Marker's *Sans Soleil* (1983)

It is for want of self-culture that the superstition of Traveling, whose idols are Italy, England, Egypt, retains its fascination for all educated Americans.... The soul is no traveler.... Traveling is a fool's paradise. Our first journeys discover to us the indifference of places. At home I dream that at Naples, at Rome, I can be intoxicated with beauty and lose my sadness. I pack my trunk, embrace my friends, embark on the sea and at last wake up in Naples, and there beside me is the stern Fact, and sad self, unrelenting, identical, that I fled from. I seek the Vatican and the palaces. I affect to be intoxicated with sights and suggestions, but I am not intoxicated. My giant goes with me wherever I go.

–Emerson, "Self-Reliance"

The map is not the territory; until you enter the realm of film. Then reality pries itself from the surface of the wall of the cave and invades the mind of the viewer. Suddenly the map itself does become the territory. Certainly at such a moment it would be wrong to say, "There is no other reality than this." But it is equally wrong to deny the reality of what we are experiencing. And we always experience the map, not the territory. Not, as Kant would have it, because of the distinction between the noumenal and the phenomenal, but rather, as Blake would have it, because our access to the real is always by way of the aesthetic. The map is the image (a representation). The Zone. Not a place but an idea, not a location but a concept. New forms of reality, not in competition with the old, but come hither to illuminate them. When commentaries become literature and the map becomes the territory, the image becomes the thing itself and we have entered the realms of cinema. It's taken over 100 years to get here.

If collage is the art form of the 20th century and cinema is the art of collage sped up to 24 frames per second, then Chris Marker's 1983 *Sans Soleil* is a reimagining of the possibilities of film, a step toward putting the fragmented world back together again.[145] When Humpty Dumpty fell off the wall (pushed, some say, by the vertiginous forces of Futurism, Dada, and Marcel Duchamp in the early decades of the last century), no one could have imagined that when all the king's horses and all the king's men finally got around to putting him back together again (rumors to the contrary notwithstanding) he would end up looking like this. No one except for Marker, because he's the one whose eye engineered the reconstruction project. Fragmentation doesn't give way by means of some Hegelian dialectic to a new affirmation of Totality. Rather it ushers us one step further along a journey on which we're still groping our way; still plunging into the darkness (the theatre) to see what lies ahead.

He wrote, "I've been around the world several times, and now only banality still interests me."

---

[145] "Another promise of fragments is that they alone will survive the catastrophe, the destruction of meaning and language, like flies in the plane crash which are the only survivors because they are ultra-light. Like the flotsam in Poe's maelstrom: the lightest items sink the most slowly into the abyss. It is these one must hang on to." –Baudrillard

Banality is the precondition of the rebirth of the Imagination. Stimulation, gratification, entertainment, suspense, excitement, surprise: these are soporific placaters of imagination. Banality itself is true stimulation, true opportunity. The purpose of art, as Samuel Johnson said about Shakespeare, is to make the strange seem familiar and the familiar seem strange. Hence Marker's narrator's fascination with the banal (which is also Richard Linklater's fascination in his 1988 *It's Impossible to Learn to Plow by Reading Books*), for with the banal rises the opportunity to see again. But who is Marker's narrator? Who is Sandor Krasna? (Who is Keyser Soze?) Another self? A fictional self? A self immune to fiction?

To see, we must have images. But what if those images began in our head? The film presents us with images. Even so-called "slow cinema" moves by at more frames a second than we can see individually. But at how many frames a second can the imagination operate? In the 19th century we lived in a world of fiction without images. In the 20th century during the era of silent film, we saw the power of images given movement on the wall of the cave. In the 21st century we are again turning inward. Virtual reality means a reality wholly contained within our own consciousness. If only we could imagine vividly enough we wouldn't need the screen. We wouldn't need the machine. We wouldn't need the game or the interface. All we would need is the ability to live completely inside our own heads, where reality will be free to unfold at our command. The only problem is, if we ever get there, are we going to be alone? Who would share such worlds with us? The inner world is of vital importance, but what will become of us if we ever leave behind the outer world for good?[146]

In Modernity the literary eye focused on the creative possibilities of writing (Henry James, Conrad, Joyce, Woolf, Proust, Stein, Williams, Eliot, Pound, Stevens). In Post-Modernity the literary eye focused on the creative possibilities of reading (Bataille, Blanchot, Barthes, Derrida, Foucault, Deleuze, Lyotard, Levinas). Now there is no longer such a thing as "the modern," except in our memories. (Proust had already relegated the modern to an act of memory, following up on Plato's theory of recollection a few thousand years earlier). And there never was such a thing as the "post-modern" except as an extended postscript on the modern. To ask "Where are we now?" is just another way of asking, "When are we now?" which is just another way of asking, "What is 'now'?" What did we ever mean, when we spoke of time and distinguished between "then", "now" and "later"? Who would have thought we could turn to film for ways of thinking about such questions? Marker did, obviously.

"We do not remember. We rewrite memory much as history is rewritten."

Marker reminds us of the power of seeing. In a world overwhelmed by images nothing disappears more quickly than an appreciation of the power images once held for us. Cinema has always been an education in seeing, and as

---

[146] Stevens is certainly right to observe that, "It is a violence from within that protects us from a violence from without." Nevertheless, we must be capable of reversing his adage that "the world about us would be desolate except for the world within us" (*Adagia*) and we must recognize that the worlds within us would be equally desolate without the world about us. Marker's gift is to be equally at home in all of these worlds. His films are constantly building bridges between them for us to cross.

our relationship to images and seeing changes, the cinema itself must change. Not to keep up with the world it captures, but to keep ahead of it. Cinema is in a race with the past. It must outstrip it. In any event, there is no danger of it being left behind, any more than the sea can rush past the waves. But if cinema is to the world as the wave is to the ocean, there is still the responsibility of the artist to craft those peaks that will carry us. Otherwise we wallow in the troughs.

Looking itself can become an art. Why not? Nothing new needs to be created. Surely we've had enough of that by now. All we need do now is see. Sei Shonagon made an art of such seeing. She wrote a book which is a record of her various acts of seeing. It is a diary of awareness. A journal of her sensitivity to the world around her and the worlds within her.

Look and look and look. Look 24 frames a second and you've made a movie. Speed it up or slow it down, the rate is irrelevant. What matters is the act of looking as it gives rise to seeing. If seeing doesn't follow looking, we're just being entertained. Henry Miller called it the air-conditioned nightmare. William S. Burroughs called it the Slow Death. But surely that's better than the Fast one. Or is it?

The world is rich beyond comprehension. Human acts of memory, creation, and imagination impose a limited (artificial) comprehension on that too-vast world. We are all of us like the scientists orbiting around the mysterious sea in Stanislaw Lem's *Solaris*. That sea is the world, both inside us and outside us. Two worlds, one incomprehensible mystery, one never-ending story about the stories we tell to parse out small pieces of it, make sense of a handful of details, wonder about what lies beyond.

"The magical function of the eye is at the center of all things."

Whereas certain Americans, possessed no doubt with a sense of guilt or chagrin about their nation's declining intellectualism and thoughtfulness, rush to preempt criticism by calling TV "the idiot box" and pasting "KILL YOUR TELEVISION" bumper-stickers on their automobiles (unaware of how illiberal the very use of bumper-stickers to foist political, social, and aesthetic opinions on passersby itself is as a practice), Marker, more comfortable and confident about his relationship to the role of intelligence and creativity in a changing world, calls his TV set a "memory box." And perhaps he's such a radical filmmaker in part because he has such good taste in television. Marker said in a 2003 interview with Samuel Douhaire and Annick Rivoire,

> I feed my hunger for fiction with what is by far the most accomplished source: those terrific American TV series like *Deadwood*, *Firefly*, or *The Wire*. There is a knowledge in them, a sense of story and economy, of ellipsis, a science of framing and of cutting, a dramaturgy, and an acting style that has no equal anywhere, and certainly not in Hollywood.

Along with Whedon's *Buffy* and *Angel* series and Britain's 1967 to '68 17-episode series *The Prisoner* with Patrick McGoohan, Marker is praising some of the best television shows ever made. And having fed his "hunger for fiction" he frees his own creative impulses to do something else, for once television has perfected the arts of storytelling and character development, the movies have to find something else to do. (And this is even truer of literature—the future of the novel depends on its ability to discover and exploit what it can do that the movies and TV cannot.[147]) Marker is on the trail of this "something else." And part of this involves the very notion of "aboutness."

Sans Soleil isn't a movie "about" Japan. It's not a movie about Guinea-Bissau or Iceland or Paris or San Francisco or Hitchcock's *Vertigo*. It's not even, as has so often been suggested, a movie about memory. It's a movie about the possibilities of the movies themselves. A movie about sounds and images and our ability to record them and imagine them and remember them and create them. It's an epistolary movie in the tradition of the 18th century epistolary novels of Aphra Behn, Montesquieu, Samuel Richardson, and Choderlos de Laclos.

The novel was the art form of the 19th century, despite the fact that some of the greatest examples of the genre, from Conrad to Gaddis and Proust to Pynchon, were created in the 20th century. The movies (as a particular form of collage) were the art form of the 20th century, despite the fact that many of the greatest examples of the genre were and will continue to be created in the 21st century. We don't yet know what will emerge as the art form of the 21st century. That's what we're here to find out. But where is here? Or when?

---

[147] As Greil Marcus put it, "To believe that the present day novel will be read in a hundred years is not to praise the novel but to condemn the world" (*Lipstick Traces*).

Sans Soleil (along with Wim Wenders' 1991 *Until the End of the World* and a handful of 21st century movies like David Cronenberg's 1999 *eXistenZ*, Charlie Kaufman's 2008 *Synecdoche New York* and Christopher Nolan's 2010 *Inception*) tries to imagine that art form (which seems often to take the form of or a reimagined relationship to our own acts of dreaming). Marker's film may be the last example of one form of art and the first example of another, as Proust's novel was simultaneously the last novel of the 19th century and the first novel of the 20th century.

The movie opens with an "image of happiness" (but can happiness ever be an image?) followed by a long piece of black leader. Marker's narrator wonders, will we (the audience for the film he imagines making) see the happiness or the black? The enigmatic, fictional, autobiographical, narrative "he" of the film wants to link this image of happiness to other images, but writes (to the equally enigmatic and mysterious female narrator, recipient of his letters), "It never worked." Worked? What sort of work is "he" trying to accomplish? What is work in a movie like this? Since there has never been a movie "like this" before, the movie itself will have to discover and reveal the answer to that question. It's not an answer we can bring with us to our viewing; it's an answer we'll have to discover in the act of watching. Will we see happiness? Will we see the black?

"*Small fragments of war enshrined in everyday life.*" The letter writer (who both is and is not the filmmaker) sees the world around him through eyes he offers to share with us. Now we too can see with the eyes of an artist. He is writing to us. He is seeing with us. He sees refugees where we might only see commuters. He sees beauty where we might only see advertising, technology, and repetition. He sees hands and faces where we might not even see people. Pauline Kael referred to cinema as "an extraordinary education of the senses."[148] "He" is offering to be our teacher in the extraordinary education. When they do not deaden our sensibilities and overwhelm our senses the movies can be a tool for the intensification of consciousness. *He wrote* to show us how. But that's not a movie, it's a rhapsody. OK. So maybe this isn't an essay, but a rhapsody-in-response. Surely we've had enough movies and essays by now that we can afford a rhapsody once in awhile.

Beyond movies, beyond essays, we'll have only the image left when the image is the mirror Alice looks into the moment before she steps through. Where is she going? Where is she taking us? Through the mirror, down the rabbit hole.

"Fragility of moments suspended in time." Time, emus, young girls, a temple consecrated to cats. He speaks of Sei Shonagon, author of *The Pillow Book* (a contemporary of Lady Murasaki, who invented the novel) while an image of a rocket emblazoned with the word "Polaris" shoots across the screen. The movie seems to jump about. Parataxis and non sequitur. Leaps of faith.[149] But the connections are there. We just have to see them (or imagine them into existence). Such acts of seeing occur as much in our imaginations as in our eye. In fact linking these images is the act by which eye and imagination communicate. It is part of that education of the senses

---

[148] "Movies, the Desperate Art," 1955.
[149] "Obstinately cross-referential and of cryptic interconnective syntax. Nonlinear. Discontinuous. Collage-like. An assemblage." –David Markson, *Vanishing Point*

"he" (either Chris Marker or Sandor Krasna, it doesn't really matter which) is inducting us into.

Marker is like Alice, gone down the rabbit hole. Or is he the rabbit, playing guide to our Alice? Or is he the smile that lingers after the cat has disappeared? Where is he taking us? What kind of rabbit hole is his movie inviting us to drop into? (And where does Alice go, when she plunges through the mirror, if not into the depths of her own imagination?)

"To repair the web of time where it had been broken." It's a movie about cats. But what is a movie about cats about? It's a movie about Sei Shonagon's observations of

Things that Make One's Heart Beat Faster

Sparrows feeding their young. To pass a place where babies are playing. To sleep in a room where some fine incense has been burnt. To notice that one's elegant Chinese mirror has become a little cloudy. To see a gentleman stop his carriage before one's gate and instruct his attendants to announce his arrival. To wash one's hair, make one's toilet, and put on scented robes; even if not a soul sees one, these preparations still produce inner pleasure.
It is night and one is expecting a visitor. Suddenly one is startled by the sound of raindrops, which the wind blows against the shutters.[150]

What is Marker's film, if not a series of images that

---

[150] *The Pillow Book*, #16 (Ivan Morris, trans.).

comprise his own visual equivalent of such a list? Who among us would not want to compile such a list and live in accordance with the poignancy it evokes? (Who would not want to write their own version of *A Diary of the Future*?)

More than Rousseau's *Reveries of a Solitary Walker*, more than Hitchcock's *Vertigo*, more than Roland Barthes' 1970 *L'Empire des Signes*, the best clue to understanding *Sans Soleil* may be Shonagon's *The Pillow Book*. References to her reoccur throughout the film; she is the film's presiding spirit. In fact, *Sans Soleil* may be to cinema what Sei Shonagon's book is to literature, something virtually sui generis. Is *Sans Soleil* a movie? Or is it something else, something that looks like a movie but is already on its way to becoming something new? (Marker's experimentation with CD-ROM for his *Immemory* project and other multimedia pieces suggest his desire to move in this direction.)

"The creator of the new composition in the arts is an outlaw until he is a classic."

–Gertrude Stein, "Composition as Explanation"

Lady Murasaki and Sei Shonagon are two of literature's most innovative authors. How do you write a novel when the novel as a genre doesn't even exist? How do you invent a new form of art? *The Pillow Book* isn't fiction, poetry, philosophy, cultural criticism, history, or journalism; so what is it? A series of moving snapshots from life? Word portraits? The earliest ancestor of Gertrude Stein's *Tender Buttons*? A movie in words 800 years before the movies were invented? There has never been another book quite like it in the history of literature. It's something like a series of letters she's written to herself, which isn't quite the same thing as a journal, a diary or a notebook. *Sans Soleil* is also constructed as a series of letters the filmmaker has written to himself. One self writing to another self. Marker's film isn't photo-journalism, documentary, sci-fi, horror, comedy, romance, a Western, a martial arts or a gangster film; so what is it?

In the movies we are each of us many selves, and Marker's movie offers to introduce us to a few of those other selves we sometimes are. But that suggests to us what the movie does, not what it is. But why should we concern ourselves with questions of being in the face of aesthetic doing?

The movie suggests we should no longer privilege being over nonbeing. We evoke the memory of what is yet to come and honor our ability to create the past before the future erases it. Heraclitus would say, "It both is and is not." Parmenides would say "'It is not *is*.'" If you can get your head around that you'll have drawn a bead on the very origins of Western philosophy.

"I begin to wonder if those dreams are really mine, or if they're part of a totality..."

What happens when a work of art makes that which should be most familiar to us—our own selves—feel radically strange and unfamiliar? Marker's camera takes us to strange and exotic lands in Asia, Africa, Europe and North America. (His most unsettling device: a freeze frame pause which makes one wonder for a moment if the film has stopped.) But where does the exoticism reside—in these places themselves, or within us, the viewers, and in our imaginations?

Literature has long been recognized as a form of tourism,[151] but if literature is tourism then the cinema is potentially a means of transdimensional travel (into the Zone and beyond) that takes us outside of time and space. (The French version of the film opens with a quote from Racine's *Bajazet*, "The distance between countries compensates somewhat for the excessive closeness of time.") What is travel when space does not exist (when a single film can move with impunity from Iceland to Japan and from Africa to California with a single cut)? What is memory when everything that has ever happened is present to us in the now of the image?

As we're told in the *Tao Te Ching*,

Without stirring abroad
One can know the whole world;
Without looking out the window
One can see the way of heaven.
The further one travels
The less one knows.
The sage therefore knows without having to stir
Identifies without having to see,
Accomplishes without having to act. (XLVII)

The further one travels, the less one knows. Might we then travel beyond knowledge altogether, into realms of unknowing? Language and reality are always in tenuous relationship with each other, to the extent that we often feel more at home with language and its multifarious permutations that with reality itself, which seems nearly always up for grabs, indeterminate, and uncertain. There

---

[151] "When people ask me why I travel, I usually answer: 'I do not know what I am looking for abroad, but I know well enough what I am escaping from at home.'" –Montaigne

is at least the impression that we have some control over language (this at least is Humpty Dumpty's lesson to Alice). With reality who knows where we stand? Add image to language and motion to them both, propel them through time, project them onto a 2-dimensional surface (called a screen), and the movies are born and reality will never be the same again. "Good riddance," you might say. But even in our wildest praise of fiction and illusion we must acknowledge the need for some counterpoint to fantasy.

"Laceration must be a feast."

This isn't art imitating reality or reality learning from art. This is the point at which any distinction between such categories collapses. The fraying of the selvage.

The filmmaker is more concerned with speech and images, with *representing* what is, than with a direct encounter with what is. But if we are honest we have to admit that there is never a direct encounter with *what is.* All we ever have is speech about what is. It's the problem of the map and the territory all over again. Language (and in this sense film is a form of language) constantly inserts itself between us and reality. There is no getting at it directly and without mediation. Why not? Because it (reality) doesn't exist as such? Because, as Protagoras said around 450 BCE, *man is the measure of all things?* (We might say not the measure but the *measurer*, though it comes to more or less the same thing.)

"More and more my dreams find their settings in the department stores of Tokyo."

The movie is a kind of dance (and also a kind of poem),

not because it lingers over long scenes of street festivals, neighborhood celebrations, parades and sequences of people dancing, but because the film itself is dancing. Along with Terrence Malick, Marker is one of the great cinematographer-choreographers of the cinema. The movie is full of cats, whose every movement is a kind of dance; owls, who seem virtually immobile except for their eyes; monkeys, who seem childlike versions of ourselves; panda bears, who are simultaneously familiar and exotic; trains (an homage to Ozu); cemeteries, temples, and the life of the streets, which we are simultaneously a part of and spectators to. When we watch these scenes of life on the streets of a city which like the panda is both familiar and strange (because all cities have this in common: they are cities, and cities are places where even foreigners feel at home and even natives feel like strangers), we are watching our own life, close-up but as if from a distance. The love of Marker's camera for Tokyo is unmatched in cinema until Bennett Miller's 1998 documentary *The Cruise*, a film about New York and a double-decker tour-bus guide in Manhattan who is also one of the great poet-philosophers of America in the classic tradition of Walt Whitman and Hart Crane. In these films the camera doesn't film the city, it dances with it.

"The entire city is a comic strip."

There are no actors in Marker's film, but it's not a documentary. It's a story, a fiction, but fiction which rather than be content to unfold in service to reality (what we often hear justified as "the truths fiction tells"), reverses the order and enlists reality in its service. Now truth will serve fiction. Real people will serve as actors, real neighborhoods will serve as sets, reality itself becomes a movie so that movies no longer have to pretend to be real. This is more than Marker's innovation in *Sans Soleil*. It is his "memory of the future" with which he anticipates the new art forms of the 21st century. (Different possibilities of virtual reality as art?) He shows us that no matter how much technology changes the world we live in, art will always be (since Plato's cave and the *Phaedrus*) an uneasy dance between two equally unreal concepts, one of which we name "reality" and the other "image" or "representation."

"Will there be a last letter?"

What does the future hold for art? What does art hold for the future? In the 21st century, or the 22nd, or the 23rd (if we make it that far), even if we have perfected the technology that will make what we now call "virtual reality" as "real" and accessible as television and the internet are today, we will still need artists and storytellers, designers of our fantasies and shapers of our imagination. Why? No matter how accessible, available, and ready-to-use currently unimaginable forms of art and technology become, there will still be audiences, participants, spectators, readers, watchers, and listeners. There will always be those of us who use our senses to respond to those of us whose work will challenge and help us expand those senses. For example, the cinema: a new kind of language, a new kind of handwriting. *"The handwriting each one of us will use to compose his own list of things that 'quicken the heart'"* [152]

---

[152] *Things that Quicken the Heart*. The smell of rain in the desert. The films of Sergio Leone. Walking home at 3:00 a.m. Black coffee and cigarettes before the sun comes up. A paperback copy of a favorite novel that's been read so often the cover is coming off. Recognizing a friend from a distance who you hadn't expected to see. The poetry of John Donne. Pappy Van Winkle 20-year old Bourbon Whiskey.

Seven Ways to End the World:
The Films of Bela Tarr

Nothing is so insufferable to man as to be completely at rest, without passions, without business, without diversion, without study. He then feels his nothingness, his forlornness, his insufficiency, his dependence, his weakness, his emptiness. There will immediately arise from the depth of his heart weariness, gloom, sadness, fretfulness, vexation, despair. The only thing that consoles us for our miseries is diversion. And yet it is the greatest of our miseries. For it is that above all which prevents us thinking about ourselves and leads us imperceptibly to destruction. But for that we should be bored, and boredom would drive us to seek some more solid means of escape, but diversion passes our time and brings us imperceptibly to our death.

–Pascal, *Pensées*

Everyone who knows who Bela Tarr is (and this already assumes a certain enthusiasm for the more obscure masters of cinema) knows that Tarr is the master of the long take. No one has ever seen cows as lovingly with the camera as he does in the opening 9 minutes of *Satantango*, or people as despairingly as he does for the

---

Watching movies alone on a Friday night when you could have gone to a party instead. The music of John Coltrane, Robert Johnson, and Sonic Youth. A favorite line from a favorite movie, like *"Poetry will be made by everyone and there will be emus in the zone."*

next 7 hours and 10 minutes. But the longer the take, the more fragmentary the thinking it provokes. You can't watch Tarr's movies the way you settle down to read a novel (despite the fact that many of his best movies were produced in collaboration with Hungarian novelist Lazlo Krasznahorkai). It's more like reading favorite passages from a very long poem, or like reading the *Bible*. No one sits down and reads the *Bible* from start to finish. Some people even start with *Revelations*.

Cinema of the Apocalypse

> [Mankind's] self-alienation has reached such a degree that it can experience its own destruction as an aesthetic pleasure of the first order.
>
> –Walter Benjamin, "The Work of Art
> in the Age of Mechanical Reproduction"

Cinema, and Hollywood in particular, has made a good thing out of the end of the world. From Abel Gance's 1931 *End of the World* (his first sound film) and Bryon Haskin's 1953 *War of the Worlds* to the three film versions of Richard Matheson's novel *I Am Legend* (between 1964 and 2007, starring Vincent Price, Charlton Heston, and Will Smith respectively) and Paul W. S. Anderson's *Resident Evil* franchise (between 2002 and 2015), cinematic visions of the Apocalypse have been as diverse as Kurbrick's 1964 *Dr. Strangelove*, Thom Eberhardt's 1984 *Night of the Comet*, Michael Haneke's 2003 *Time of the Wolf*, John Hillcoat's 2009 adaption of Cormac McCarthy's *The Road*, Roland Emmerich's *2012* (also in 2009), and Lars von Trier's 2011 *Melancholia*; whether by comet, zombie, plague, war, natural disaster, or unnamed mystery, the movies have been imagining the end of the world with great anticipation. The catalogue of end-of-the-world movies is extensive and ranges from the comedy to the romance to the horror and from the sci-fi to the art house film. The fascination these movies have on us is intriguing in its own right.

When Bela Tarr ends a film, it's like the entire world has come to an end. (And in his final film there is the strong suspicion that it has.) But Tarr's cinema of the apocalypse is far more intimate than your typical end-of-the-world fare, and for that reason far more unsettling. He doesn't need to end the entire world in some sort of cataclysmic catastrophe (though *Werckmeister Harmonies* certainly has elements of the American zombie film); he just brings the worlds of particular individuals to a state of personal doom: a depressed housewife, a hopeless helpless pathetic romantic, an agoraphobic alcoholic doctor, an innocent boy with a fascination for astronomy, a father and daughter trapped in a farm house when the water runs out and the light disappears. In Tarr's movies there are no global disasters. The world ends one person at a time, just like it will for each of us.

Perhaps no one ends the world more beautifully (or more comically) than Samuel Beckett, but Tarr gives him a good run for his money.

Imagine Beckett without the Chaplin-influenced sense of the comic absurd. Tarr's humor is more Nietzschean than Chaplinesque, but Nietzsche is most often funny when he doesn't intend to be, which is always a little embarrassing for his readers. Tarr rarely embarrasses his viewers, but he does make us squirm.

A day in the life of Bela Tarr

> "We have some ontological problems and now I think a whole pile of shit is coming from the cosmos." –Bela Tarr

Even though Tarr made his first movie at 22, he is one of those artists, like Beckett, who seems to have never been young. He looks out at the world through the eyes of a man always and already old, weary, and disillusioned. He was still in his 30s when he made *Satantango*. But what difference does that make? He's always been ageless.

Imagine if *Endgame* were 7 ½ hours long. Or *Krapp's Last Tape*.

If you sat down one morning at 6 a.m. and started watching Bela Tarr's 1977 *Family Nest* and kept on more or less without pause through all 9 of Tarr's feature-length movies, you'd be finished with his 2011 *The Turin Horse* almost exactly 24 hours later (as long as you didn't take too many bathroom breaks). 34 years of moviemaking in 24 hours. Nine movies in one day. There's probably something in the Geneva Convention that makes this sort of viewing of Tarr's oeuvre illegal. Something resembling a crime against humanity, which is what many of his movies seem to be documentations of.

Beginning at the age of 22, between 1977 and 2011, Tarr made 9 feature-length films (if 7+ hours counts as feature length) in addition to a version of *Macbeth* for television, a handful of short films and a documentary. Anyone who has seen his early films, including *Family Nest* (1977), *The Outsider* (1981), and *The Prefab People* (1982) will hardly be surprised that he started fantasizing cinematic versions (not so much portrayals as reenactments) of the end of the world in his later films. We're left with the feeling that the only thing worse than the end of the world as we see it in these early films would be its continuation. But continuation, duration, and repetition are the culminating and enduring themes of Tarr's work. This is Nietzsche's Eternal Return with a vengeance, because despite being the great poet that he was (except when he tried to write actual poems), here, even Nietzsche's imagination fell short: the Eternal Return is not the worse thing man can suffer, rather it's the Eternal Continuation. Faced with a horror like this, the End (any kind of end) would come as a relief. It may be the only relief we have in store for us.

As a general principle of aesthetics, I have a hard time accepting the idea that taste is just a matter of personal preference and there is no such thing as absolute standards in the realm of art, but when it comes to Bela Tarr it's hard to imagine anyone insisting on universal assent. There are some people who don't like his movies, won't like his movies, and I can't think of any argument or experience in the world that would be likely to change their minds, any more than Aquinas's proofs for the existence of God have ever led anyone to faith. Just as long as such people are willing to admit that these movies they dislike are so often marked by moments of profound devastation and beauty as to be absolutely staggering. Not everyone likes to be staggered. Fair enough.

When it comes to the raw image on the screen, no one, in my experience, is more stunningly beautiful than Tarr.

And no one is more relentless in tormenting his audience with a level of tedium that allows us to fully enter into the predicament of his characters. It's not that the boring becomes beautiful, but that we're led to discover new levels of beauty by being carried *through* the boring into something that feels like an altered state of consciousness. New levels of awareness become possible due to the assault on our senses Tarr's films subject us to.

People who tend to dislike Tarr complain that his movies are too long, with confusing (or no) storylines, and that they sacrifice narrative development for endless shots of bleak faces and blasted landscapes. The beauty of these images, people who like Tarr contend, makes up for everything. In fact his dark beauty *is* everything. It's not part of an aesthetic debate; it's a visceral response. Tarr was the first to admit, "I despise stories, as they mislead people into believing that something has happened." But people like stories. A filmmaker who is going to impose his disdain of stories on the audience has to replace them with something. But rather than replace, Tarr takes away. He takes away more and more (happiness, hope, dignity), from his characters as well as from his audience, until eventually the nothing we're left with is so light it feels like another one of Tarr's endless dances. You can hear the grinding accordion music breaking out in what's left of your soul.

No doubt there's something perverse at work in people who like Tarr's movies. Such people like to be messed with. They believe that's part of what art is for: not to comfort the afflicted, but to afflict the comfortable, to shake us out of a complacency born of too much good entertainment.

People object that Tarr movies are boring, and this criticism is leveled as often against his 1982 75-minute *The Prefab People* as the infamous 7 hour and 20 minute *Satantango* (1994). How can there be such a thin line between boring and enthralling? Yet there it is.

Faces in the Rain

> "I just think about the quality of human life and when I say 'shit' I think I'm very close to it." –Bela Tarr

The story of Tarr's movies can be told in the faces captured by his camera (his 2005 5-minute documentary *Prologue* is a one-take shot of a long line of faces waiting in a welfare line in Hungary). He may be intent on ending the world, but no director since Dreyer has loved the faces of the men and women he trains his camera on more than Tarr. He doesn't use actors; he uses human beings to a degree that would have blown Bresson away. He casts people who appear so used up, it's amazing the use he can get out of them, and the beauty he not only sees in them, but shows us. My favorite sequence in any Tarr movie is a camera pan on a rainy afternoon in *Damnation* that shows groups of people, separated by stretches of plaster wall, staring out at the camera and staring at us, the movie viewers, in a moment of reciprocal watching as the rain beats down between us. I feel these are the most human faces a movie has ever shown me, and no moment in cinema has ever made me feel the weight of my own humanity more acutely.

Tarr's art is the art of despair. Human despair, raised to an art form. Which transforms it into what, exactly?

Dancing and the Immobility of Stationary Things

Nearly all of Tarr's movies feature long dance scenes. In *The Man from London*, two men dance around a billiards table to the music of an accompanying accordion. One man balances a cue ball on his forehead, between his eyes. The other man dances with a chair suspended above his head, moving it in circles. A third man looks on, holding his billiards stick. The scene has nothing to do with the plot of the film, which means it has everything to do with the movie itself.

Sitting under the dryer at the hairdresser's, a woman complains that her husband never takes her dancing; that "he can't really read [her] mood." She goes on at length about her love of dancing when she was younger. It is only scene in the movie (*The Prefab People*) in which her face reflects any kind of joy—the joy of past happiness. (Is it remembered, or imagined?) In the next scene she's in a dance hall with her husband. Everyone dances except for her, and her husband dances with everyone except for her. Tarr's movies revel in these long dance scenes in which what should be an act of physical celebration is transformed into an interminable torture sequence as much for the viewer (the tango scene in *Satantango* is 25 minutes long[153]) as for the dancers themselves. The actors dance on and on, but the viewer, like the woman in *Prefab People*, feels trapped; helpless onlookers not to other people's happiness, but to a level of painful

---

[153] About as long, in other words, as a typical American sitcom once the commercials have been taken out. And without a doubt length is the only thing this scene has in common with a sitcom.

repetition that has sapped the joy out of what should be one of life's great pleasures. Later her husband drunkenly sings a sentimental love song, "my heart burns for you"; but he's not singing to her. Her face registers all the loneliness and despair that Tarr will dedicate the next 29 years of his movie-making career to capturing and exploring.

This series of close-ups of the woman (starting 45 minutes into the movie) are among the most devastating images I've ever seen captured on film, even though they're simple shots of a woman's face. The camera doesn't relent. It stays trained on her as the minutes drag on, and it feels like each minute she lives through under the camera's gaze is a miniature eternity of hopelessness: there will never be any time for her beyond these hopeless minutes. There will never be a time when she is happier than she is now, and she is not happy at all. She's not an actress. She's a human being, utterly devoid of hope, of dreams, of anything, her face tells us, to live for at all. She's beyond boredom. There is nothing in life that could possibly interest her, ever again. She is alone. Her husband, across the table from her—drunk, singing, oblivious to her pain—is a symbol of the world's indifference to her very existence. Nevertheless, she's devastated when her husband leaves her, though there were never any signs of happiness in their lives when they were together. Apparently he comes back to her. They go out and buy a washing machine and ride home with it together in the back of a flatbed truck. What joys life still has in store for her!

Despite his fascination with capturing dance on film, Tarr is a director with a nearly perverse taste for the static (his camera constantly roving past frozen faces, buildings, and landscapes), and he is the most infamous director of the long take and the emotion of immobility. But the despair on the woman's face in *The Prefab People* is so dynamic that a single frame can't capture it. She only reveals the depths of her emotion in the subtle changes of her face; changes fellow Hungarian filmmaker Bela Balazs called microphysiognomy when he wrote of "the polyphonic play of features" and "mute dialogues" in his *Theory of Film*.

If she is an actress, she is one of those women who can only play herself, infinitely and throughout the eternity of her hopelessness.

Twenty-five years later Tarr films *The Man from London* with Tilda Swinton; all her brilliance as an actress cannot outdo the intensity of the emotion of this unknown Hungarian woman, because no matter how good Swinton is, we know we're looking at her playing a role. With the woman in *The Prefab People*, it feels like we are simply looking on at her witnessing her own life in ruin. As Tarr said of his first movie, *Family Nest*, "this is a true story; it didn't happen to these people, but it could have." And the truth these stories tell is written on this one woman's face, this one night of her life, which is the worst night of her life, but also the best night of her life, because it's never going to get any better than this. We look on at the moment of her realizing this fact: this is not the despair of a single night of being bored and neglected; it is desolation born of a sudden and utter clarity about the rest of her life.

When he moves away from the documentary style of his early films, Tarr begins more deliberately to aestheticize the shots of the faces of his actors. Agi Szirtes, who plays

Brown's wife in *The Man from London*, commands the final shot of the film before it fades to white (Tarr's films usually end in black). Here we have something between the raw realism of the woman in *Prefab People* and Swinton's hollow-eyed but professional depiction of stunned anguish. But it's still a look that reminds us that there are no words for what the human face can say.

Dance of the Cosmos

> "I just wanted to make a movie about this guy who is walking up and down the village and has seen this whale." –Bela Tarr

The hero of *Werckmeister Harmonies* (2000) is Janos, who opens the movie by orchestrating a cosmic dance in a barroom, using the drunken patrons as sun and planets. He closes the movie in a state of shocked and deranged stupor, beaten into submission by the horror he has witnessed and been unable to intercede against or prevent. Again, it is his face that tells the story of what has happened to him. The stories, in Tarr's film, are always interior crises that can only be expressed visually. There are no words for what Tarr wants his characters to tell us.

Werckmeister's intimate portrayal of how one innocent boy's undoing stands in for the end of a world entire is all the more powerful because of this opening scene of cosmic choreography. Here we have the creation of the universe as a bookend to the descent into madness of one lone boy unable to accept the world that has come to be.

Ecce Homo

At a crucial moment in the film a mob of violent men

destroy a hospital, attacking patients, overturning beds, wrecking everything in their path. Suddenly they come across an old man, naked, alone, standing in a shallow tub with his arms helplessly dangling at his sides, his head bowed. The shot is paralyzing, to the mob as well as to the audience. The men silently disperse, somehow brought back to earth by this vision of human frailty. But it's too late for Janos. He has seen it all, a witness to the horror and destruction from his hiding place in the hospital. As Nietzsche warned, he has looked into the abyss, and the abyss looked back into him. The camera shows us his face staring out from the shadows, hardened with anger, his eyes burning. This gentle dreamer has just witnessed the end of the world, from the outside in. It is a journey he can't make his way back from.

The Endless Return: *Satantango*[154]

The doctor in *Satantango* may be the most twisted version of Emily Dickinson ever captured on film. Alcoholic, agoraphobic, he is holed up in his dilapidated house with his notebooks in which he keeps detailed records of the other members of the collective. After his housekeeper quits, he ventures out in the rain to buy more brandy, collapses, and is hospitalized at the very moment when the village is abandoned. When he returns

---

[154] Peter Hames described *Satantango* as "a slap in the face of consumerism and corporate taste," but in fact the film is a slap in the face of every one of us trying to cling to our dignity in the face of a cosmos whose indifference so closely resembles hostility it's hard to tell the difference. Jonathan Rosenbaum described *Satantango* as "a slap that returns us to our senses." Hames and Rosenbaum are both right about the sensation of being slapped. Repeatedly. But is it a slap in the Buddhist tradition of the blow that delivers sudden enlightenment, or in the Marx Brother's tradition of slapstick enlightenment?

home he doesn't even realize he's returned to a ghost town.

The last 30 minutes of *Satantango* follows the doctor's return from the hospital. Back in the village he doesn't know is deserted, he boards up the window of the room from which he has spied with his binoculars on his neighbors (a particularly perverse version of Hitchcock's Jeff Jefferies), keeping detailed records of their comings and goings in his notebooks. Shutting out the outside world, or shutting in the inside one, the screen grows darker with each nailed-up board until finally he, like the viewer, is left in the final and absolute darkness of a black screen. We can still hear his hammer and his labored breathing, and then the sound of the doctor narrating to himself what he is writing, which is the account of Futaki and the bells with which the movie began. In this film the world does not end—it repeats itself.

The Eternal Return was the most horrible thing Nietzsche was capable of imagining; he thought the will to affirm it, to say "yes" in the face of the most horrible cosmic possibility, was the only way man could overcome Nihilism. Tarr gives vivid life to Nietzsche's challenge: we've just watched 435 minutes of beautiful but painful cinema. But if we really want to affirm life we have to be able to start over again from the beginning immediately. (Structurally the film resembles *Finnegans Wake* in this respect.) There is no pause in life. We either affirm it or admit defeat, and Tarr's film is almost certain to defeat us. Like the doctor, it is easier to board up our windows than enter into the fray again.

Man Bites Dog: *Damnation*

In *Damnation*, Karrer grasps futilely for love, stands in the rain, stands helplessly by, betrays himself, then the woman he loves (or thinks he loves, or lacks the courage to love). In the final moments of the film, after confronting a wild dog on its own terms, he enters a desolate field of mud battered relentlessly by the rain (as the movie has relentlessly battered us for the past 2 hours) from the right side of the frame. The camera tracks, but more slowly than Karrer, who is at first followed by the dog, then left alone, so that he quickly disappears off the left edge of the frame (abandoned in the end even by the camera). The camera, having lost the human element, continues to track across the battered landscape of rain and mud and debris, coming to rest in a final shot of a mound of dirt and twigs. Perhaps it's a visual echo of the mound of skulls in the mist Washizu comes across in *Throne of Blood* after encountering the witch. Or perhaps it's just a pile of dirt, drenched by the rain, another image of the end of one man's world in a world where one man is every man.

Universalism aside, it's hard to tell whether Karrer is some sort of romantic tragic hero or just a flake off the cosmic turd. Does anything in Tarr's movie stir sympathy, empathy, or even a sense of our own self-loathing? Or are we simply wildly stunned, beaten into a spiritual submission, as much by the torturous artistry of Tarr's eye as by the objects he relentlessly trains that eye (and thus by extension our own eyes) on?

If all of Tarr's themes, obsessions, and despair can already be seen in the face of the woman in *The Prefab People* watching her husband at the dance as she realizes that her life is nothing, that she has nothing to look forward to, and that she will never dance again as she did when she was young and still capable of believing in the future, this is still Tarr is the documentary phase of his filmmaking style (his Lumière phase). With *Damnation* the journey he began in *Almanac of Fall* of aestheticizing this style reaches a highpoint he continues in his last four films.

"This Fucking Movie": The Melancholy of No Longer Being Able to Offer Resistance

In a sense, all of Tarr is contained in every moment of Tarr. The whole is always present in the part. Perhaps this is why he reached the conclusion, at the end of *The Turin Horse*, that to make any more movies after this would only be a form of vain repetition; and perhaps this is why a dominant theme in *The Turin Horse* is precisely the soul-crushing burden of vain but necessary repetition in human life[155]: we must get up and get dressed in the morning, we must go to the well, light the lamp, feed ourselves; in the midst of such a grind even a shot of homemade brandy isn't part of a celebration; it's just another act incorporated into the relentless repetition that life has been reduced to. Here Sisyphus's heroic smile is swallowed by a grimace of endurance. Hold on. Cling. But to what? Surely when the world comes to an end, despite their struggle and resistance, the man and his daughter must feel something of a relief.

The Turin Horse is an account of the end of the world in

---

[155] About *The Turin Horse* Tarr wrote, "Do you remember, Milan Kundera wrote this book about the lightness of being? We just wanted to show you the heaviness of being. You are doing always the same thing every day, but every day is a little bit different, and the life is just getting weaker and weaker, and, by the end, disappears. This is what this fucking movie shows you."

the most literal sense that Tarr's anti-symbolism can bear. It's not *about* the end of the world. It *is* the end of the world. Six days, and each day sees the undoing of one of God's original acts of creation. There is no 7th day because there's nothing to rest from. Or no one left to rest. God seems to have undone himself at the beginning of the process. He's the first to go. The horse senses this from the beginning and is the first to follow suit.

"Tomorrow we'll try again," the father says. It sounds like a quote from *Waiting for Godot* because it is. But the God Vladimir and Estragon are waiting for isn't coming, and the God the father and daughter are waiting for has already left. What tomorrow? Tarr has brought time to an end. The silent music John Cage introduced to the world with his *4'33"* in 1952 has finally found its echo in the final moments of Tarr's last film: not silence, but the deafening roar of the abyss, closing in around us.

Tarr said in an interview, "I don't believe in God. That is my problem." This is Tarr in a nutshell. Not his atheism, which is common enough in the modern world, but the fact that he recognizes this atheism as a problem. The death of God is nothing to be complacent or smug about, as Nietzsche's madman knew (*The Gay Science* #125). He who isn't terrified in the face of his own denial of God's existence hasn't really repudiated God; he just hasn't thought about it very much.

Shooting the final scene of *The Turin Horse*, Tarr already knew (or believed) he was making his last movie. This last shot then is his last word on film to future audiences.

The end of *The Turin Horse*, like the end of *Satantango*, leaves the characters, and the audience, in final darkness.[156]

The light that is the very stuff of cinema has either disappeared or been eradicated from the world. The darkness we are left with is Tarr's last word on world and cinema alike. (Surely for Tarr the world is cinema, and cinema the world.) It would feel like a far more despairing word if not for the wrenching beauty of the images that precede it. But because of that beauty, Tarr's last word is not Kurtz's "the horror" or "the heart of an immense darkness" with which Conrad ends his novel, but rather the beloved's "cry of inconceivable triumph and unspeakable pain." For as Adorno, who had intended to dedicate his *Aesthetic Theory* to Samuel Beckett, had his world lasted long enough for him to complete that work, observed,

> Artworks detach themselves from the empirical world and bring forth another world, one opposed to the empirical world as if this other world too were an autonomous entity. Thus, however tragic they appear, artworks tend a priori toward affirmation.

In other words, Tarr can end all the worlds he wants at the end of each of his movies so long as the movies themselves keep affirming the existence of an aesthetic realm that may always constitute the best that any world has to say for itself. No matter how dark Tarr gets, he can't get darker than the light that simultaneously emanates from and illuminates the work of art. This light is the very stuff of cinema. Because even though the endless rain in *Damnation* and *Satantango* is fake and the

---

156 When we're not left in darkness, we're left with the residual carnage of the desperate human urge to obliterate the self. But on the other side of that obliterated self, who knows what new worlds we might discover, invent, or create.

relentless wind in *The Turin Horse* is made by a machine, the despair these movies expose is real, and art may be all we have to combat it with.

EPILOGUE
Going to the Movies
(Miscellaneous Notes on the Metaphysics of Cinema)

I like the movies too. And after all, only Whitman and Crane and Williams, of the American poets, are better than the movies.

–Frank O'Hara, "Personism: A Manifesto"

It is a weird and wonderful feeling to write a booklet about something that does not in fact exist.

–Sergei Eisenstein, *Film Form*

He wished to become totally absorbed in the film no matter how trivial or artificial it was, in order to free his mind temporarily from the philosophical thoughts that tortured and exhausted him.

–Norman Malcom, *Wittgenstein: A Memoir*

Introduction to the Epilogue: Sequels to Other People's Movies

In 1986 I was invited to deliver a lecture on the philosophy of cinema at an academic conference on aesthetics in Ottawa, Canada. During one of the receptions, a Texas Hegelian asked me how I thought a person intent on living well should spend his time. Would such a person watch movies? Before I could respond we were interrupted by a short, agitated man, holding a drink in each of his hands (which gave him the look of being on his way to deliver one of them to someone else, though over the course of the ensuing conversation I watched him drink from both of them, if not simultaneously then in such close succession as to give the impression that he was capable of doing so), who took over the task of answering the question for me.

"Would a person intent on living well spend his time watching movies?" (His first move in answering was to repeat the question.) "Or, in other words, to what extent has watching movies become a possible, perhaps even necessary part of "the good life" as we move towards the end of the 20th century?" (His second move was to restate it in slightly different terms.) "Have you ever seen . . ." (His final move was to turn the question back on the inquirer, only this time in terms of a specific moment in a specific film in the belief that a detailed interpretation and deeper understanding of this one scene was far more interesting and important than vague and general answers generated in response to vague and general questions.) This, I was to learn over the course of the next 20 years, was how he engaged in conversations. He always wanted to talk about specific movies, rarely his own, as if other people's movies were the vocabulary with which he populated his conversations.

That was almost 30 years ago. I remember him now with that same relationship to memory that he embodied in his own life when talking about the past, which he described as if he were recalling fragments of a movie he had once started watching but had left the theatre before seeing the end of. I remember him with a kind of nostalgia for something I always felt was missing from my own life, but that I could detect in the contours of certain fictional lives I had read about or watched or imagined. He had a remarkable capacity for being silent, which seemed to open up vast spaces around him. When you talked to him the words swirled around but never quite filled these spaces. He seemed to be saying more than his words conveyed. He was for me almost but not quite an object of the imagination itself.

Judging from an album of pictures he showed me once, he was short and heavy and bald even as a young man. But he was handsome in his own way and exuded a certain confidence that belied the merely physical details of his appearance. In fact he had many ways of appearing, and the physical often seemed the least interesting way in which he manifested his presence.

He was a brilliant conversationalist, but those of us who knew him agreed that his writing never lived up to the promise suggested by his ability to speak. We suspected that he was capable of great things, but we never found them in his books; and it wasn't until much later, when he turned to making movies, that he confirmed in the play of light and shadow, sound and silence, and the illusions of time and space projected in two dimensions, what we had always known must be true about his vision of the world.

It seems he lived many lives all at the same time, or at least in close enough succession to one another that they appeared simultaneous to those of us who stood on the outside looking in at each reinvention of himself as another facet of the whole: a dishwasher, an adjunct philosophy professor at a California Community College, a failed novelist, a cab driver in L.A., and finally a successful filmmaker. Finally discovering the one thing he seemed destined to, it was also the thing he put off the longest, perhaps hoping to avoid a destination he had been rushing towards all his life. All his lives.

He asked me once which I thought were more intelligent, cats or dogs. I told him I didn't know and he agreed saying, "That's right. And in fact we can't know. Because any test of intelligence we might choose to administer would only tell us which species displayed features of what *we* consider intelligence, but such tests would tell us nothing of the intelligence of cats and dogs proper to cats and dogs themselves.

"How do we know that what counts as intelligence for a cat resembles what counts as intelligence for a dog? Is the fact that dogs are more easily trained and more obedient a sign of more intelligence, or less? How do we measure intelligence? The fact that we can't say whether cats or dogs are more intelligent tells us more about our own limited understanding of intelligence than it tells us about cats and dogs.

"We think we understand the world we live in, but we don't even understand the one perspective from which we are capable of viewing it. If we were capable of more than one perspective, we might be capable of true understanding. That's why I make movies: they increase the number of perspectives from which we can see the world. The greatest movie ever made would allow us to finally understand the world of cats and the world of dogs, and liberate us from the illusion that these creatures do no more than share a common world with us."

When I started writing for *Cinema Critique*, I asked him if he would do a series of interviews with me about his work as a filmmaker. He said No, but he agreed to share with me some of the director's notes he had assembled over the years; a collection of meditations on the metaphysics of cinema he had never intended to publish, but that I might do with as I wished. Written over the course of a 20-year career as a filmmaker, he described these notes as the theoretical compliment to a body of creative work that included eight films, two never-produced TV pilots, and a handful of shorts shown privately to friends and eventually disseminated over the Internet.

We would meet at a downtown bar and sit over gimlets talking about his work in the movies, but he never let me use a tape recorder or write anything down. When we finished drinking he would hand me a stack of notecards with a rubber band around them, we'd agree on a time to meet the following week, and he would say goodbye. When I learned that he had been killed in a car accident I decided it was finally time do to something with the stacks of notecards I had been accumulating over the several years of our weekly meetings. Editing them, it seemed to me, was out of the question. They were not dated and there was no natural order to put them in. But I wanted to do something.

Many of the notecards were about the relationship he saw between his voracious reading and his work as a filmmaker. Other cards spoke of other people's movies: his favorite films, his favorite directors. Some were descriptions of his work as a director, and others were about his work—and his play—as a voracious moviegoer.

Although they ranged greatly in theme as well as quality, in the end I decided simply to reproduce them (omitting some of a more personal nature, especially those dealing with his relationships with actors, writers, directors, and other people in the movie business who are still alive). I wanted to give as accurate a portrait as possible of the mind that had produced them, rather then impose on that mind a clarity of expression his own words often lacked. Still, it took me several years before I got around to completing the project. I could never bring myself to admit that time had imposed an artificial limit on his work and had brought it so abruptly to an end. My inability to finish my portion of this work may have been my own feeble protest against the premature termination of what I saw as the incomplete body of his work. I wanted there to be more. We always do, when confronted with an end that still feels like part of the beginning.

Along with these notecards he left a sheaf of production notes and a treatment for the project he was working on at the time of his death: a film he intended to call *Fragments of Paradise*, which was to be a re-visioning of Milton's great epic. He described the film-in-progress as "my latest attempt to realize in the poetry of film the essential solitude of man's struggle with the threat of the

Divine."

* * *

I still think of him often. He was the kind of man who scuttled out of a room with the sort of furtive swiftness one associates with the experience of being interrupted in the act of doing something shameful; as if he were endeavoring to escape from the scene of his embarrassment with as little dignity as possible. But when he reached the parking lot, his entire demeanor changed and he sat behind the wheel of his automobile with a kind of intimate comfort one normally accords only to other living beings. Indeed, he drove his car as it if were alive, and in turn it responded to his touch with something like the air of a neglected lover grateful for the return of his attentions. He told me he always enjoyed the years he spent working as a cabdriver, and he responded with mixed emotions when he realized his first movie was going to make enough money to allow him to give it up. Indeed, he had no choice, for the work on his second movie would quickly become so all-consuming as to allow him no time for anything else. Certainly no time for driving other people around L.A., as much as he enjoyed the work. He often attributed to his hours in the cab the inspiration for some of his best creative insights.

He told me once that he had started making movies because he wanted to design soundtracks for the images he carried around with him in his head. He spent hours putting together the mixed tapes he played in his cab, as much for his passengers as for himself. These tapes were the soundtracks of his long nights behind the wheel. They gave shape and contour to the city he was constantly moving through. The city of music and movies.

290

He told me that when he was young he had fallen in love with a girl whose family had moved to Chicago. Over the course of several years he wrote her letters, sometimes as many as one a day for weeks on end. He wonders, from time to time, what became of those letters, and even more strangely, what became of the man who wrote them. He told me he still thought of those adolescent letters when he sat down to work on the treatment for one of his scripts.

"These scripts are like letters I'm writing to a forgotten self, not as part of an effort to remember, but simply in order to say goodbye. Perhaps I'm saying goodbye to someone who never even existed. That seems to me a good description of the movies."

This is how I remember him: a small man in a large automobile that he maneuvers with skillful ease. Standing on the sidewalk outside of an L.A. bar on a Wednesday afternoon I can still see him pulling out into the flow of traffic as if stepping onto a dance floor.

For two years he lived on a Melanesian Island in a small bungalow without electricity, surrounded by notebooks swollen with the damp sea air and old paperbacks that fell apart after a few readings. "Glue holds things together; nature takes them apart. And nature always wins out in the end," he told me once. For two years he did not watch a single movie or ever leave the island. He swam in the ocean, tolerated the mosquitoes, listened to the music of the native villagers, learned to fish and picked fruit in the jungle. He told me a story the villagers used to tell about a goat that lived on the moon. At night it would crane its neck down towards the sea to drink.

Because it tried to drink up the sea the people who lived on a neighboring island called the Moon Goat a voracious creature, bent on its own destruction. Although they suspected that it was divine they felt no need to appease it, because they knew that eventually the salt water would destroy it, and it would leave them in peace.

The villagers on his island told him that these people from the other island had forgotten how to pray, and as a result their destruction was as assured as that of the Moon Goat that they both feared and disdained. Having forgotten how to pray, the breath they drew was ultimately as self-destructive as the salt water the Sea Goat drank every night.

He told me that was why he started making movies: "To help people who have come to disdain the world around them remember how to pray."

He used to recite to me that line from Aimé Césaire's *Return to My Native Land*:

Those whose only journeys were uprootings...

In my memory he's always driving away from something. There was always somewhere he needed to go, and as far as I know he never got there. Sometimes I think the notecards he left me might help me explain why. Or where.

* * *

Ways of watching. Reaching a destination without going there.

*

An interesting phrase: *to go to the movies.* In what sense are we *going* somewhere? Are the movies a place we travel to? A destination we pursue? We want to go somewhere. We choose the movies to take us there.

*

How far we've come from those words of Séverin-Mars (and how many remember his movies today?) quoted by Walter Benjamin in his "The Work of Art in the Age of Mechanical Reproduction" about going to the cinema: *Only the most high-minded persons, in the most perfect and mysterious moments of their lives, should be allowed to enter its ambience.*

*

Where does the lens end?

*

Imagine light as a place.

*

In order to make a movie
close your eyes
and then
look.

*

Explanation is the death of art, but interpretation is its life.

*

Editing a movie is like cutting 300 pages out of a 200-page book.

*

"The movies are a world of fragments." –Godard

*

Since there is no such thing as *the* world, the task of the filmmaker (as of the poet) is to bring *a* world into existence.

*

A great movie always leaves the door open. Even when it's not clear whether there's a room for us to enter.

*

"Seeing with the entire eyeball is all-inclusive study." –Dōgen

*

All those movies. What were we hoping to gain by watching them? (Wasn't it something we already had?) Or what were we hoping to lose? (Was it really something we could get rid of simply by watching movies?)

*

For the Romans soul is *anima*, that which moves (animates). Like the movies.

*

Di-minish-stract-vert the eye by means of the camera. Teach it to see (either in new ways (physiological change) or new things (naturalistic or metaphysic vision). Camera as bridge between the familiar and the unfamiliar. A pathway towards the new.

*

Chaplin described the silent films of Josef von Sternberg as works of visual poetry. Like other forms of poetry, our understanding, appreciation, and enjoyment of movies can be deepened and enhanced by cultivating our skills as readers/viewers. The act of seeing is not passive and it is not strictly natural. It is a learned skill, like eloquence in speech and reasoning in thought. We can learn to see better. And by seeing more we expand not only our experience of the movies, but of the world around us. In this sense film is an opportunity not only to see more, but to experience more.

*

Movies introduce us to new forms of seeing and hearing (what Michel Chion calls the *audiovisual* experience). To see more and to hear more is to experience more. Thus cinema is capable of expanding our experience not only of the movies, but of the world. We can learn many things from going to the movies. For example, how to pay attention.

*

On the one hand, I have never tried to make what people call "philosophical films." But on the other hand, I think philosophy presents itself to us as both a promise and a threat, and I think that movies are like that too. But this is something that movies have in common with philosophy, not something that makes them "philosophical."

*

"A man who has nothing more worthwhile to show us than the works he has written, or rather put together, spending hours twisting phrases this way or that, pasting in this and pruning that–such a man you would, no doubt, be right to call a poet..." –Plato, *Phaedrus* 278

Or a filmmaker.

*

It's not right to say I don't trust beautiful women, but rather that I don't trust myself when I'm around them, which amounts to the same thing. If you think that working with actors resembles working with professionals in any other business, you're kidding yourself. Which is why I will never make a movie starring a beautiful woman. Instead, I allow my movie to transform an average looking woman into a beautiful person. In this way, I start from what is possible, rather than from what is already given.

*

The radical fungiblity of existence. No matter who the main character is, a successful movie inevitable draws the audience into a sense of identity with that character (cf. Travis Bickle in *Taxi Driver* or Willard in *Apocalypse Now*). The audience is always the protagonist because we come to see the world through the protagonist's eyes, and seeing what he/she does, we come to think as and sympathize with that character. Thus movies create a sense of our own universal identity. In this sense, cinema may be the ultimate fulfilment of Schopenhauer's moral philosophy.

*

With so little verbal language at its disposal, the silent film must resort to the poetry of images.

It is a strange fact about art, time, mortality, and the movies that the world we live in today is a world which, for the majority of moviegoers, will not include the experience of watching some of the greatest films ever made, simply because they are silent movies. In part this is because we are gradually forgetting the language in which they speak to us. We are losing the ability to understand what they say. We have been so overwhelmed with sound that we can no longer hear the poetry of images.

*

When I am making a movie I am not trying to tell a story, but to engage in a rhapsody. It is not ideas, but feelings I am trying to unleash. It's important to understand that feelings are not the same as emotions. The idea that a work of art is intended to provoke emotion is the 19th century prejudice of naïve audiences who never stopped to think through the implications of a work of art. Anything can provoke an emotion: being cut off in traffic, being complimented at work, losing one's keys, breaking a favorite coffee mug, getting stuck at a red light, waiting in line at the grocery store, being accidently bumped into on a busy street. These things are not works of art. The *feeling* involved in one's encounter with a work of art is simultaneously more active (more reflective) and more passive (experiential) than the provoking of emotions. Provoking emotions lacks the necessary intellectual component of feeling (feeling involves a kind of self-awareness capable of seeing beyond the self, whereas emotion is its own form of awareness and is therefore not an aesthetic response). It also lacks the potentially spiritual dimension a work of art must be capable of revealing.

*

In Plato's Allegory of the Cave, the enchained audience has become so enraptured by the show that they have forgotten how to distinguish between fantasy and reality. Socrates asks Glaucon to use his imagination not only to picture the captive audience, but to become one of them—to try and envision the truth through an act of the imagination. He goes on to describe the actions of one restless member of the audience, freed from his chains (Plato is deliberated vague about how this original act of liberation occurs), who leaves the cave to seek the cause of these enchanting images that dance on the wall before them. He does not encounter the filmmaker or the cameraman, the actors or the director, but instead stumbles across the light itself, that which makes all images possible. Light which for thousands of years has served as a metaphor for knowledge, for truth, and for understanding. But the rest of the audience stays put. They are enjoying the show. They do not need to understand the magic to be enchanted by it. In fact perhaps they suspect, as filmmakers since Georges Méliès have known, that explaining the magic doesn't bring us closer to the truth, it just makes the reality created by the cinema feel like an illusion. No one is trying to fool anyone here. It is delight, not deceit that is at stake when we go to the movies. This is metaphysics on a different level entirely.

*

"...the image stretches out into infinity, and leads to the absolute..." –Tarkovsky

*

"Well, there you have the secret of good work: to plod on and still keep the passion fresh." –George Meredith, *The Egoist*

*

Every book I've ever written has been the best book I was able to write at that time, and no book I've written has ever been as good as I wanted it to be. In this sense, every book I've written has been a failure, but also the closest to success I've been able to come. For this reason, although my writing is important to me, the books I have written are not. In inverse proportion to the importance of writing in my life, my books, once they are finished, are of virtually no importance since they never embody what I had hoped to achieve in writing them. They are symbols of my aspirations, not marks of my accomplishment. As Wallace Stevens observed, "It is not what I am, but what I aspired to be that comforts me." This remark has guided me as a filmmaker as well as a writer.

*

Writing is a conversation I'm having with my own imagination. And what is this imagination but a name I give to the miraculous place whence ideas come. I don't know where it is, or how ideas travel from there to here. I don't know where ideas come from; I only know that with patience they do come, and if I'm sufficiently attentive I can receive them when they pass near, like the gravitational pull a planet exercises on a close-passing asteroid. Some miraculous gift from outer space.

*

The restless philosopher is apparently the only one to mistake the show for an attempt to perpetrate a false reality on the audience. What he took to be chains may have only been aids to our wandering attention. After all, it takes a great deal of concentration to really *watch* a movie, to try and enter into it as if it were a portal to another reality—which in fact is what it might be. What it *can* be. The light that makes the movies possible, the philosopher's great discovery—do we see more when we try to stare directly at it, or when we look intently at that which is visible by virtue of its power in order to contemplate the images its presence makes possible?

*

"Art's office is to render visible the Divine." –Hegel

*

Even today the movie theatre is something like a cave; and long before Socrates, caves from uKhahlamba to Kakadu and from Lascaux to Altamira have been home to the earliest acts of human creation preserved as images. If we no longer go to the movie theatre, it's because we have learned to transform some corner of our own homes into a cave where we can give ourselves over to works of cinematic art. Today we are recapturing the ancient practice of homes that once had domestic altars, places for private acts of devotion. There was a time when every house had an area set aside for worship, reverence, contemplation, and meditation. A place where images and icons were given a home and the sacred was still considered to have a place in our daily lives. These corners were the sites of worship, adorned with idols and images of holy objects, domestic shrines. Today this is where we place the screens on which we watch our movies at home. The image has regained its ancient status in our contemplative lives. Through acts of the imagination we again reach out for the Divine.

*

To be sure, not all movies are works of art, nor is all watching an act of giving oneself over to our hope for the Divine. Reverence and contemplation are perhaps the rarest modes with which we encounter a movie. For the movies, like any art form, exist largely in the potential of what they can be, or what we can be, while watching them. Nothing is guaranteed.

*

In the *Republic* Socrates says,

> The power to learn is present in everyone's soul and the instrument with which each of us learns is like an eye that cannot be turned around from darkness to light without turning the whole body. This instrument cannot be turned around from that which is coming into being without turning the whole soul until it is able to study that which is and the brightest thing that is.... Education is the craft concerned with this turning around, and with how the soul can most easily and effectively be made to do it. It isn't the craft of putting sight into the soul. Education takes for granted that sight is there but that it isn't turned the right way or looking where it ought to look, and it tries to redirect it appropriately.

If the instrument with which each of us learns "is like an eye", are we not right to ask: What kind of education might "going to the movies" constitute? For going to the movies provides us with the opportunity for various forms of seeing, and "watching" a film turns out to be a complex act which involves far more than just sense perception. Going to the movies might turn out to be a kind of education for the eye, and the eye a necessary tool of the mind, which Socrates calls the soul.

*

The movies exist outside of time. In the instant of its unfolding, the movie liberates the viewer from past and future, setting up an eternal now. Time is created as an artificial construct within the movie (decades can pass in 90 minutes); but outside of it, for us as watchers, it does not exist. Until the lights come up and we are grudgingly restored to "reality."

*

The movies replace Time & Space, those oppressive Kantian categories of reality, with infinite possibility. For although they unfold within Time & Space, they take them over, violate their constraints, and reveal that behind them are other forms of reality we have known about all our lives, but have only been able to visit through the power of our imagination. This is where we "go" when we *go to the movies*, even when we're sitting in our own living rooms. It's not a time or a place, because the movies happen within a version of Time & Space beyond the laws of physics: how can years unfold in just 90 minutes? How can we visit so many cities, countries, and planets without moving from our couch?

*

We must be careful, however, to distinguish such travel from what is often called "entertainment." The former is a kind of radical motion; the latter is an ever-deeper sinking into our selves and our local limitations. The movies liberate us from ourselves not to transform us into someone or something else, but to free us from the restrictions of identity altogether; entertainment chains us to the sloth of identity and the familiar comforts of stultifying certainty.

*

Tarkovsky observes that the film *always turns out to have more thought, more ideas, than were consciously put there by its author*. How does the artist move aside so as not to get in the way of the potential realization of his own work?

*

How do we understand the relationship between form and content, style and subject in a film, and why is this relationship more complicated in the cinema than in other works of art? In music the form and content are identical. In literature the style unfolds in a single dimension: that of language; and while the literary style of each great writer is unique to that author, that style is always a matter of his or her use of and relationship to language. But in film, there are many styles at work all at once, and each of these styles has a direct and profound effect on the content—the story, the plot, the narrative, the psychology and development of the characters—of the movie. There is the style of the camera work: consisting of angle, light and shadow, motion (panning shots, tracking shots, close-ups, deep focus, etc.), and other qualities of stasis and dynamism. There is the style of acting and directing; the style of scene and scenario, of landscape and setting, or perspective, of sound and music. Forms of form...

*

The secret of good writing is simple: make every sentence such a pure pleasure that the reader cannot put the book down. But you cannot falter even for a single sentence. If one sentence flags, the whole game is up. It is no different when making a movie. Every shot must be perfectly compelling, so that the audience does not want to look away even for a moment.

*

I was nothing, so I could do anything, Witold Gombrowicz writes. This is what the movies give us: they turn us into nothing (take us away from ourselves) so that we can do/be/go anything or anywhere (even if only for an hour or two—but that is another thing the movies do: they destroy time, replacing it, not with eternity but with an all-consuming omnitime that only lasts an instant but goes on forever, the eternal Now of the movies). By means of erasure the movies restore to us the infinite possibility of the indeterminate, uncertain, and inchoate.

The writer who counseled his readers to . . . stop identifying themselves with what defines them, Susan Sontag said about Gombrowicz. Beyond the limits of the self movies might help us discover the possibilities of the not-self. (Not the Other, which is simply another self, but that which is beyond selfhood altogether.)

*

A staircase in Luc Besson's *Leon, The Professional* is the perfect representation of a staircase in a low-income urban setting. And while it is undoubtedly such a staircase, it's appearance in the film lifts it out of any specific context in which we would ever encounter it in "real life" and raises it, as if in a gesture of reaching towards that notion of the Platonic form (cf. van Gogh's paintings of peasants' shoes and of the bed where he slept in Arles), toward something neither more abstract nor more concrete, neither more nor less real, but something wholly *other* than any staircase we have ever experienced before, or perhaps have even had the ability to experience. In this sense the movie expands the realm of our possible experiences, expanding it to allow it to encompass the experience of a staircase which both does and doesn't exist (the staircase filmed by Besson's cameraman exists, but the staircase in the film does not exist outside of the film; thus the film appropriates an object (in fact an entire locale) and draws it into itself, erasing it's "real world" existence and bestowing on it an existence unique within the film, which we as viewers are temporarily drawn into. We can never climb those stairs ourselves, and yet they are somehow more real to us that the staircase we climb every night back to our apartment on our way home from work.

*

Reality comes about in unreal ways. A lesson from fiction borrowed by the movies.

*

"Although human beings are incapable of talking about themselves with total honesty, it is much harder to avoid the truth while pretending to be other people." –Akira Kurosawa

*

306

I turn to art from a frustration with the limitations of my own individuality. For this reason, the collaborative quality of filmmaking is particularly important to me. Of course the auteur theory and the star system hold up individuals as examples of creative genius, fame, wealth, and power; but what I'm after is something beyond these illusions. "What I'm after" probably doesn't exist. But that's no reason not to pursue it.

*

In the midst of one's daily duties and responsibilities it is difficult to maintain a sense of the profound mysteries that underlie reality. It may even be that a kind of spiritual schizophrenia is required of the person who tries to maintain a faith in these two incompatible senses of reality (the visible and apparent "real" versus the invisible and elusive "ideal"). Perhaps this is the essential schizophrenia of the artist in the world.

*

Listen, my friend, this is the dream I dreamed last night. The heavens roared, and earth rumbled back an answer; between them I stood before an awful being, the somber-faced man-bird; he had directed on me his purpose. His was a vampire face, his foot was a lion's foot, his hand was an eagle's talon. He fell on me and his claws were in my hair, he held me fast and I smothered; then he transformed me so that my arms became wings covered with feathers. He turned his stare towards me, and he led me away to the palace of Irkalla, the Queen of Darkness, to the house from which none who enters ever returns, down the road from which there is no coming back.

–The Epic of Gilgamesh

The movies, obviously, have been around as long as literature itself. As long as dreaming. How can anyone say they are an invention of the 19th Century?

*

Man is that being that bursts forth spontaneously from mud and light. Ultimately the mystery of life submits to no clearer explanation than this.

*

Where does seeing begin?

We have to learn to see the movies through the eyes they teach us to see with, not with the eyes we unreflectingly bring with us.

*

"The film is the art form that is in keeping with the increased threat to his life which modern man has to face..." –Walter Benjamin, "The Work of Art in the Age of Mechanical Reproduction"

*

The machines used to make movies are secret intermediaries. With their help the gap between Reality and Imagination is not closed but widened to the point where everything that falls in between becomes the object of our contemplation and wonder.

*

Look for the solution where the enigma is deepest.

*

Is nature itself (the universe) essentially valueless? If there are no values inherent in atoms or planets or anything in between then where does value come from?

*

If we value something like honesty, but then tell a lie, it can only be because we value something more than honesty. We always act in accordance with our highest values. If we want to achieve self-honesty, we need only look carefully at our actions and determine from what values they stem. If we know *why* we do what we do, we know what we value, and if we know what we value, we know who we are. This is not Existentialism, but Axiological Aesthetics.

*

The camera's goal is to make us forget it's there. But we must resist this illusion in order to help the camera realize an even greater goal, which is to make us aware that we are not here either. The camera, superficially a means of presencing the world around us, is ultimately a means of erasure.

*

"Thought that does not have a dead fragment as its object has the inner existence of flames." –Georges Bataille, "The Sacred Company"

*

Books you thought you'd read but never opened, places you thought you'd go but never visited; music you thought you'd listen to, things you thought you'd learn to do, films you thought you'd one day make. Youth is a time for accumulating things you believe there will be time for in the future. Old age is a time for getting rid of those things you didn't have time for in the past.

*

Each list is an attempt at a perfect distillation of that sense of self which I am continuously trying to obliterate through repeated acts of affirmation and repetition. Hopefully, eventually, under the weight of this oppressive repetition, I(t) will simply disappear.

*

Can a film be made of a man's life? Of his entire life, minute by minute, day by day—a film that lasted exactly as long as the life itself did? And would someone choose to watch that film rather than live his own life (or rather, allow the watching of that other life to become his own?)

*

Cinema as appetite.

*

The language in which it might have been given me to write, and even to do my thinking, is neither Latin nor English, nor Italian, nor Spanish, but one of which I know not a single word, one used by the dumbest of things in speaking with me, and one in which, perhaps, I will someday be called to account for myself from my grave before an unknown judge.

–Hugo von Hofmannsthal, *The Lord Chandos Letter*

It is in this way alone that I have found it possible to speak of the language of cinema.

*

Montaigne said about wine, "Only good things can be abused." The same is true of the movies.

*

"In my opinion, the cinema more than any other art is particularly bound up with love." –André Bazin, "De Sica: Metteur-en-Scène"

*

"I believe that the essence of the cinema lies in cinematic beauty." –Akira Kurosawa, "Notes on Filmmaking"

*

Awareness is a particular form of attentiveness. We can be bored by living life, but not by paying attention to the living of it. When we pay attention, boredom retreats— for boredom it is the result of a lack of concentration (a lack of awareness). The movies are a school for watching, watching is a prelude to seeing, and seeing is a form of paying attention, of being aware.

*

The seeing involved in watching a movie is a form of awareness, and awareness itself is a mode of being. When we see better, we are more aware, and when we are more aware, being becomes more than what it was. Awareness is different from knowledge, different from experience. It is neither a cognitive nor emotional state. Watching is a form of awareness, and *awareness* replaces selfhood so that it's not "me" watching the movie, it is the act of watching taking over the "me" that limits my understanding of the self. The movies combat this limited understanding by means of the awareness made possible by watching as a creative act in which will disappears under the force of seeing.

*

In his *On the Advantage and Disadvantage of History for Life*, Nietzsche describes a herd of animals that are "enthralled by the moment and for that reason are neither melancholy nor bored." This is how we are when we enter into the film we are watching. Not that it is impossible to be bored *by* a film, but we are not bored when we are *in* it. (When our ability to be aware has been awoken by the movie). This is not self-conscious awareness: the awareness of ourselves being aware

(aware of ourselves as watchers of a movie), but an awareness so all-consuming we are not aware of ourselves as subjects performing the act of watching. Then we become *enthralled by the moment*. If there is a happiness in oblivion (and the human desire for drugs, daydreams, sleep and alcohol seems to suggest there is), this is it. The oblivion that does not raise self-consciousness but razes it.

*

Cinema is the night through which the Owl of Minerva flies, but it is not the wings that carry him.[157]

*

---

[157] "The moment has probably come to designate the crucial element toward which an obscure and uncertain search was directed, through the detours of the creation of forms of verbal invention. The great 'quest' of what has been given the poor name 'modern spirit' was certainly not obsessed with a 'grail' as easily accessible as the 'beautiful'; it distanced itself with distrust, and sometimes even with an ostentatious distrust, from all paths leading to the 'true,' and seemed to have only equivocal feelings about 'the good,' going from profound modesty to insulting rage, from affirmation to an equally trenchant negation. The conditions of the search were, moreover, obscurity and the limitless character of the goal that it had resolved to attain. Long torment and abrupt violence alone bore witness to the fundamental importance for all life of this 'quest' and its indeterminable object ... It is decisively important in this movement that the search, intellectually undertaken at the promptings of unsatisfied desire, has always preceded theory's delineation of the object sought. The belated intervention of discriminating intelligence certainly opened up a field of possibilities for empty error, whose extent became discouraging, but it is no less certain that an experience of this nature would not have been possible if some clairvoyant theory had tried to fix in advance its direction and its limits." –Georges Bataille, "The Sacred"

The most effective watching requires a certain kind of forgetting. We must forget we are watching—in effect *become one* with our own activity of watching so that we are no longer a subject (audience) performing a verb (watching) on an object (a movie). That grammatical structure must explode under the pressure of an entirely different logic. (Raúl Ruiz speaks of "a cinema capable of inventing a new grammar each time it goes from one world to the next.") The impossible logic of an audience who becomes the object of its own act of forgetting and thus relinquishes its agency. Watching is not passive, but neither is it active—it is a kind of forgetting beyond action. Awareness. A forgetting that carries us away to something we remember even as we experience it for the first time.

*

To be worthy of what we lose is the Supreme Aim- Emily Dickinson

And what we are trying to lose in the cinema is ourselves.

*

Sartre said that Hell is other people. In my work I have explored the possibility that Hell is an absence of Imagination. This is more than Hell on earth—this is the very possibility of Hell taking over our sense of Being. However, there is something paradoxical about this possibility, since Hell itself is one of the most powerful manifestations of the human imagination.

*

All film, in one sense or another, is about our relationship to death. When the movie begins, a world comes into being and that is a kind of birth. Everything that was born to life with the beginning of that movie dies 90 minutes later. Unless it lives on in our imagination. Perhaps that is why sequels and prequels and sequels of sequels (franchises) are so popular (from the Lone Ranger to *The Fast and the Furious*)—people don't want the characters they've grown attached to in the movies to die, and they don't want to bother with keeping them alive in their imaginations. They want the studios and the actors to do the work for them.

*

What does it mean when we ask whether or not *death* has a meaning? What kind of meaning? What do we *mean* when we ask about meaning in relation to death? Tolstoy remarked that death has no meaning for a *civilized* person. But perhaps one of the tasks of the movies is to restore us to that state of pre-civilized purity we associate with the enchantment of wonder. Before progress displaced wonder we were still subject to enchantment (of which Don Quixote is the greatest symbol in literature). If the movies can still enchant us, they can, despite their reliance on technology, restore us to wonder and free us from the chains of a belief in progress that renders Death meaningless.

*

Interviewer: Does the past explain the present?
John le Carré: No, these are ghosts that we must fight.

Interviewer: At what date did life cease being

incomprehensible for you?

le Carré: Oh, I think I may safely say that has never happened.

*

There is a difference between what I call imaginative fantasy and imaginative reality. John le Carré gave voice to this difference when he said, *I want people when they open my book and begin to read to feel, "God, this could be me!" When they are reading this other type of heroic book* [by Ian Fleming], *I think they are saying, "Oh, gosh, I wish this were me," and that is a sharp difference.* (Interview with Leigh Crutchley, 1966)

The filmmaker must be aware of this difference, and must decide from the outset what sort of film, and what sort of hero, he wants to create: a film of imaginative fantasy (from *James Bond* to *The Bourne Identity*) or a film of imaginative reality (virtually any of Bresson's works or the best of American cinema of the early 1970s). Both sorts of movie have their unique pleasures as well as what might be called their *aesthetic uses* (a peculiar form of utility). But they are different kinds of movies with different stakes associated with watching them.

*

Max Weber writes,

> Abraham or any other peasant of olden times died "old and fulfilled by life" [*Genesis* 25:8] because he was part of an organic life cycle, because in the evening of his days his life had given him whatever it had to offer and because there were no riddles he still wanted to solve.

Hence he could have "enough" of life. A civilized man, however, who is inserted into a never-ending process by which civilization is enriched with ideas, knowledge, and problems may become "tired of life," but not fulfilled by it. ("Science as Vocation")

It is this kind of elusive fulfillment I am trying to achieve when I make a film. I am trying to provide my audience with a glimpse of it, and I am trying to experience it myself through the process of making a movie. This experience is in large part a negative one: it is the freedom from idea, knowledge and problem, rather than the addition of yet more to the ever-growing pile.

*

A movie is not deemed a success or failure in terms of semantic accomplishment, but simply in terms of different forms of pleasure and frustration. Movies are not part of a dialectic unfolding. It is not that they are previous to or beyond dialectics, but that they are too naïve in their own pleasures to embrace the abstract sophistication of dialectics. This is why, ultimately, all psychoanalytic or semiotic "readings" of movies always seem somehow beside the point. Not necessarily wrong, but somehow not touching what we know is most important about the work.

*

Let the silence do its work.

*

Create your own legends, so long as you are not a part of them.

*

There is no film large enough to contain the entire world, but a successful film can be an intimate portrait of a single moment in the mind of its creator, which in many ways may be much larger than the entire world.

*

Beauty can be quiet and virtually still, so long as it moves the viewer. It need not shock, but it must animate.

*

In cinema there is no Truth with a capital T until there is Life with a capital L. It is that sense of life the camera must expose.

*

Walter Benjamin observed, "It is likely that no one ever masters anything in which he has not known impotence; and if you agree you will also see that this impotence comes not at the beginning of or before the struggle with the subject, but in the heart of it." This is how I have felt about my life as a filmmaker. None of my films have allowed me to satisfy the ambitions I brought to them as I was making them, but without each of their unique failures my life would have been much less than it is.

*

The gods remain mute. And yet we yearn to hear from them. If the movies cannot force them to speak, they will presume to speak for them. This would be an unforgivably audacious act of presumption, if not for the longing that inspired it.

*

Writing stimulates the imagination by means of the linguistic consciousness. Movies stimulate the imagination by means of the auditory and visual consciousness.

*

"A composer most usually creates parallel to the soundings of the inner ear—the primary thought of sounds; I, similarly, now work with the electric synapses of thought to achieve overall cathexis paradigms separate from but 'at one' with inner lights, The Light at source, of being human." –Stan Brakhage, "Influences"

*

Joyce boasted to a friend that he once spent an entire day working on a single sentence of *Ulysses*. But Brakhage has him beat. Describing a film he was making he wrote, *I've been working two years now and have three seconds done.*

*

"The camera is the eye of the marvelous. When the eye of the cinema really sees, the whole world goes up in flames." –Luis Buñuel

*

In filmmaking, the line between longing and despair should be almost impossible to distinguish.

*

In the modern age of secular materialist sybaritic hedonistic technocracy, nothing is more difficult to approach seriously in a work of art than the Sacred. The Scylla and Charybdis of this elusive quality is a vague mysticism on the one hand and saccharine self-satisfaction on the other. The only ship I have found that can sail between these two failures to approach the Sacred is an honest depiction of torment and despair. If a character, in his or her struggle with life, portrays a sincere relationship to despair, whether that is portrayed religiously as in Dostoevsky or comically as in Beckett, then the work can portray our yearning for the Sacred without sinking into flaccid vagueness or smug self-satisfaction.

Thus Antonio Porchia wrote, "I believe that the soul consists of its sufferings. For the soul that cures its sufferings dies" (*Voices*).

*

More and more often we watch movies alone, listen to music alone, read books alone. When we talk about these experiences it is in terms of our own personal reactions (our taste, our opinions, our insights and evaluations), not in terms of a communal activity. Art has become a private affair we write about or talk about, but rarely share. It takes place between us and the object (the book, the painting, the song or the movie), not between us and other people. This inability to engage in shared aesthetic experience has impoverished our notions of what the life of the Spirit might be. Spirit has become a personal matter where once it was the very essence of community.

*

The movies occupy a complex dialectic in terms of their relationship to the rational. In one sense, they are wholly dependent on the technology which makes their physical existence a possibility; a technology which itself is wholly dependent on the accomplishments of scientific rationalism. On the other hand, the ambitions of the movies are beyond rationalism and beyond materialism. As with all art forms, their plastic limitations strain against their spiritual ambitions.

*

If life poses us with irrational questions, what good are rational answers? This is why the cinema, although tied to the strict rationality of its technical means of production, must constantly reach beyond rationality and beyond technology if it is to provide any sort of meaningful response to the challenges we face in simply being alive. The movies are not irrational, but they strive to be transrational. Movies take place in a *surrational* realm beyond the appearances of mere physical reality. (Plato with a movie camera.) Since all film is fundamentally illusion, from what better place are we likely to be able to access the truth about the illusory quality of all appearance posing as reality?

*

Reason is the enemy of all greatness: reason is the enemy of nature: nature is great, reason is small. I mean that it will be more or less difficult for a man to be great the more he is governed by reason, that few can be great (and in art and poetry perhaps no one) unless they are governed by illusions.

–Leopardi, *Zibaldone* 15

*

"Does Death have a meaning?" (Weber asked.) What makes things meaningful is our ability to value them; either to find value in them or to place value in them. Man is the axiological being. Axiology is an aesthetic phenomenon. If we ask, "what is the meaning of meaning (of our need for meaning)?" we are not asking a philosophical question, but an aesthetic one. A question, therefore, for the movies.

*

"Release from the rationalism and intellectualism of science is the fundamental premise of life in communion with the Divine." –Max Weber

*

There is no monotheistic cinema. The movies, even the most radically Christian of them, are always fundamentally polytheistic. No one deity can contain all the possibilities of the cinema. It is no coincidence that India, the nation of the richest polytheism in the world, is also the country that produces the most movies. And after that, the United States, the country that has erected and pursued more idols than any other.

*

"My soul is not a soul, it is a conflagration." –Malcolm Lowry

"Can I take fire from so benign an ash?" –Wallace Stevens

*

When we ask about "the meaning of life," or "the meaning of Death" (which may be the same thing), we need to go back to the fundamental question: What do we mean by *meaning*? What is meaning? When we tell a story, do we want to know what the story means? But that's what a story is: the imposition of meaning on events in the world. In contrast, think of the physical landscapes in David Lynch's *Eraserhead* or of the words that make up Gertrude Stein's *Tender Buttons*—here meaning is something quite different, if it is present at all.

Here meaning is not the answer to a question, but a way of asking it.

*

"In fact I cannot totally grasp all that I am. Thus the mind is not large enough to contain itself: but where can that part of it be which it does not contain?" –Augustine, *Confessions*

In other words: where do ideas come from? Do they come *from* the imagination, or *to* it? When we work to cultivate the imagination, are we trying to develop a productive faculty or a receptive one? Despite all our recent advances in the fields of biology, chemistry and cognitive science, the fact is we really don't know *where* an idea comes from, or how it is even *possible* to "have an idea" in the first place. What kind of "having" is this?

"The mind is not large enough to contain itself." This itself is among the most fascinating ideas that have occurred to the mind. But how was the mind capable of thinking it?

*

Why do self-forgetting, loss of control, and oblivion so often feel like forms of pleasure? I am enlightened every moment of the day during which I am content not to be myself. It is only when I insist on clinging to the illusion of my own sense of self that enlightenment retreats.

*

At first I thought life would be much easier after I achieved enlightenment—to live like a Bodhisattva among men, I thought to myself—but then I realized that being enlightened did not mean I no longer got hungry when I didn't eat, or no longer grew cold in winter, or even that I no longer became angry or impatient or frustrated when the circumstances of the world conspired against me. I began to wonder if in fact I had achieved enlightenment at all. But of course I had. I merely had to remember that even enlightened beings inhabit the world. We are all embodied beings, until we pass beyond.

I realized that being enlightened is not a matter of never again becoming cold, hungry, angry or impatient. It is merely a question of how we respond to these states when they rise up in us. It is a matter of observing them as phenomena rather than of being controlled by them. It has been my work as a filmmaker, more than anything, that has taught me how to become an observer, even of myself. Observing, in this sense, becomes a form of self-knowledge.

*

When Gertrude Stein remarked to Picasso that the portrait he had painted of her did not look like her, he replied, "don't worry, it will." So too with the camera—use it not to capture the objects as you see them, but as they will appear once the reality of the film has brought them to life.

*

Film is not a language, but a way of speaking the languages of sound and image.

*

I believe that the inner needs of a human being with the "music" of religion in his veins will never be served if the fundamental fact that his fate is to live in an age alien to God and bereft of prophets is hidden from him and others by surrogates in the shape of all the professorial prophets. The integrity of his religious sensibility must surely rise up in rebellion against this.

—Max Weber, "Science as Vocation"

Weber recognizes that this "music of religion" flows through the veins of some of us, but not of others. It is not a choice we make, but something we are born with. Or without. What do we do about this fact? Weber speaks of man's "inner needs," but we do not all have the same needs. The music of religion (the cinema of the soul) is not like food or oxygen.

Those who turn to the movies not for the comfort of false prophets but to reveal and explore the hidden truths of the human condition are looking for something quite different from those who seek entertainment, pleasure, distraction, and a surrogate to religion in the mysteries of the cinema. In the modern world it is embarrassing to speak of our spiritual needs (we have equated need with weakness) and commonplace to extoll the gratification of our desires (we have equated the ability to gratify a desire with strength and power). But when this leads to an inability to confront the reality of our inner needs or the impulse to turn from them in shame, we do not free ourselves from them but merely resign ourselves to leaving them unfulfilled.

In order not to appear weak, needy, vague, soft-headed, sentimental or blinded by wishful thinking, we find it better to scoff at the very notion of the soul than to devote to it our most serious and earnest thought and effort. In today's world, better a hedonist or a biological materialist than a mystic; this is taken for honesty: the denial of anything we do not have the currency to pay for.

*

If it's not in frame, it doesn't exist, Elias Merhige has his imagined version of F. W. Murnau (John Malkovich) say in

Shadow of the Vampire. This is more than an imagined version of Murnau's attitude toward film. For certain filmmakers questions of ontology are always subsumed under the creative rubric of the metaphysics of cinema. Or simply of the camera.

*

Weber observes, "Our age is characterized by rationalization and intellectualization, and above all, by the disenchantment of the world." Cinema's task is to help restore this sense of enchantment, as Don Quixote did in the lives of those he met along his journey riding out from La Mancha. Enchantment (a form of the power of the Imagination) is the great theme of Cervantes' novel. Film pursues the idea that philosophy not only begins in wonder, but should strive to end there as well; it should not resolve the mystery (by answering the questions it rises in response to), but celebrate it (by deepening our asking of them). Philosophy as a phenomenon of the cinema.

*

Instead of asking whether the cinema can be philosophic, why not insist on a cinematic philosophy? Instead of measuring everything by its own unquestioned yardstick and centuries old rubric, what if philosophy were to challenge itself to *be* something different, to *do* something different. What if the activity of philosophy itself were radically re-envisioned?

*

When I think back to my work as a writer, I realize that the struggles I had with language were every bit as collaborative as the struggles I have now with other human beings as a filmmaker (with editors, cinematographers, sound engineers, lighting specialists, actors). Language too played a role in shaping and influencing my vision, in revealing to me what was possible and in challenging me to confront the impossible. So in that sense, writing is every bit as much a collaboration, although done in solitude, as making a movie is.

*

My movies come as much from the process of working with people as they do from the interior vision of my own mind. After all, what is that mind? Not a black box. Not a closed system. It is a mystery, even to me. One mystery at work trying to create, through its collisions with other mysteries, a new mystery altogether. This is a good description of what making a movie is like.

*

When I was still writing, my ambition was to write a book that the reader would constantly be tempted to put down, but somehow not quite be able to. I wanted every page to hold the reader on that border between boredom and suspense, tedium and anticipation, so that she would be driven nearly mad from the almost excruciating act of reading, and yet nevertheless not be able to lay the book aside. Pleasure, pain, and provocation in equal measures.

I believe something similar can be accomplished by the movies. In the extraordinary beauty and tedium of Bela

Tarr's *The Turin Horse* for example.

*

There is a particular relationship between the boring and the beautiful that I have not yet fathomed. But I know it's there. Boring things are often beautiful, but the moment we realize their beauty we cease being bored by them. This is because the boredom lies in us, not in the thing itself. If the object succeeds in carrying us outside ourselves the boredom disappears at the same time we do. To be replaced by what?

*

For me, working on a movie is something like prayer—an intensely private affair. Therefore, it is surprising (to me at least) that when I am done with the work something intended for public consumption has been produced. Perhaps it is more like going to church than prayer. (Is this why there have been a number of great Catholic filmmakers, but fewer interesting Catholic novelists or poets?) The public manifestation of a private impulse. The sharing of that impulse with a like-minded (or like-spirited) community.

*

On the skeptical cinema. The skeptic is not a denier, but a questioner, a seeker—one who *wants* to know, not one who denies the possibility of knowing. In this sense, the cinema is a tool of skepticism.

*

The resemblance between dissimilar objects. Are there metaphors in cinema? Symbols? No doubt the Freudian critic has a great deal to say about Terry's caged birds in *On the Waterfront*, just as the Marxist has much to say about the plight of the dockworkers and the feminist critic reads significance into Edie's collapse against the wall under the force (passion) of Terry's kiss. (This is how Zizek "reads" much of Hitchcock: through the lenses of Freudian and Marxist concepts of repression and alienation, desire and power, analysis and ideology; he imposes readings on the movie, finding evidence for the presence of nothing more than what he has brought with him.) As a filmmaker, I am interested not in these "vocabularies" (symbols) of the cinema but in the power of certain images—in the gold of Edie's hair captured on black and white film and by the cut of her negligee and the fur on the collar of her brother's jacket. Not the Freudian or economic signifying power of the jacket throughout the film (its symbolic value) but its sensual and aesthetic weight. The symbols in the movie—birds, grappling hooks, the jacket, the guns—are less interesting as symbols (which point outside the movie) than they are as objects that constitute the sensual world these characters live in (pointing to the movie's interior, and perhaps to our own).

*

Frame by frame, the movies frames. The movie frames the act of experiencing it, and thus frames experience itself, drawing attention to the experience of experiencing and thus lifting the act of experiencing out of time. Ironically, the careful attention demanded by the movie's frames, carefully crafted and aesthetically staged, resists the *enframing* Heidegger associates with technology. In its place experience of the frame frames our experience as aesthetic subjects. We are aware of ourselves as taking part in something—as being a part of something that is not the work of art itself (for we are not a part of the movie we watch), but something the work of art reveals to us. The movie, in this instance, functions with the power Heidegger attributes to certain poems (by Trakl, Hölderlin, Rilke).

*

Parker Tyler, in his thoughtfully revealing "Hollywood's Surrealist Eye" (1944), calls the movie camera "a kind of monster capable of projecting marvels" and "the very soul of the cinematic medium." The camera is a piece of technology that "retains permanently the faculty of creating the wonderful" and thus leaves its status as technology behind because it enters (and allows us to enter) the wonderful. The wonderful is that which sets itself up against the powers of disenchantment, as rife in the modern world as they were during the time of Don Quixote.

Deprived of the movie theatre, Quixote had to make up his own movies, conceived in his head but played out in the world around him, with every person he encountered (including priests, prisoners, and hapless barbers) a potential extra in his drama. Perhaps he was better off. His experience at Gines de Pasamonte's puppet show suggests that too often the creative figure makes a poor audience for another artist's work.

*

Tyler observes, "the beauty of the camera may seem most eloquent just when its material is most incongruous and trivial." (A fact Bresson was a master of exploiting.) He bemoans the fact that we do not "measure our enjoyment by equating the effect of the physical mode with that of the spiritual and emotional mode." The power of the camera when it speaks in the language of small things seen. Not the plot, the action, and the character portrayals in Elia Kazan's *On the Waterfront*, but the shot glass raised to Edie Doyle's lips or the scar over Terry Malone's right eye. Not the heroism (laugh at it if you will, especially in light of Kazan's dark political compromises) of Terry's final lurching walk up the dock, but the cuff of his trousers, revealing the top of his dockworker's boots.

*

The danger of the overwhelming power of movies today is that too often "looking" is absent from "watching." The best movies are part of the process by which we learn to see when we look. Looking is active; watching passive. We must be alert to the distinction between cinema's power to educate our vision and its ability to shape and form our tastes and expectations. It's aesthetic power versus its ideological power. These two are inseparable from one another, but pull in opposite directions.

*

The audacity of vision.

Certain films are nearly always theological statements.

Sensuous immutability of the sign.

*

If a film achieved the status of a great piece of music, we would not ask, "What is it about?"

*

> Ideas, meaning-structures that are produced in individual persons and have the miraculous new way of containing intentional infinities within themselves, are not like real things in space... –Husserl, "The Vienna Lecture"

Husserl's "are produced" is a great mystery and a telling use of the passive voice. What produces these ideas? Where do they come from, and how do they come to us? Do we receive them, like some sort of divine gift, or do we produce them? Even planets and stars are produced from the cosmic dust that fills the universe. How do we gather the cosmic dust that becomes our ideas?

In Husserl's sense, movies are a kind of idea brought into motion through the arts of representation. They do not so much exist "in space" as they bring a new conception of space into being along with their creation. They are the result of those "intentional infinities" we associate with human acts of creation.

*

The Grammar of Cinema. Spiritual movies are made almost entirely out of nouns, especially faces and the objects that make up landscapes (as one might call the features of a person's face the landscape of that face). Such landscapes are a combination of light and shadow.

Entertaining movies are made almost entirely of verbs. The best movies are both spiritual and entertaining and harmoniously bring nouns and verbs together. Adjectives are unnecessary in movies because of the power of the human face to show us what cannot be said and of objects to present themselves as they are (which is indeterminate outside of the phenomenological act of seeing).

*

Art and entertainment both give the audience something; but art provides its audience with something that entertainment does not, and that is the opportunity to be more than simply an audience.

*

The Drunken Lord. When watching a movie is a kind of meditation and a holding of one's self in the timelessness of a perpetual present, it requires the kind of concentration that at the same time is an effortless forgetfulness. It is a particular form of trying. Where is the effort? We must be unaware of it, but it must be constantly present.

*

It has become popular, since the valuable work of Balazs and Bazin, to speak of a *film language*—a language we can enrich ourselves by learning the particular grammar and vocabulary of. But in fact film is not a language, because, with the exception of the filmmaker, it is not something we speak, but something we experience. In this sense it is more like a text than a language. And as a text, we must learn, not how to speak it, but how to read it. And more importantly, how to inhabit it. Of course it also makes sense to speak of "inhabiting a language" or "being inhabited by the language we speak" (this sounds vaguely Wittgensteinian), but to call film a language is merely a metaphor. Of course language itself is "merely a metaphor," and nothing is more complex, linguistically, that to be a metaphor, so perhaps in this sense it is correct to speak of film as a language after all.

*

Where does the reality of a movie reside—in its images, or in our memory of them? Ask yourself what you remember about a film after you've seen it: an hour after you've seen it; a week after you've seen it; a year after you've seen it. Is Tomas Alfredson's *Let the Right One In* shot in black and white or color? Why can't I remember? Because of the snow? How does a movie change after the second, third, or fourth viewing? Do we remember more of it each time, or does our memory simply change with each new viewing? (Or does the movie change because of our earlier memories of it?)

*

The complete history of the world has been recorded in a book, and that book is the world itself, whose author is God. Movies are images of this book, which simultaneously contain the whole of it while representing only a part of it.

*

What is sacred if not the desperate imagination—the imagination made desperate by our overwhelming need to find or impose meaning on the world around us?

*

The greatest theological question is not whether or not God exists but whether God is rational.

*

Are man, nature, and the universe fundamentally rational or irrational? Will all things ultimately submit to rational, law-based explanations, or are there non-reducible things in the universe (consciousness, quantum phenomenon, the relation of gravity to space and time) that will never be explained in rational (that is, scientific and material) terms?

Theologically, this question is even more fundamental than the question of whether or not God exists. For after all, even if we knew that a God did exist, we would still have to wonder if this God were a rational (as human beings understand rationality) or an irrational Being. Theologians have struggled to understand the mysteries of God's justice, but justice itself follows from a certain form of rational thought. If God is not rational, as we understand rationality, what would it mean to speak of his justice? Love, on the other hand, is not rational. Is this why it is easier to associate God with Love than with Justice?

*

Superficially, it appears that the universe is rational—objects from electrons to planets seem to obey predictable laws. But it turns out that upon inspection these laws are mere probabilities. It is only statistically likely that an electron will jump from one energy state to another, or that a planet will continue in its orbit. Of course even probability itself may prove to be governed by strictly rational laws. Gravity looks like a law independent of statistical probability, but we don't understand what gravity is, how it works, or how it is related to other forces in the universe, like electricity or magnetism. At bottom, the functioning of the universe is a vast mystery to which the laws of probability give the appearance of rational predictability. But what if behind these laws lies a vast chaos of unpredictable chance, hazard, and non-rational whim?

"What if"? What would the discovery of such a "fact" (the fact that facts themselves are only an illusion) change about the way we live or lives? Very little. Filmmakers would still make movies and people would still go to see them. In other words, all the important things about the world would go on unchanged.

*

The Christians and their philosophers and theologians, from Aquinas to Hegel, have assumed that God is rational; that he is capable of sharing (indeed responsible for instilling in us) our concepts of "justice", "right and wrong", and "good and evil." The Christian believes that God holds certain values in common with mankind because it is from God that we get these values. But how do we know that God is rational? If there is evidence for his rationality in the careful ordering of the cosmos and in the existence of supposedly universal laws, there is also evidence to the contrary in the life of man. Man asserts his irrationality at every turn. And was he not created in the image of his God?

*

The rationalist says, "The world is a rational place," but he has no absolutely rational grounds for this assertion (because there's no final evidence to prove the claim; there's only a pile of evidence that looks like it suggests it *might* be true). The *surrationalist* says, "The world is not a rational place." And paradoxically that *is* a rational claim because it doesn't draw final conclusions from the presence of limited evidence.

The rationalist is irrational because from local and specific evidence he draws general and universal conclusions about the way the world is. The surrationalist is rational because he acknowledges the local evidence for specific forms of rationality but does not leap to the conclusion that therefore everything in "the world" will necessarily behave the same way.

The filmmaker who sees the world in strictly rational terms will always be limited in terms of the kind of movies he can make. The surrational filmmaker will always seek to work on the edge of a disaster that just might lead to a great triumph.

*

I am not talking about Surrealism, or the subconscious, or the unconscious. The surrational realm is the realm of the Unsubconscious, not the realm of dreams (where we go when we dream), but the realm from which dreams come to us. Or perhaps where they might lead us.

Experiments in automatic writing are useful in showing us how active a role the subconscious plays in our aesthetic productions, but they remain experiments. A movie cannot stop at being "experimental." It must be fully executed.

*

"While it is true that commercial art is always in danger of ending up as a prostitute, it is equally true that noncommercial art is always in danger of ending up as an old maid." –Erwin Panofsky, "Style and Medium in the Motion Pictures"

*

Tarkovsky observes, "people are limited in their capacity for knowing the world by the organs of the senses that nature has given them"; this is surely true on one level and explains why the cinema tries to engage as many of those senses as possible. But the most important faculty engaged by the cinema is the imagination. The imagination allows us to experience a form of "knowing the world" that goes beyond these organs. In fact it is the only means by which we can go beyond and expand the realm of the senses and their limits.

As Lewis Carroll knew, in addition to the "organs of the senses" there is the "organ of non-sense", and this organ in particular is often associated with the activity of the imagination.

*

Woody Allen is to cinema what John Updike is to fiction. Despite some early successes (or perhaps because of them), their work quickly devolved into rather unfortunate self-parody. They are both practitioners of a kind of pseudo-serious work that strives for intellectual popularity—works that pander to the worst aspects of our self-important intellectualism; works that make us feel smart for being cynical and indulge an obsession with the contortions of our own egos. Artists who create such works incrementally debase the genre in which they work until its potential has been impaired through the ravages of their ambition. Not that there is anything wrong with the egocentrism or ambition of an artist—but when the ambition is for something mediocre the whole art form suffers. The barbarians are always at the gates. Some artists choose to entertain them.

*

Updike and Allen fail to understand that the courage of self-exposure through the dramatization of one's own insecurities and delusions of grandeur in itself does not amount to art. If it did, there would be far more good poets in high school.

*

> Whether we like it or not, it is the movies that mold, more than any other single force, the opinions, the taste, the language, the dress, the behavior, and even the physical appearance of a public comprising more than 60 percent of the population of the earth ... If all the serious lyrical poets, composers, painters and sculptors were forced by law to stop their

activities, a rather small fraction of the general public would become aware of the fact and a still smaller fraction would seriously regret it. If the same thing were to happen with the movies the social consequences would be catastrophic.

–Erwin Panofsky, "Style and Medium in
the Motion Pictures" (1934)

*

Does it take courage to express sympathy for the Mystic and Divine in a world of rational materialism? No, because if one feels the presence of such things in the world around us (and therefore beyond that world as well) then one has no choice but to confront those feelings and try to understand them, even to give them expression (perhaps through works of art). Not to do so would be like not shivering when you feel cold.

*

In film, just because something isn't true doesn't mean it's false. In the realms of art, these alternatives don't exhaust the possibilities of being.

*

How does human consciousness perceive phenomena? The filmmaker doesn't need to ask himself this question. He doesn't require an answer in order to practice his craft (doesn't need a cognitive theory in order to work). But the question lurks behind every assumption he makes which allows him to make a movie.

*

Because the entire world and all phenomena are a painting, human existence appears from a painting, and Buddha ancestors are actualized from a painting. Since this is so, there is no remedy for satisfying hunger other than a painted rice-cake.

–Dōgen, *Gabyo*

The movies are a painted rice-cake.

*

How do we see, without allowing the preconditions of thought to interfere with our vision?

*

There is a difference between thinking *about* film and thinking in the wake of an experience of film. One is the thought we bring to bear on a film; the other is the thought made possible by the film.

*

Regardless of the genre (Western, mystery, action, comedy, romance), there are works of art made from the perspective of conviction, and works of art made from a position of extreme doubt and uncertainty. And this doubt encompasses everything, from the artist to the world around him. The work of doubt is something quite different from the work of conviction. Two Westerns, for example, may have less in common with each other, if one is a work of doubt and the other a work of conviction, than a Western and a romance if they are both works of doubt or both works of conviction.

*

The idea of personifying Death as a kind of literary character, some *one* (rather than some *thing*) that haunts humanity, but who can be argued with, bargained with, (engaged in a game of chess with), perhaps even interceded with, appeals to me. I like the old fashioned images of Death cloaked in black rags leaning on his scythe, his claw-like hand extending from his tattered sleeve to beckon with one bony finger that cannot be avoided or denied. When the time comes, all must heed the call. And yet I like to imagine to myself the arguments I might have with Death if I were given a chance.

*

Poetry is born of insecurity, wrote Sandor Krasna to his unnamed correspondent. Is this why I have sometimes thought of my whole life as a kind of poem?

*

The question of whether the Sacred is something unique to each of us, or whether it is necessarily the one thing that all of us must share (must be capable of sharing) is one I have taken up repeatedly in my films.

*

If the book of the world teaches us all that we need to learn, how can it help but render all other books superfluous? Cinema, which is nothing but a photocopy of the book of the world, renders not just other books but perhaps all other art unnecessary.

–Raúl Ruiz, "For a Shamanic Cinema"

Ruiz said of *Poetics of Cinema* that it was written for those who use the cinema "as an instrument of speculation and reflection, or as a machine for travel through space and time." And perhaps not only *through* time and space, but beyond them as well. For a movie is better than a time machine—it not only allows us to travel through time, a movie can create time. Movies unfold in dimensions all their own; their two dimensional projection in space and their 90-120-minute duration in time in no way limit the full extent of their existence, for they occupy imaginary space and time as well.

*

What is God's relation to chaos? (A question for filmmakers.)

*

His dark materials. Can the filmmaker illuminate them?

*

A movie can either restore us to a primal state of daydreaming, or it can replace that state with a kind of ersatz fantasy that overruns the imagination and narcotizes it. Movies should show us enough to stimulate the faculty of daydreaming, not overwhelm it. Simply put, movies should make us dream; otherwise they are simply replacing our dreams with something else. The conclusion we should draw from this is that the activity of watching a movie does not end when the movie ends. In so far as our facility for dreaming has been quickened, the activity of "going to the movies" begins in earnest only when the film is over. The movie exists in its most potent state as a kind of memory, stimulating our imagination. While we are watching it, we are storing up for these future experiences.

*

By the end of the 20th century the movies had become so familiar that we no longer doubted our right to them, nor our ability to understand (and thus judge and evaluate) them immediately and intuitively, without effort. Therefore, the idea that movies were a form of art that demanded (and deserved) a particular kind of effort was lost within the first few decades of their existence. This is the price they paid for their immediate success and immense popularity. The more we loved them, the more we presumed that they possessed a kind of absolute accessibility. Until, despite their indisputable magic, they lost all sense of that effort in response to mystery that other forms of art more obviously demand.

So enervated have certain muscles of the creative imagination become as a result of the easy pleasures we associate with watching movies that learning how to *see* what we have grown accustomed to merely watching is more difficult than ever.

*

Talking about the movies. When we tell what a movie is about—when we retell the story or describe the film to a companion—we are doing something very different from what we do when we recount the plot of a novel. In the latter case we are moving from the written word to spoken words and our own words are a pale reflection of the words that are the very being of the writing itself. But when we convert our experience (our memory, interpretation, reaction, pleasure or dislike) of a film into words, we are performing an act of transformation. We *say* what we *saw* and *heard*, and transform images and sounds into words. We transform time and space into language. This act of description is always revealing, for there is no neutral seeing, and certainly no act of neutral *saying* about what we have *seen*. Therefore, even the plainest retelling of a movie reveals something not only about the film, but about our experience as watchers as well.

*

In the movies only the present tense exists. No matter how many years or centuries, worlds or galaxies are traversed within the film, for the viewer the movie unfolds in a perpetual present. When the movie is over we are an hour or two older, but in that hour a lifetime has passed, and we have been carried forward not from one moment to the next but on a perpetual and ever self-renewing wave of *Now*.

*

Personal density is directly related to temporal bandwidth. "Temporal bandwidth" is the width of your present, your *now*. It is the familiar "Δt" considered as a dependent variable. The more you dwell in the past and the future, the thicker your bandwidth, the more solid your persona. But the narrower your sense of Now, the more tenuous you are.

–Thomas Pynchon, *Gravity's Rainbow*

The goal of the movies is to make us as tenuous as possible. The unreality of the movies shows us something about the reality of Time & Space. In this reality selfhood is an illusion we are trying to overcome, a nightmare (as Joyce said about history) from which we are trying to awake.

*

If we are happy when we are at the movies ("at the movies" a spatial metaphor for a temporal experience that removes us from both time and space), it is that particular form of atemporal happiness that does not suffer awareness to taint it. As Nietzsche describes it:

> With the smallest as with the greatest happiness ... there is always one thing which makes it happiness: being able to forget, or to express it in a more learned fashion, the capacity to live *unhistorically* while it endures. (*On the Advantages and Disadvantages of History for Life*)

Among the various gifts given to us by the movies one of the greatest is that of forgetting: to forget everything except the movie that has drawn us inside itself, that has taken over Time & Space and has relieved us, temporarily, of the onerous burden of being self-aware.

*

Only ghosts watch TV. We are citizens of worlds that do not exist. The Princeton Plainsboro of *House*; Portwenn of *Doc Martin*; Harlan, Kentucky of *Justified*; Sunnydale of *Buffy*; Baltimore of *The Wire*; New Orleans of *Treme*; The Village of *The Prisoner* are simultaneously real and fictional places. When we watch, we are inhabitants of these places, but we never really go there. We're ghosts who haunt their environs, living among their citizens without really living. We live peripherally—we are not another of the characters who inhabit these TV shows but neither are we merely ourselves while we watch them. We are no one. Free from identity but somehow still involved.

In the moment of watching, we are no one at all. We are the divine observer, like God looking down on his creation. Only better than God, because although we may judge (indeed it is one of the great pleasures of watching), we do not carry out the sentence (unless we terminate the program by turning off the TV). We are not the creators of the worlds we watch and therefore we can observe without the burden of responsibility for what we're seeing.

*

"Why would I want to make a movie when I can spend my time watching them?" –Anonymous Moviegoer

The movies have no creator. We can point to the producers, the writers, the director, the editor, the cameraman, the actors, and set designers, the casting agent, and the different members of the technical crews, and say, *they brought this into being*. But in fact the movie emerged as if magically from their collective efforts. A movie, being greater than the sum of its parts, can never simply be created, any more than the author who writes a poem can take credit for inventing the language in which it was written. He can only take partial credit for the magic of the poem. A movie is a magical entity, and as its audience we participate in this magic. Indeed, perhaps the magic only exists for us, free from the behind-the-scenes pettiness, intrigue, compromises, strife, and frustrations that were also part of its creation. (Creation without a creator—like the world itself?)

*

No matter how sophisticated they are, movies provide us with an opportunity to return to the state of being children—the purest, and also the most dangerous of conditions; the one full of the most possibilities, and therefore also of the greatest risks.

*

Renoir, Kurosawa, Bergman—great directors who start their autobiographies with accounts of their childhoods. Why should people who care about the movies be interested in the childhoods of people who make movies? For one simple reason: childhood itself is like the movies. As Bergman writes:

The prerogative of childhood is to move unhindered between magic and oatmeal porridge, between boundless terror and explosive joy. There were no boundaries except prohibitions and regulations, which were shadowy, mostly incomprehensible. For instance, I know I did not grasp the concept of time. *You really must learn to be punctual. You've been given a watch and you know how to tell the time.* But time ceased to exist... (*The Magic Lantern: An Autobiography*)

This is what going to the movies is like. Time ceases to exist. There are no boundaries (except those prohibitions and regulations against which it is the job of the artist to strive, and beyond which it is the task of the movie to carry us). We move unhindered. We are children, not again, but still.

*

I cannot repeat too often: the cinema should be an education in seeing, and since seeing is a form of experience, learning how to see more is a means of increasing the realm of one's experience. So cinema itself is an increase in experience.

*

The Final Truth. Just as the purpose of all religions is ultimately to free us from religion and deliver us over to a realm of higher spirituality, so is the purpose of all cinema to free us from the movies and yield us up to the power of our own imagination, where we might dwell as part of the greatest movie never made—the one never filmed that exists in us as we exist within it.

*

Film is fire and shadow, light and dark, an invention of the 19th century that stems from the very dawn of time.[158]

*

Diaries, movies, and mysticism all share a common question—what is reality? What is "real life" or the truth about that life? The metaphysics of cinema. The poetics of a life recorded. If movies are an image of human life, if a diary is a record of that life, then mysticism asks, what if life itself were only an image of something else? What would that "something else" be?

*

---

[158] It can be said that a person who is fascinated does not perceive any real object, any real form, because what he sees does not belong to the world of reality, but to the indeterminate realm of fascination. A realm that is so to speak absolute. Distance is not excluded from it, but it is excessive, being the unlimited depth that lies behind the image, a depth that is not alive, not tractable, absolutely present though not provided, where objects sink when they become separated from their meaning, when they subside into their image. This realm of fascination, where what we see seizes our vision and makes it interminable, where our gaze solidifies into light, where light is the absolute sheen of an eye that we do not see, that we nevertheless do not leave off seeing because it is the mirror image of our own gaze, this realm is supremely attractive, fascinating: light that is also the abyss, horrifying and alluring, light in which we sink." –Maurice Blanchot, "The Essential Solitude"

For when man understands, he extends his mind to comprehend things; but when he does not understand, he makes them out of himself and, by transforming himself, becomes them.

–Giambattista Vico, *The New Science*

Description of the filmmaker: a man who does not understand. Or, as Jean-Pierre Melville said, "a man constantly open, constantly traumatizable." Art as a kind of trauma. Or sometimes, a form of triage.

*

The movies are a kind of poetry, and "the proper subject of poetry is a believable impossibility" (Vico, *The New Science*).

*

Newton called mathematics the language spoken by God in his creation and regulation of the universe. Film is the language in which man strives to imitate the God he needs to believe in; a God who not only created but continues to care about his creation. When we watch a movie it reflects, shapes, and guides our desires—we want to see evidence of justice, love, and the possibility of redemption in the fate of the characters we watch. We want good things to happen to the characters we like and bad things happen to the characters we dislike. In the movies we play out our fantasies about the existence of a God we despair of finding evidence for anywhere else. And this is nowhere more true than in those movies that superficially deny God most explicitly; those movies which appear, on the surface, to be wholly and entirely "of and about this world." These movies depend on our superstitious fantasies about God as much as or more than any others.

*

How do the images in a film reach out from within the world of the film to draw us in and make us a part of it?

"Your film's beauty will not be in the images (postcardism) but in the ineffable that they will disengage." –Robert Bresson

If I were a critic, I would want to write about the beauty of movies, not about their meaning.

*

All movies should be ghost movies—not horror movies, but haunting movies.

*

After the philosopher has asked, "Why is there something rather than nothing?" the filmmaker steps in to show that *if* there *is* anything then there must *be* everything. (Even if that "being" is part of an illusion.)

*

Art and violence. Film analysis is fundamentally violent to the work it examines. Movies are made to be watched in the amount of time in which it takes them to unfold on the screen before us. When we watch them scene-by-scene, pausing the image to linger over its details, and scrutinizing certain moments over and over again, we are subjecting the work of art to a particular form of violence that masquerades under the name of appreciation. On the other hand, the unity and coherence of the work of art is itself a masquerade. The artists who produced the film lingered with minute care over the details of every shot and scene. What appears, in the final product, as a smooth and natural flow of events is a carefully constructed and artificial whole. For art by its very nature is always artificial. The techniques we employ, not when watching, but when analyzing a film (not unlike the techniques we employ when we analyze a poem: counting its syllables, identifying its meter and rhyme scheme, looking up alternate meanings of its words, lingering over the relationship between its sounds and images, paying especial attention to its structure and form) are equally unnatural, but for that very reason are equally true to the nature of our aesthetic experience. If our goal is to deepen that experience, and to allow it to enrich our encounter with the work, then violence is a necessary part of that encounter.

*

There is no so thing as neutral watching. There is something like a quantum effect at work when we read a book or watch a movie, for the act of reading/watching transforms the object of our attention, just as the act of paying attention has the potential to change us. We are never simply the subjects who perform the act of watching; we are the objects of that act as well.

*

Other seeing. When it comes to watching movies, our seeing is not natural. We have been trained, over time, by the very movies we watch, in how to see them. Early audiences did not understand, instinctively, effects like the close-up or certain editing choices. The notion of narrative continuity depends on an audience's ability to understand how cuts that shift our attention from one time and place to another work. How do we know, when a cut takes us from a room to an exterior shot, what has just happened in the film? This is not something our own visual experience in the world can have taught us, for we have never experienced such a thing "in the world," but only in the cinema. Outside of the movies, we cannot shift our point of view so suddenly or radically. In fact, outside of the movies we are always confined to our own point of view. We can turn our heads, look out a window, close our eyes. But the camera commands a far greater range of possibilities than this. When we watch a movie, we see not as people do, but as the camera has taught us how to see while looking at the screen. This is a wholly other kind of seeing. We are so used to certain conventions of the cinema by now, in terms of cuts, editing, camera angle, the close-up and other techniques, that when these conventions are violated we feel that something unnatural has occurred. But there was nothing natural to violate here in the first place. Only our expectations have been defied, and these are precisely what the movies should be cautious about showing too much respect for in the first place.

*

In constructing a tragic plot there is only one rule: give them a ray of light, that it may be extinguished.

*

"The film can be a true art because in it the author takes fragments of reality and arranges them in such a way that their juxtaposition transforms them." –Bresson, *Notes on the Cinematographer*

"Cinema is the one art form where the author can see himself as the creator of an unconditioned reality, quite literally of his own world. In cinema man's innate drive to self-assertion finds one of its fullest and most direct means of realization. A film is an emotional reality, and that is how the audience receives it—*as a second reality*." –Tarkovsky, *Sculpting in Time*

"I found myself asking: How could film be art, since all the major arts arise in some way out of religion? Now I can answer: Because movies arise out of magic, from below the world." –Stanley Cavell, *The World Viewed*

*

Increasingly, "going to the movies" has become a private experience. We watch alone, perhaps in our bedrooms (even in our beds). We have our own private screens. We pause, rewind, freeze a frame. We can skip over (as we sometimes do when we read). Furthermore, we can *own* the work of art. Just as we can own a copy of a novel, or a recording of Beethoven's *Quartets*, or a print of a favorite painting. Ownership of the work of art changes our relationship to that work. (A movie that costs tens of millions to make can be owned for a few dollars.) The *experience* of watching a movie has entered the realm of the private. Eventually this dislocation of the cinematic experience from the public (the theatre) to the private (from the home entertainment system to the personal screen we control or our phone or tablet) will change not only the way we watch movies, but the kind of movies that are being made.

*

"A half-baked idea like humanity," Zukofsky said in his essay on Chaplin's *Modern Times*. But humanity, which may have failed as an idea, succeeds as body: bodies in space and time, bodies with faces; faces which may constitute the greatest works of art of all, not only in the movies (from Dreyer's *Joan of Arc* to Bela Tarr's *Damnation*), but also in fiction. For example, in William Gaddis's *The Recognitions*:

> Benny had hardly looked at the face of the man who was talking to him: in contrast to his own it was a detailed fortification, every rampart erected with definite purpose, their parapets calculated to withstand repeated assaults from any direction, tried in innumerable skirmishes where many had approached so close as to tumble between scarp and counterscarp, an arrangement so long in the building that, though every bit of it had been erected for defense, in finished entirety it assumed aggressive proportions; inviting strategy, it might only be taken by storm. (pg. 600)

Have we seen faces like this while watching a movie? Has going to the movies taught us how to recognize faces like this one? Taught us how to read them?

*

The power of the cinema operates in contrary directions, usually simultaneously. How do we contend with the tension between the fascination of language and the fascism of language? Word as fetish and word as fanaticism? The image that liberates and the image that enslaves, especially when it is the same image?

*

Barthes understood the difficulties that oppose the keeping of a journal, so that when he writes, in a 1979 diary entry (less than a year before he was killed by a laundry van), "The evening's pathetic failure has impelled me to begin, at last, the reformation of my life which I have so long had in mind," he knows that the journal is uniquely suited to hold for us precisely these kinds of lies; lies we tell ourselves in the hope that someday that person for whom we have searched all our lives (if only in our imaginations) will read them and believe they were true. This is the fantasy of love, no less true in the written expression of our most private thoughts than it is in the movies that cast their spell over us. In this way the movies we watch constitute another kind of diary.

*

Kafka used his *Diaries* as a way of effacing the distinction between life and his vision of a possible life. When he writes,

> I was considering the hopes I had formed for life. The one which appeared most important or the most affecting was the desire to acquire a way of seeing life (and what was related, of being able, by writing, to convince others) in

which life would keep its heavy movement of rise and fall, but would at the same time be recognized, and with a no less admirable clarity, as a nothing, a dream of a drifting state.

it is not clear if he is describing literature, his life, or the experience of going to the movies (*a way of seeing life*).

*

Chaplin, as a comedian and metaphysician, captures the fundamental quality Barthes ascribes to the journal keeper:

> What the Journal posits is not the tragic question, the Madman's question: "Who am I?", but the comic question, the Bewildered Man's question: "Am I?" A comic—a comedian, that's what the Journal keeper is. ("Deliberation")

Seen in this light, Chaplin is not the *keeper* of a journal, but the very stuff of each of our own private diaries. He is a choreographed version of our own questions, doubts, uncertainties, and insecurities about self and identity.

Samuel Beckett built as teetering a dark tower on the work of Chaplin as literature was capable of supporting. Chaplin himself, who along with Buster Keaton and Harold Lloyd was one of the three great stars of silent comedy, spoke the body's eloquent language that allowed him to maintain that verbal silence aspired to by Beckett. Small wonder that Beckett turned to Keaton when he needed an actor for his single foray into the cinema. The fact that he insisted that Keaton be filmed from the back—that the audience never see the face for which Keaton was so justifiably famous—was simply another attempt at groping for that Silence which Beckett sought it all its forms.

*

James Agee described Chaplin's genius in a kind of journalistic prose poem honoring the comedian's uniquely corporeal poetry of motion (and thus honoring as well the idea that poetry comes in many forms):

> With *Tillie's Punctured Romance*, in 1914, he became a major star. Soon after, he left Sennett when Sennett refused to start a landslide among the other comedians by meeting the raise Chaplin demanded. Sennett is understandably wry about it in retrospect, but he still says, "I was right at the time." Of Chaplin he says simply, "Oh well, he's just the greatest artist that ever lived." None of Chaplin's former rivals rates him much lower than that; they speak of him no more jealously that they might of God.[159] We will try here only to suggest the essence of his supremacy. Of all comedians he worked most deeply and most shrewdly within a realization of what a human being is, and is up against.[160] The Tramp is as centrally representative of humanity, as many-sided and mysterious, as Hamlet, and it seems unlikely that any dancer or actor can ever have excelled him in eloquence, variety, or

---

[159] As Fats Waller was to speak of Art Tatum around the same time.
[160] Again we see signs of the profound influence he had on Beckett.

poignancy of motion. As for pure motion, even if he had never gone on to make his magnificent feature-length comedies, Chaplin would have made his period in movies a great one singlehanded even if he had made nothing except *The Cure* or *One A.M.* In the latter, barring one immobile taxi driver, Chaplin plays alone, as a drunk trying to get upstairs and into bed. It is a sort of inspired elaboration on a soft-shoe dance, involving an angry stuffed wildcat, small rugs on slippery floors, a Lazy Susan table, exquisite footwork on a flight of stairs, a contretemps with a huge, ferocious pendulum and the funniest and most perverse Murphy bed in movie history—and, always made physically lucid, the delicately weird mental processes of a man ethereally sozzled. ("Comedy's Greatest Era")

*

Why has eroticism disappeared from literature? He may wonder if there are true and false ways of being bored, and he can ask himself finally why writers don't want to do anything anymore but make movies.

–Roland Barthes

What is the "true way" of being bored? (A way explored by artists like Gertrude Stein, John Cage, and Bela Tarr intent on revealing truths about human consciousness and aesthetic experience.) Exciting movies are engrossing, but often their excitement, which constitutes a kind of pure pleasure of distraction, distracts from something alien to pleasure in the ordinary sense. There is a form of boredom that doesn't distract our attention but rather stimulates and focuses it. This kind of boredom forces us to pay attention to things that action, adventure, mystery, and suspense often obscure. The movies provide us with an opportunity to *pay attention* in ways that "real life" does not, because real life is not lived with the calculated aesthetic intensity of a 90-minute experience. One of the challenges of watching a certain kind of movie is discovering this "true way" of being bored and experiencing what lies on the other side of (the side we reach by means of) these aesthetically calculated forms of boredom.

*

Octavio Paz writes,

> Drugs provoke the vision of the universal correspondence of all things, arouse the powers of analogy, set objects in motion, make the world a vast poem shaped by rhymes and rhythms. Drugs snatch us out of everyday reality, blur our perception, alter our sensations, and, in a word, put the entire universe in a state of suspension. ... drugs take us to the very heart of another reality: the world has not changed, but it is now seen to be governed by a secret harmony. (*Alternating Current*)

Granted that the movies do all this and more, this is not to say that the movies are a kind of drug. Or are they? For just as the use of drugs has gone from rite and ritual (in Ancient Greece, Sacred India, and with the natives of North, Central, and South America) to recreation, we have seen the potential *use* of (the ambitions associated with) the movies decline from enlightenment to entertainment.

Are movies a drug (a means of altering our cognitive experience of reality)? Can viewing them become a kind of ritual? Are there private rituals, or must rituals always be sanctified by the solemnities of communal practice?

Why this persistent temptation to try and say what movies are (other than themselves): a kind of language, a form of prayer, a kind of meditation, a drug...

*

The use of drugs betrays the fact that man is not a *natural* being; he experiences not only thirst, hunger, dreams, and sexual pleasure, but also a nostalgia for the infinite. The supernatural—to use a convenient but inaccurate term—is part of his nature. Everything he does, including his simplest physical acts, is tinged with a yearning for the absolute. Imagination—the power to produce images and the temptation to incarnate these images—is part of his nature. Imagination: a faculty of our nature to change itself. (Paz, *Alternating Currents*)

The movies are precisely this "power to produce images." They are the fulfillment of this "temptation to incarnate these images." But as the potential of the movies declines (due to the other uses to which we put them: commercial, ideological, cultural, political, hedonistic), what happens to our "nostalgia for the infinite" and our "yearning for the absolute"? What are these impulses replaced with? Is it possible that we risk losing them altogether? Will they be taken away from us, or will we simply give them up, exchange them for the gratification of more immediate pleasures?

*

In cinema there is no substitution. Not "image" for "word" or "vision" for "language."

*

This Absurd Undertaking. What Paz says of poetry is true of the movies as well, because the movies are a kind of poetry:

> Poetry is an attempt to do away with all conventional meanings because poetry itself becomes the ultimate meaning of life and of man; therefore it is at once the destruction and the creation of language—the destruction of words and meanings, the realm of silence, but at the same time, words in search of the Word. Those who dismiss this quest as "utter madness" are legion. Nonetheless ... a few solitary spirits, among them the noblest and most gifted human beings who have ever trod the earth, have unhesitatingly devoted their entire lives to this absurd undertaking.

*

If the movies do not become a form of poetry, what will become of the modern counterparts of those great poetic geniuses of the past, from Baudelaire to Mallarmé, Holderlin to Lorca, Pierre Reverdy to Paul Celan, Osip Mandelstam to Emily Dickinson? If these men and women do not learn to work in the medium of cinema, in what language will they speak to us?

*

Whether you are consciously aware of it or not, you are either completely satisfied with your life right now, or you are waiting for something. In which case the only question is, what are you waiting for?

*

When even despair isn't safe from the marketplace, where are we?

*

One of the great revelations of silent films, 100 years later, is that it doesn't matter what we say. We know it already. We've always known it. The words don't have to be said, and in fact in the movies, as well as in life, often more is communicated when they are not said.

*

> While all the other arts were born naked, this, the youngest, has been born fully-clothed. It can say everything before it has anything to say. It is as if the savage tribe, instead of finding two bars of iron to play with, had found scattering the seashore fiddles, flutes, saxophones, trumpets, grand

pianos by Erard and Bechstein, and had begun with incredible energy, but without knowing a note of music, to hammer and thump upon them all at the same time.

–Virginia Woolf, "The Movies and Reality"

Art is timeless, but movies, it turns out, are not. The motion pictures, ironically, are frozen in time in a way that other works of art are not. They violate the dictum that "a classic is a work that never ages." For while there are certainly "classic movies", these movies age in ways that other artworks do not, and in one sense they inevitably, and very quickly, become dated. Classics like Robert Wiene's *The Cabinet of Dr. Caligari* and Victor Sjostrom's *The Phantom Carriage* (both from 1920) are greater works of art than any of the recent blockbusters to roll out of the Hollywood studios, but it is obvious that they are nearly 100 years old in a way that does not mark *Don Quixote* as a 500 year-old novel. Paintings from the first decades of the 20th century have not aged the way films have. Why is this? What accounts for the temporal specificity of the movies, which constitutes at once part of their great power and appeal but also a significant obstacle to learning how to watch them?

One of the reasons movies seem to age in a way that music, literature, and painting do not has to do with the advances in technology that their production is tied to. As the technology we use to film, edit, and produce the movies changes, the look, the feel, and even the effect of the movies changes with it. Another reason is the incredible contemporaneity of the movies. Even when we are trying to provide a glimpse of an imaginary future, the vivid visual imagery of a film reveals how we see and portray the world around us at the time of filming. (John

Carpenter's 1981 *Escape from New York*, set in 1997, was supposed to be a terrifying vision of the future; but by the time 1997 actually rolled around the movie, while still entertaining, already felt wildly outdated; in fact, this has become part of its charm.) Movies always feel so much a part of the Now in which they are made because they are records of our visual imagination, which always betrays us to our most immediate sense of the present.

*

There is great pleasure in having an idea.

*

Bergman's *Scenes from a Marriage* is a remarkable achievement. It provides us with a portrait of two people (brilliantly played by Liv Ullmann and Erland Josephson) who have nothing to look to outside or beyond themselves and each other. There is nothing else in their lives. And so these lives, lacking any sense of what was once called "higher purpose" seem to have no choice but to devour themselves. These *Scenes* are a portrait of spiritual cannibalism where the bones are already showing through the gnawed-on flesh.

*

I don't think it makes sense to speak of favorite directors. Great directors certainly. And favorite films. But how can you have a favorite director, when any director who is truly struggling with his art will be responsible for as many bad movies as great ones. How else can he know that he is pushing the boundaries of what he is comfortable with, and trying to see farther than he has seen before? Compare Bresson's *Les Dames du Bois de Boulogne* with *Au Hasard Balthazar* and *L'Argent* (or his *Lancelot du Lac*). Is it not amazing that the same creative mind, over the span of 40 years, created all these films? Such range is possible only through constant and restless effort, and a willingness not only to risk failure, but sometimes simply to fail. As Bresson said, *The greater the success, the closer it verges upon failure.*

*

Cultural Elitism. The difference between art and entertainment? At its best, entertainment can help smart people forget their intelligence (which can be a very fine thing), and can help dull people forget their ignorance (which is a kind of mercy). At its worst, entertainment makes stupid people feel smarter than they are (for example the work of novelist Dan Brown). Art, on the other hand, succeeds when it makes intelligent people feel stupid (or stupefied).

*

Pause to wonder. When we watch a movie, the pleasure of ideas is inextricably connected with the act and the art of seeing. The irony of seeing is that, on the one hand, it is something perfectly natural, something that most of us cannot help but do, every time we open our eyes and point our head in a particular direction. We are so used to seeing, whether we want to or not, that it is easy, in fact natural, to take the images we see for granted. The act of seeing, in daily life, does not need to be lingered over, pondered, contemplated, and wondered at. It does not need to be questioned. And for the past 100 years (longer than any of us have been alive), movies have been so much a part of our "daily life," that we have grown accustomed to them in a way which has encouraged us to no longer ponder, question, contemplate, and wonder over them. We watch them. We enjoy them. We are entertained by them. But we have grown so used to them, so accustomed to them, that we no longer pause before the images we see when we watch a movie. We no longer pause to wonder: to wonder about where they came from or how they were created. We often forget—and indeed such forgetting is one of the illusions the movies are intent on fostering—that we are watching something artificial. Something wholly unnatural. But of course the movies want to draw us in, to possess us with a sense of their naturalness, a sense of our *being there*, inside and a part of the movie we are watching.

*

When we read a film we read facial expression, hand gestures, posture and body movement. We read nuances of light and shadow, camera angle, cuts and edits between shots. We read the furniture and objects in a scene, the location of windows and doors, the color and texture of the walls. We read the actors' eyes and we read what is called their "body language." Movies speak this language more eloquently than any other medium. And the better we read, the more we see; the more we see, the richer our experience and the more nuanced the layers of meaning become. It starts with learning how to read, and with knowing what reading is.

*

I dreamt about being quiet. All these people had come together in the same place, and they had promised to do extraordinary things to fall in love. But two of them realized that nothing more was necessary than to be absolutely quiet, and if you were quiet in this way you would hear the person you were meant to love talking to you, inside your head. Two of the people discovered this secret and fell in love, which no one around them noticed or realized because they were so busy performing the busy tasks they thought would lead them to love in some other way. At the end of the dream everyone was saying goodbye to everyone else, except the two people who had fallen in love by being quiet with one another. They knew they were going to stay behind and be together, after everyone else had left.

*

A philosophical movie does not set out to answer or explore the perennial questions of philosophy. (Questions like: Is the world created or eternal? What is the relation between thought and language? Is the nature of reality one or many? Is matter real? What is consciousness? What is human will? Is it free? Are human beings bodies and souls or just bodies or just souls? Why is there evil in the world? What is the best way to live? What happens to us after we die?) A philosophical movie simply has to make us think about things we otherwise take for granted.

*

Men with Guns. The cowboy, the soldier, the secret agent, the gangster, the detective, the assassin, the police officer—the movies are full of men with guns. But even for people for whom, in the real world (real soldiers, police officers, secret agents and assassins) guns are a part of their everyday reality, the image of the gun in cinema is a fantasy (perhaps for these people even more of a fantasy, as it contrasts all the more radically with their real-life experience), because the gun in the movies is not really a gun; it's not an external object alien to the hero. The gun, as it is inevitably featured in the movies, is an extension of the hero—not merely of his body, but of his will, his intent, his sense of justice or malevolence. The gun need not be aimed, but simply pointed. It obeys the will of the hero (or villain). And, like the actor's face, the gun is an object of desire for the camera and for the filmmaker.

*

Watching is a dangerous activity. It threatens to condition us, to turn our acts of watching into self-fulfilling prophecies. Seeing what is shown is the danger of watching. This is a sign of its power, and what is powerful always has potential. Therefore watching is full of potential and the potential is precisely that we might see beyond what we are shown. To go beyond the shown— this is the *task* of watching.

*

The free man has no character, since character is that part of us that determines our actions, thoughts, and beliefs, and what is determined is not free. If we were able to choose between being a person of character and being free, that would be a free choice, unless our choice to be a person of character retroactively abnegated that freedom.

In the movies, it is because the characters (played by actors) so often seem possessed by a sense of character (a particular moral quality) that there also seems to be a sense of fate or inevitable destiny about what happens to them in the film. They are rarely faced with true decisions (especially in the Western, the Gangster, or the Detective movie). Instead, they are presented with opportunities to act out the inevitable consequences of their natural (and unavoidable, inevitable) character. If these figures are role models, they model a potential absence of freedom which nevertheless strikes us as desirable.

*

"...the problem before us is that of realism. This is the problem we always end up with when we are dealing with cinema." –André Bazin, *What is Cinema?*

"The function of the camera is to portray reality, but I like to show that much reality is unreal." –Roger Corman

The problem of realism. Regardless of whether they have advanced the thesis that the movies should approximate reality or depart from it, all discussions of cinema's relation to reality thus far have suffered from the same problem: they invariably take for granted that such a thing as "reality" exists in the first place, whereas it is the task of the cinema to call such assumptions into question.

*

"The world about us would be desolate except for the world within us."

"It is a violence from within that protects us from a violence from without."

–Wallace Stevens

What is the relation of the movies to the *inner life*?

*

Watching Tarr's *The Turin Horse*: Why does the hedonist so often fail to appreciate the possibility of a *spiritual hedonism*?

If you are not capable of working for your pleasure (suffering for your pleasure), all you can ever do is repeat old pleasures—you will remain incapable of experiencing anything unfamiliar, difficult, challenging or strange. Pleasure then will be a form of death. The movies are suspended between these two possibilities: of delivering this pleasure that is a form of death (albeit a pleasant one) and the possibility of stimulating something like a means to life. The question is not whether the work is a source of pleasure, but whether that pleasure contributes to life or death.

*

There had been a time when the fear of no longer being myself had horrified me, and similarly with each new love I felt (for Gilberte, for Albertine), because I could not bear the idea that one day the being who loved them would no longer exist, which seemed like a kind of death.... For I understood that dying was not something

373

new but quite the reverse, that since childhood I had already died a number of times.... These successive deaths, so feared by the self they were doomed to annihilate, so meaningless, so gentle after they had happened and when the person who was afraid of them was no longer there to feel them, had enabled me for some time now to understand how unwise it would be to be frightened of death.

–Proust, *Finding Time Again*

Nothing demonstrates more vividly to me the truth of this passage than the experience of rewatching old movies. When I return to a film I have not seen in 20 years and it is as if I have never seen it before, I realize how irrevocably lost is the person who saw that movie for the first time. So many past selves have been lost to me over the years, each a form of death in life, that I now realize the final death that awaits me will not even come to the me I am now. That final death has been reserved for a future me I have not yet become, a me who will have already survived the death of the me I am now, and in fact will hardly have noticed his passing, much less mourned for him.

*

God is no philosopher. Knowing everything, God does not wonder. But perhaps it is not so difficult to imagine God going to the movies. Haven't we always imagined God as the perfect audience (and critic), even if all he has to watch are scenes from his own movie?

Our own philosophizing, on the other hand, stems from

our yearning for the Divine, just as our going to the movies is an expression of our wonder in the face of that Divine, which is the world itself. We go to the movies not to be entertained, but to be transported.

*

Going to the movies as a kind of perpetual tourism through the landscapes of our imagination.

www.ingramcontent.com/pod-product-compliance
Lightning Source LLC
Chambersburg PA
CBHW070312190526
45169CB00005B/1598

* 9 7 8 1 5 3 5 2 2 0 8 1 1 *